Supernatural Youth in Media

Sharon R. Mazzarella
General Editor

Vol. 36

Supernatural Youth in Media

Edited by
Ilana Nash and Rebecca C. Hains

PETER LANG
New York - Berlin - Bruxelles - Chennai - Lausanne - Oxford

Library of Congress Cataloging-in-Publication Data

Names: Nash, Ilana, editor. | Hains, Rebecca C., editor
Title: Supernatural youth in media / edited by Ilana Nash and Rebecca C. Hains.
Description: New York : Peter Lang, 2025. | Series: Mediated youth, 1555–1814; Volume 36 | Includes bibliographical references and index.
Identifiers: LCCN 2024039958 (print) | LCCN 2024039959 (ebook) | ISBN 9781636677217 (paperback) | ISBN 9783034354059 (hardback) | ISBN 9781636677194 (ebook) | ISBN 9781636677200 (epub)
Subjects: LCSH: Youth in mass media. | Supernatural in mass media. | LCGFT: Essays.
Classification: LCC P94.5.Y72 S87 2025 (print) | LCC P94.5.Y72 (ebook) | DDC 809.3/937–dc23/eng/20240920
LC record available at https://lccn.loc.gov/2024039958
LC ebook record available at https://lccn.loc.gov/2024039959
DOI 10.3726/b22359

Bibliographic information published by the Deutsche Nationalbibliothek.
The German National Library lists this publication in the German National Bibliography; detailed bibliographic data is available on the Internet at http://dnb.d-nb.de.

Cover design by Peter Lang Group AG

ISSN 1555-1814 (print)
ISBN 9781636677217 (paperback)
ISBN 9783034354059 (hardback)
ISBN 9781636677194 (ebook)
ISBN 9781636677200 (epub)
DOI 10.3726/b22359

© 2025 Peter Lang Group AG, Lausanne
Published by Peter Lang Publishing Inc., New York, USA
info@peterlang.com - www.peterlang.com

All rights reserved.
All parts of this publication are protected by copyright.
Any utilization outside the strict limits of the copyright law, without the permission of the publisher, is forbidden and liable to prosecution.
This applies in particular to reproductions, translations, microfilming, and storage and processing in electronic retrieval systems.

This publication has been peer reviewed.

This book is dedicated to the tweens and teens who bring magic to our lives each day: May, Theo, Alex, and Xavier.

Contents

Acknowledgements xi

1 Supernatural Youth in Media: The History and Meaning of a Fantastic Genre 1
  Ilana Nash and Rebecca C. Hains

Part I Adaptation and Interpretation

2 Growing Up in A Winx: Reworking a Children's Text for a Teen Audience 27
  Kyra Hunting

3 Sex Magic: Orgasm, Embodiment, and the Erotic Navigation of "the Circumstances" in *The Magicians* 45
  Cory Geraths

4	Rewriting the Past and Present: *Ragnarok*, Norse Myth, and Teen Heroes Ilana Nash and Jana K. Schulman	63
5	Mystical and the Mundane in Netflix's *The Irregulars*: Exploring Supernatural Narrative Engagement and Reception Gwendelyn S. Nisbett and Newly Paul	83

Part II Intersecting Magic and Femininity

6	Supernatural Savior or Sacrificial Lamb? The Contradictions and Cost of Young Supernatural Femininity: *Chilling Adventures of Sabrina* in a Post-Buffy Context Lori Bindig Yousman	105
7	Youth at the Border: Finding the Monstrous-Feminine in Marvel Comics Eric M. Kennedy Jr.	125
8	Saving Herself and Turning Rhetorical Tropes in Disney Films: Subverting the Monstrous-Feminine in Supernatural Genre Conventions Erika M. Thomas	143
9	A Zambian Fairytale: Shula and the Magic of Rungano Nyoni's *I Am Not A Witch* Hope L. Russell	163

Part III Confronting Exclusions in Supernatural Identities

10	Where Are All of the Black Kids?: A Contemporary Search for Black Youth in the Fantastic World Asha Winfield, Meghan Sanders, Rockia Harris, Hope Hickerson, and Tiffany R. Smith	183

11   Queering Teen Supernatural TV Dramas: Fandom's Impact on
     LGBTQ Youth   201
     Victor Evans

12   Welcome to the Witching Hour: *The Craft* as a Neuroqueer
     Allegory of Legibility   221
     Desirée Rowe

     Notes on Contributors   237
     Index   243

Acknowledgements

We wish to thank Sharon Mazzarella, editor of the Mediated Youth series, for her support of this volume and for her vision in providing a home for scholarship on youth and media. Special thanks also to Elizabeth Howard and Sweetlin Ajitha at Peter Lang press, and to our authors, whose excellent work and enthusiasm for the topic brought such joy to this project.

1

Supernatural Youth in Media: The History and Meaning of a Fantastic Genre

ILANA NASH AND REBECCA C. HAINS

In today's media landscape, supernatural tales featuring young people with magical powers abound. From the enduring fame of the blockbuster *Harry Potter* books and films to more contemporary TV series like Netflix's *Wednesday* (2022), stories about tweens, teens and young adults with mystical abilities are everywhere—and many of them have enjoyed critical, popular, and economic success. Whether using magical powers to pursue adventure or to save the world from evil, supernatural youth are popular protagonists whose stories resonate with diverse audiences, especially young people.

Prior to the turn of the millennium, stories of this type were less common. But in the 1990s, supernatural youth media exploded in such texts as the popular film *The Craft* (1996), the first *Harry Potter* novel (1997 in Great Britain, 1998 in the United States), and the debuts of popular, long-running TV series like *Sabrina the Teenage Witch* (1996–2003), *Buffy the Vampire Slayer* (1997–2003) and *Charmed* (1998–2006). In the decades since, audiences have enjoyed a multiplicity of texts featuring young heroes with supernatural powers made possible by those early media texts' successes. Network and studio executives tend to greenlight projects in genres and franchises whose recent performance indicates audience interest and therefore financial promise. On networks like the CW and streamers ranging from Disney and Netflix to Max (also called HBO Max in some markets), various contemporary texts have thus built upon one another's popularity, establishing recognizable discourses and practices surrounding tales of supernatural youth that resonate with audiences and are, therefore, commercially viable. These discourses and practices are so cohesive, so identifiable, and so enduring, that supernatural youth media (SYM) have coalesced into a distinct genre—identifiable by its texts' networks of overlapping similarities (Wittgenstein, 1953) and interconnected discursive norms (Foucault, 1972). Today, SYM continues to thrive both in reboots of the last generation's texts and in the production of new texts like Netflix's *School Spirits* (2023), suggesting that audiences have an enduring fascination with the intersections of youth and mystical or occult themes.

While many books, both scholarly and mass-market, have discussed individual texts or series in this genre, few have considered the genre as a whole—and its articulation *as* a genre has been minimal, at best. In this book, we assemble scholarly essays about disparate SYM texts, placing them together in one collection to enable readers to think further about what the persistent mediated fantasy of magical youth enables or inspires for its viewers, and how its texts address the fantasies (or nightmares) of the societies that produce them. In this attribution of genre, we consider not only the contents of the texts themselves, but also their positions in relation to their production, distribution, and audience—and to one another. As Miller (1984) argued, "A theoretically sound definition of genre must be centred not on the substance or the form of discourse but on the action it is used to accomplish" (p. 151)—emphasizing that studying genre explores historical and social aspects in a manner overlooked via discourse analysis alone (p. 151). To this end, we interrogate not just what the genre is, but *why* it is, which requires considering SYM's sociocultural relevance at the time of its emergence and to the present day. Audience matters in this exploration: As Rieder (2010) has argued, the attribution of genre promotes texts' "use by a certain group of readers and in certain kinds of ways," including the "promise that a text can be usefully, pleasurably read" in a specific way—including in conversation with other texts and readers of that genre (p. 201). By exploring SYM as a genre that spans multiple decades, we unpack SYM's accomplishments—the cultural conversations and perspective shifts it has introduced via its discourses (Rieder, 2010).

In surveying the landscape of supernaturally themed youth media, we note that texts in the genre typically include some or all of the following identifiable similarities and norms:

- A primary focus on youthful (tween, teen, young adult) protagonists who discover or develop mystical abilities as figures from legend or

mythology: witches, angels, werewolves, seers, gods, vampires, fairies, and others.
- The placement of young protagonists in youth-specific settings and situations, often as students in schools or as young adults who are not yet settled into stable careers or marriages.
- A target audience of young viewers (tweens, teenagers, and younger adults—but not, typically, younger children), reflective of the 1990s' rise of teen-targeting TV networks like the WB and UPN, which in 2006 coalesced into today's youth-focused CW network.
- Content that appeals to teen and young-adult viewers, often with soundtracks and costume designs that showcase contemporary, trendy styles.
- Protagonists who are often (though not always) specifically tasked with saving the world from evil or destruction.
- A distinct difference from the sci-fi genre (with which SYM is often superficially conflated): Protagonists' powers derive from mythical and mystical sources, not from the genetic mutations, alien planets, or technological gadgetry upon which sci-fi depends.

This last point is central to this book's focus. Timothy Shary (2014) describes a "supernatural" subgenre of teen film that includes science fiction, as its contents are fantastical and imaginary. We use the term supernatural more exclusively, separating it from science fiction. The word "science," which derives from the Latin *scire* (to know), studies the social or natural worlds with the assumption that humans can ultimately gain knowledge and power by mastering learnable, consistent systems. Even science fiction, though unreal, is rooted in this definition, for outer-space aliens conform to the natural world of their own planets—and planets, of course, visibly exist in reality. By contrast, "supernatural" literally means "above nature," and the SYM genre draws from myths and fairy tales—narrative traditions that pre-date the Scientific Revolution—about magic that comes from unobservable, uncontrollable sources, beyond scientific understanding. Remarkably, in the midst of the digital revolution that characterized the late twentieth century, SYM emerged with tales of youth whose powers are *not* rooted in systems of science or technology. On the verge of the year 2000, in the midst of rapid technological change that brought sci-fi-esque ideas into the real world, tales about supernaturally empowered youth offered audiences pleasurable escapes from both dystopian sci-fi tales and the realities of a quickly evolving world.

Millennial Concerns

Chronology and timing are relevant to our understanding of supernatural youth media as a genre, because new genres emerge in specific historical contexts or moments (Cohen, 1986). Those moments are influenced by purposes including the commercial, the social, and the aesthetic (Cohen, 1986). Taking a long view of SYM's history, we see significance in the timing of its coalescence into genre in the years approaching the turn of the millennium, as observable through the release of ever-more texts sharing similar traits, purposes and audiences. The SYM genre that emerged in the 1990s typically featured teenage characters and targeted teenage audiences. Adolescence and the millennium itself both share a position of liminality, an emotionally laden threshold between two states of being. Teens have long been understood to occupy a transitional space between childhood and adulthood, marked by rites of passage. In the words of anthropologist Victor Turner (1987), who studied rites of passage, "Liminality may perhaps be regarded [...] as a realm of pure possibility whence novel configurations of ideas and relations may arise" (p. 7). Additionally, liminality—often figured as a crossroads—features prominently in the myths and folklore from which SYM texts often draw, as a space where the barrier between the physical and mystical worlds dissolves. Puhvel (1976) noted that the crossroads motif, prevalent in numerous cultures' folkore, is "associated with the appearance and activities of various, generally uncanny creatures—ghosts, witches, and demons of many kinds. They are a place where mysterious preternatural phenomena occur and magic rites of multiple sorts are performed" (p. 167).

The turning of centuries and millennia can similarly be read as a liminal space, a threshold between the known and the unknown, igniting hopes and fears about changes and "novel configurations" on the horizon. In the 1990s, many of those hopes and fears attached to the digital revolution, which dramatically changed both the media landscape and our world with the explosion of personal computer use, the mainstreaming of the internet, and widespread adoption of cellphones. While people celebrated these digital media for their opening new realms of information and communication, the innovations also sparked worries—just as electric communication technologies did upon their introduction in the late nineteenth century (Marvin, 2000). Unknown negative potentials included people's fears of being unable to keep up with rapidly changing technology; disruptions to personal relationships; and a concomitant fear of adult authority being challenged or replaced, as children and teens quickly became more adept with technology than their elders.

The pre-turn-of-the-millennium fear of technology was quite prevalent. In fact, after conducting a survey in 1993, the Dell Computer Corp. found that more than 50% of Americans were uncomfortable with electronic devices, leading the company to conclude that "Fear of technology may well be the phobia of the '90s" (Boyd, 1994, p. 6). Media reports widely enhanced that phobia. In the summer of 1997, as SYM texts were enchanting consumers, *Newsweek* magazine ran a variety of articles about scientific breakthroughs and the life-altering consequences of modern technology: animal cloning, identity theft on the internet, global warming, and especially, the widely feared specter of the "millennium bug" or the "Y2K bug"—a flaw in computer programming that threatened to wreak global havoc when the world's clock shifted from 1999 to 2000. *Newsweek*'s special report on the topic, titled "The Day the World Shuts Down," asked, "Could the most anticipated New Year's Eve party in our lifetimes really usher in a digital nightmare when our wired-up-the-wazoo civilization grinds to a halt? Incredibly, according to computer experts [and] corporate information officers [. . .], the answer is yes, yes, 2,000 times yes!" (Levy & Hafner, 1997).

In these very years, as Americans worried about new technologies and saw news reports of impish young hackers wreaking havoc with computer systems, popular media began proffering fantasies in which young people save the world by turning chronologically back to a time of mysticism and magic, not forward to scientific or technological discovery. There are, for example, no computers in J. K. Rowling's *Harry Potter* novels; the magical environment of Hogwarts interferes with electricity, disabling all Muggle electronics. Rowling's creation of a world where letters are written with plumes on parchment, and delivered by owls, offered readers a pleasurable alternative to their "wired-up-the-wazoo civilization." With a few exceptions, most SYM texts from the 1990s and early 2000s similarly marginalized or dispensed with modern technology, as their teen protagonists gained knowledge and power from the more familiar, traditional practices of reading books and reciting words in prayers or spells. Better the devil you know than the one you don't.

Even in more recent years, despite society's increasing comfort and familiarity with the technological "devil," many SYM texts continue to share this tendency; for example, the animated tween series *Owl House* (Disney, 2020–2023) depicts magical teens in a world without smartphones or similar human technology. As these young characters are not constantly in touch with (or digitally surveilled by) parents or caregivers, unlike their hyperconnected real world counterparts, this adds more drama to their fantastical adventures. Such omissions may also contribute to or reflect the widespread nostalgia for the not-yet-digitally-connected

1990s among today's young people, a phenomenon that many commentators have observed (Hoffower, 2022).

Reflecting producers' and consumers' understanding of the "in between" states of both adolescence and the millennial shift, with its anxiogenic cultural innovations, the SYM genre places its protagonists in liminal spaces, at crossroads between identities and states of being: human and not-quite-human, child and adult, mundane world and mythic world, old millennium and new. In this context—the emergence of a large new generation of youth, situated at the cusp of a new millennium at a time of rapid technological change—supernatural youth media truly emerged as a genre in its own right. But the millennial blooming of the SYM genre had roots in earlier stories.

Supernatural Youth Media: The History of A Fantastic Genre

The link between youth and the supernatural is far older than the decades preceding the millennium; teenagers have been "raising hell" for centuries. In 1692 a group of Puritan girls, who would today be called teens and tweens, dabbled in the occult to have their fortunes told. The resulting Salem Witch Trials led to deaths and imprisonment for dozens of townspeople falsely accused of trafficking with the Devil. In more modern times, scholars have noted the cultural rituals of teenagers seeking thrilling and occult experiences as informal rites of passage within their social groups. Examining such well-known practices as visiting graveyards or haunted houses ("legend tripping"), using Ouija boards, or playing the familiar Bloody Mary game of evoking a spirit by chanting her name into a mirror, Ellis (2004) found that "self-consciously diabolical rituals have been a common element in children's and adolescents' folk culture for a long time" (p. 11).

But although youth and the supernatural have long intermingled, popular media only started pairing them in the later twentieth century. Representations of youth in media reflect a variety of influences, including market considerations, current cultural anxieties, and the prevailing contemporary attitudes about youth. Adolescence has long been understood as a separate period of development, distinct from both childhood and adulthood, and marked by emotional turbulence. As the large Baby Boomer generation was growing up in the 1950s, businesses began courting teens as a distinct consumer market, producing more products aimed specifically at teenage tastes and interests. At the same time, a social panic focused on juvenile delinquency among the generation of children affected by WWII (Gilbert, 1986). The discourses of youth as both dangerous and endangered converged with the new emphasis on marketing to youth when American International Pictures (AIP) released teen-focused horror films that juxtaposed youth and monstrosity. One of their more profitable films was *I Was a Teenage Werewolf*, closely followed by *I Was a Teenage Frankenstein* and *Blood of Dracula*, all released in 1957. These hastily produced exploitation films did not launch a mainstream trend in SYM, and therefore can only be read as SYM texts in hindsight—calling to mind Geraghty and Janovitch's (2008) insight that texts can "change meaning as they are classified or reclassified in relation to [changing] definitions of genre at different historical moments" (p. 4). These films did, however, set the stage for another property soon to emerge in a similarly youth-oriented medium: comic books.

In 1962 "Sabrina the Teen-Age Witch" debuted in a single story in Archie Comics, and immediately became popular with readers; by the early 1970s, Sabrina had earned her own comic book and her own animated TV series (Gorelick, 2017). Inspired partly by the successful 1958 film *Bell, Book and Candle*, about a sophisticated adult witch, Sabrina was the first mainstream media character to embody witchcraft in a specifically high-school-aged girl. Sabrina has had an unusually long life-span for a teen media character; she reemerged in a live-action sitcom, *Sabrina the Teenage Witch* (1996–2003) and was later rebooted again, this time in the horror genre, in the 2014 Archie Comics series *Chilling Adventures of Sabrina*, as well as a Netflix series of the same name (2018–2020).

But apart from the long-enduring Sabrina, the 1960s and 1970s did not offer a wide representation of supernaturally gifted teenagers. Instead, that period of American media introduced a small but potent group of frightening films about youth as agents of Satan. We might see this as reflective, during a period of youth-driven rebellions and social upheavals, of adults' view of youth as harbingers of doom—a theme reflected in these hit films, which targeted adult audiences. A dark fantasy about Satanic youth was born in Roman Polanski's film *Rosemary's Baby* (1968), in which a coven of witches coerces an unsuspecting woman to bear Satan's child. A few years later, top-grossing films terrified audiences with more stories of children-as-Satan: *The Exorcist* (1973) and *The Omen* (1976). These films' "R" ratings reflected not only their explicit horror imagery, but also the films' presentation of youth, not as subjects, but as objects of adults' legitimate terror. At best, in these films, "youth" is an abstract notion to provide an affecting contrast between innocence and evil. At worst, it is evil incarnate. The sympathetic protagonist in Brian DePalma's film *Carrie* (1976) seems an exception, as she has no connection to the Devil; but her powers of telekinesis are seen as Satanic by her religion-obsessed mother, and Carrie's powers do have horrific results, causing deaths—including her own—at the film's end.

If the 1970s offered adult audiences a handful of high-profile films focused on youth with darkly supernatural identities, the same cannot be said of the 1980s. While an explosion of youth-focused films emerged in the 1980s (Shary, 2014), the majority of them placed their characters in realistic settings and plots. Youth-centered films with fantastical premises, when they appeared, more often used a framework based on science or technology rather than mysticism; average human kids are swept-up in sci-fi adventures in films like *E.T.* (1982) and *Back to the Future* (1985). When young protagonists have an unusual "super" power themselves, that power is often rooted in science. In *Firestarter* (1984), for example, the young heroine's pyrokinesis results from scientific experiments conducted on her parents. Some films featured male protagonists with the "super" power of an intellectual gift for scientific or technological discovery, signaling the gender bias that associates STEM and masculinity. Thus, in films like *War Games* (1983) and *Weird Science* (1985), teenage boys create unintended chaos with computer hacking and scientific experiments, nodding to the cultural stereotype that youth have greater technological affinity than adults have.

The pairing of youth and magic was not wholly absent; it continued (as it long had done) to appear in children's and "family entertainment" based on fairy tales and children's fantasy literature—as in *The Neverending Story* (1984), the TV musical *The Worst Witch* (1986), or Disney's *The Little Mermaid* (1989), which initiated the magic-inflected Disney Princess films that flourished in the 1990s and beyond (Hains, 2014). Such films' protagonists accessed magic to defeat evil, with relatively simple storylines and themes appropriate for their target audience of younger children. For older youths, the subgenre of teen horror or "slasher" films often presented human madmen as the killers, rather than mythical beings. When supernatural figures do appear in teen horror films—like the dream-stalking spirit of the *Nightmare on Elm Street* (1984) franchise, the vengeful ghost of *Trick or Treat* (1986), or the teen vampires of *The Lost Boys* (1987)—occult forces are figured as menacing. Teen protagonists seldom embody autonomous supernatural identities; they are more often the victims or intended victims of a supernatural force that threatens to possess or kill them. With a few exceptions—as in the third *Nightmare on Elm Street* film (1987), where one character psychically draws allies into her dreams to defeat the monster—the supernatural is presented as an exterior threat, not as a positive, empowering benefit intrinsic to a teen's identity.

These trends are striking when we consider the 1980s emergence of the Satanic Panic, a social anxiety about children's and teens' vulnerability both to alleged Satanic ritual abuse, and to supposedly Satanic themes in popular culture. From heavy metal music to the tabletop game Dungeons & Dragons, youth-targeting entertainments with dark or occult themes were widely criticized for supposedly luring children to the dark side (Richardson et al., 1991; Victor, 1993; Janisse & Corupe, 2016). This social context seems to have put a damper on adult audiences' taste for films about youth wielding occult powers, or overcome by demonic forces; while *The Exorcist* had been one of the 1970s' top-grossing films, for example, none of its three sequels was released during the 1980s.

Notable exceptions to the 1980s' general dearth of magical teens include *Teen Wolf* (1985), loosely inspired by *I Was a Teenage Werewolf*; *My Best Friend Is a Vampire* (1987); and *Teen Witch* (1989). Strikingly, these films are comedies with sympathetic supernatural protagonists, reversing the prior cinematic portrayal of supernatural youth as either menacing or fatally endangered. In the years that followed, that shift in perspective stayed consistent, and grew stronger. The 1992 release of the film *Buffy the Vampire Slayer*, though not a critical or financial success, presented a mystically gifted heroine able to conquer vampires, and with a much more comedic tone than the popular television series that later followed. Two SYM texts that appeared in 1996—the popular film *The Craft* and the live-action *Sabrina the Teenage Witch* TV series—posit the existence of good teenage witches, with *The Craft* explicitly noting that magic is intrinsically neither good nor bad; its moral value depends on its practitioners' motives. After *Buffy the Vampire Slayer* debuted as a TV series in 1997, it added positive witchcraft in the character of Buffy's best friend, Willow.

To be sure, some 1990s media continued to present witchcraft as negative; the popular horror film *The Blair Witch Project* (1999), for example, presented a trio of non-magical college students victimized by supernatural forces. Leaving only "found footage" from their camcorders to tell their tale, the hapless young heroes fatally learn that ancient magic is a greater, more powerful force than modern technology. But in SYM texts, where teens themselves naturally wield mystical powers, the 1990s' biggest innovation was to present such protagonists as morally good: wiser, more altruistic, and more capable than others around them. This representational shift allowed such characters to function as positive, likeable heroes rather than as wreakers of havoc, tragic victims, or harbingers of Hell.

The Satanic Panic of the 1980s was a classic moral panic, meaning that in response to an intensely felt and overstated perceived threat, the threat's alleged agents were classified as deviants who were stereotyped and attacked (Goode & Ben-Yahuda, 1994). Evangelical Christianity's growth in the United States fueled this panic, which accused all manner of pop culture representations of being "satanic" and thus threatening to young people, and assumed that literal Satanic rituals were regular occurrences. Scholars have noted that, as a powerful and widespread religious movement, Evangelical Christianity—which focused on such mystical themes as the Rapture and the horrors of Hell—unwittingly created its own worst nightmare in the following decade: It inspired mainstream media producers to capitalize on the popularity of supernatural themes while jettisoning the Christian framework, leading to a youth-targeting media landscape filled with demons and witches (Clark, 2003; Ellis, 2004). Although anxieties about real-life Satanic ritual abuse faded in the early 1990s, the fears of a spiritual evil, spread through entertainment, continued—recalling Goode and Ben-Yahuda's (1994) insight that, unlike mere fads, moral panics always leave a legacy.

To some degree, those fears had a grain of truth to them; the release of *The Craft*, about a coven of high-school witches, influenced many teen viewers to explore Wicca, the pagan religion represented in the film. While Wicca is entirely different from the modern religion of Satanism, it is also entirely different from Christianity. Paganism and Wicca gained popularity in the later decades of the twentieth century among young people who sought a spiritual path less rigid and less judgmental than traditional faiths (Clark, 2003; Berger & Ezzy, 2007). Surmising that "no other contemporary film had as great an impact on the modern witchcraft movement as *The Craft*," Peg Aloi noted its effect on viewers: "Enthralled by its dark glamour, countless young girls were compelled to learn more about witchcraft and paganism, many turning to the nascent pagan internet for information and networking" (Aloi, 2020). Spurred by *The Craft*'s success among teen audiences, and by the growing number of teens interested in learning Wicca, several instructional books were published for teenagers, like Silver Ravenwolf's *Teen Witch: Wicca for a New Generation* (1998), thus lending some credence to the overwrought fear that popular media were enticing youngsters away from Christianity.

But the majority of 1990s' SYM texts showed a purely imaginary, fantastical form of magic, not rooted in the real-life practices of Wicca; thus, they did not encourage young viewers to change their religious affiliations. Nonetheless, these texts came under scrutiny and criticism from a wide variety of Christian groups. J. K. Rowling's globally successful *Harry Potter* books drew the sharpest response. As Ellis (2004) noted, "An especially embarrassing moment in the anti-Potter crusade was the wide circulation among Christian youth counselors of a chain letter that alleged that Rowling's books had inspired millions of children to join Satanic organizations" (p. 2).

Lingering anxieties about Satanic themes in popular culture influenced the texts of the emerging SYM genre in the 1990s, which wanted to attract, not repel, as broad a viewership as possible. The TV series *Charmed*, about three young-adult sisters who discover that they descend from a long line of witches, took pains in its first season to emphasize its heroines' mission to fight evil and protect the innocent. In the series' second episode, one sister, Piper, hears a legend about a witch struck by lightning while entering a church. Fearing that she too might suffer Divine punishment if she attempts her charity work at a local church, Piper is relieved to find that she can enter unscathed. "I'm good!" she joyfully shouts (Kern, 1998). This explicit assertion of the heroine's righteous morals seems tailor-made to answer viewers' doubts. In a characteristically snarkier fashion, *Buffy the Vampire Slayer* also addressed the Satanic Panic, in its third-season episode "Gingerbread" (1999): Under the spell of a demon who specializes in whipping-up moral panics about children and witches, Buffy's own mother co-founds a violent vigilante group, "Mothers Opposed to the Occult," with the acronym MOO—a sly suggestion that hysterical moralists are dumb cows.

The depiction of youth as virtuous supernatural heroes allowed teen viewers—people who do not yet enjoy the freedom and authority granted to adults—to see images of themselves as intrinsically and effectively powerful. This attitudinal shift in SYM texts reflected producers' interest in creating products designed for and marketed to teens, a sizable demographic in the 1990s. The millennial generation, also known as Generation Y, consists of those born from approximately 1981 to 1996 (Bennett et al., 2022). This population is of such a substantial size that at the turn of the millennium, a full 26% of the U.S. population were people younger than age 18 (Meyer, 2001)—the largest generation of adolescents since the earliest Baby Boomers became teens (Morton, 2002). Between 1990 and 2000 alone, the number of U.S. residents ages 10 to 14 grew by nearly 20%, and the 15-to-19-year-old group increased by almost 14%. They were the first generation for whom growing up with cable television (Paul, 2001) and the internet (Herring, 2008) in the home were normal—or, as Cray et al. phrased it in 2006, Gen Y are "a technological generation that takes computers, emailing, text messaging, and the internet for granted" (p. 7). Along with these data, it's noteworthy that teen spending at the turn of the millennium was significant—$155B in 2000 (Meyer, 2001)—and that this cohort had "more money to spend than any teens to date, 51% more than 1995 teenagers" (Morton, 2002). In fact, during millennials' youth in the 1990s and early 2000s, marketers created and solidified the concept of "tweens" as a target audience, just as "teen" had been devised as a target audience during the baby boom years (Hains, 2012). During this period, "tween extravagance" became an increasingly commonplace phenomenon, in which pre-teens and their families spent lavishly on products and experiences. Some marketing experts promoted millennial tweens to their clients, lauding their ability to "create a $100+ million brand" through their collective purchasing power (Quart, 2003, p. 64). Indeed, Quart notes, "The movie version of *Harry Potter and the Sorcerer's Stone* [. . .] was a gold mine of a tween product, and its success guarantees that studios will redouble their efforts to work the seam between kid films and teen movies" (p. 65).

Overall, the demographic's size, impressive discretionary spending power and influence, and comfort with newer media technologies made young millennials an appealing demographic to marketers, advertisers, and media producers alike—even to the detriment of an Emmy-nominated supernatural series that drew adult audiences: *Joan of Arcadia* (CBS 2003–2005), about a teen girl who can see and speak with God. Despite its critical success and a loyal fanbase that included some younger adults, the median age of the series' viewership was 53.9 years old, leading CBS to cancel it after two seasons and replace it with *Ghost Whisperer*, about a young married woman who can converse with the dead. As CBS' Chairman put it, "I think talking to ghosts may skew younger than talking to God" (Bauder, 2005).

The eagerness to "skew young" led to a plethora of essays about how best to target the millennial generation, with *Public Relations Quarterly* noting—among other things—that in their media choices, millennials liked "the mysterious. Blatant and obvious means nothing to them" (Morton, 2002, p. 47), and that with an average of 62 cable channels available in their homes, their media choices were significantly more complex than those of previous generations (p. 47). In this context, the runaway success of supernatural youth texts with members of this generation has arguably continued to influence the types of stories that the media tells to young people for decades.

Both *Charmed* and *Buffy* debuted on the fledgling WB network, a product of the niche-marketing trend in the media industries of the 1990s. As one of the 62 channels Morton (2002) noted had made media choices more complex for Gen Y than for previous generations, the WB network built its success on teen-focused TV series, banking on the power of the lucrative millennial market. In 2006 the WB merged with UPN to create the youth-oriented CW network, which has continued to thrive by airing series targeting a similarly young audience— including such SYM texts as *Supernatural*, which ran for a remarkable fifteen seasons (2005–2020); *The Vampire Diaries* (2009–2017) and its spin-offs, *The Originals* (2013–2017) and *Legacies* (2018–2021); and a modestly successful reboot of *Charmed* (2018–2022). At the same time, networks targeting younger viewers had success with SYM offerings for children and tweens. Key examples include Disney's *That's So Raven* (2003–2007) and Nickelodeon's *Winx Club* (2004–2009), which successfully fused SYM themes with girl power content—which had previously focused mainly on girls with *sci-fi* powers, as seen in *The Powerpuff Girls, Kim Possible, Totally Spies,* and other shows of the era (Hains, 2012).

Today, nearly thirty years after the SYM genre's rise, its texts continue to emerge not only in original stories for a new generation of viewers, but in revisions or sequels of popular 1990s texts. For example, the streaming service Max announced in 2023 that it is adapting the *Harry Potter* novels into a TV series, promising to bring new life, and new fans, to this durable franchise. The chapters assembled in this book treat just a sampling of the past and present texts in the SYM genre, but there are far more texts to be studied, and far more contexts of production, distribution, and reception to be considered.

Interrogating Supernatural Youth Media: A Novel Approach

The chapters in *Supernatural Youth in Media* come from scholars in both humanities and social science fields, and their approaches vary accordingly—greatly enriching this interdisciplinary volume. We have organized these diverse explorations of the supernatural youth media genre into three parts: Adaptation and interpretation; intersecting magic and femininity; and confronting exclusions in supernatural identities.

Adaptation and Interpretation

The supernatural youth media genre has featured a diversity of adaptations, through which original source materials are (re-)interpreted and (re-)created (Hutcheon, 2006). Although critics have long denigrated adaptation as inferior to original works, placing for example original literary works above their media adaptations, adaption studies scholars argue against such hierarchical thinking. Hutcheon (2006) posits that through adaptation, "multiple versions exist laterally, not vertically" (p. xiii)—and asks: "If adaptations are [...] inferior and secondary creations, why then are they so omnipresent in our culture and, indeed, increasing steadily in numbers?" (p. 3). She notes that "the constant appearance of new media and new channels of mass diffusion" have helped drive adaptations' popularity as a site of pleasure (p. 3).

The turn-of-the-millennium context in which SYM emerged informs our understanding of the role of adaptation in the genre: As a multiplicity of cable channels became standard in U.S. households, audiences became fragmented. While on the one hand this presented challenges to those seeking to capture as "mass" an audience as possible, it also allowed for more skillful audience segmentation—including works targeting the unusually large audience of tween and teen millennial viewers. It makes sense, then, that adaptation is a through line in the genre. SYM have often been adapted from book series, such as the *Harry Potter* and *Percy Jackson* franchises, the CW series *The Secret Circle* (2011–2012), and Syfy's *The Magicians* (2015–2020). Some, like *Sabrina the Teenage Witch* and *The Chilling Adventures of Sabrina*, began as comic books. Netflix's *Wednesday* offers a particularly robust history of adaptation: its characters were first created by artist Charles Addams, whose cartoons of the ghoulish family appeared for decades in *The New Yorker* magazine before their adaptation as a TV sitcom, *The Addams Family* (ABC, 1964–1966). The popular 1991 film *The Addams Family* sparked a major revival of the Addams characters, leading to numerous live-action and animated films over the following thirty years.

In Part I of this volume, our contributors offer diverse perspectives on adaptation and interpretation in the SYM genre. Chapters 2 and 3 consider adaptations of more recent source materials, dating from the early 2000s, while Chapters 4 and 5 examine adaptations based on more historical source materials. In "Growing Up in a Winx: Reworking a Children's Text for a Teen Audience" (Chapter 2), Kyra Hunting presents an in-depth and thoughtful analysis of Netflix's *Fate: The Winx Saga* (2021–2022), a live-action teen drama adapted from the popular turn-of-the-millennium tween SYM cartoon *The Winx Club* (2004–2009). Hunting argues that this adaptation demonstrates both the potentials and perils of aging-up children's programming. In "Sex magic: Orgasm, embodiment, and the erotic navigation of 'the Circumstances' in *The Magicians*" (Chapter 3), Cory Geraths explores the Syfy network's adaptation of Lev Grossman's youth fantasy novel trilogy of the same name. Geraths interrogates the series' adaptation of Grossman's concept of sex magic, which instantiates another subdivision in the "youth" demographic, denoting older youths of college or graduate-school age rather than teenagers.

The next two chapters consider modern SYM adaptations that draw upon much older sources. In "Rewriting the Past and Present: *Ragnarok*, Norse Myth, and Teen Heroes," Ilana Nash and Jana Schulman (Chapter 4) examine Netflix's series *Ragnarok* (2020–2023), which is inspired by (and deeply intertwined with) the medieval texts that contain what we know of Norse mythology. Nash and Schulman consider how ancient narratives are made relevant to modern audiences as the series blends the genres of myth, superheroes, and teen drama, suggesting that the key to navigating modern life lies in eroding traditional categories and hierarchies of identity.

The exploration of identity in an adapted SYM work is also a key feature of Chapter 5, "Mystical and the Mundane in Netflix's *The Irregulars:* Exploring Supernatural Narrative Engagement and Reception." In this chapter, Gwendelyn Nisbett and Newly Paul explore Netflix's *The Irregulars* (2021), set in the Sherlock Holmes world created in the late 1800s by Arthur Conan Doyle. Analyzing the series' content and reception, Nisbett and Paul argue that media narratives can play an important role in increasing audience members' understanding and acceptance of diverse experiences. Collectively, the chapters in this section demonstrate some of the ways that SYM works creatively to revise older texts to suit the needs and tastes of the contemporary moment, and the desirable demographic of teens and younger adults.

Intersecting Magic and Femininity

The relationship of magic and gender in SYM has an interesting history, and it continues to evolve. In its earliest iterations, such as *I Was a Teenage Werewolf* (1957) and the debut of "Sabrina the Teen-age Witch" (1962), the SYM genre relied on traditional American gender-coding. Male werewolves and female witches reflect ideologies associating masculinity with brute strength, and femininity with mysterious, "bewitching" magic. The reality of gender in relation to magic is, of course, more complex. In the real world, the practice of witchcraft (as Wicca) includes men and women alike. In fantasy media, a British context—where the legacy of the Arthurian legends and the wizard Merlin remains strong—produced SYM texts with young male magicians at their center, like the *Harry Potter* books and films (1997–2011) and the BBC television series *Merlin* (2008–2012).

In the United States, however, the witches who burst on the scene in the 1990s followed the lead of Sabrina in all being girls—a trend encouraged by the rise of girl power, a pop-culture form of feminism which, as a media trend, presented girls and women on screen in a wide assortment of heroic roles (Hains, 2012). Younger children enjoyed girl power-fueled witches in TV series like *Winx Club* and *That's So Raven*, parallel to older youth and young adult audiences receiving supernatural girl power stories from series like *Charmed* and *Buffy the Vampire Slayer*. This was a notable change after the decades in which teen girls, even as protagonists in teen-focused narratives, had their agency routinely contained, thwarted, or outweighed by patriarchal authority (Nash, 2006). But the 1990s' concept of girl power was strongly intertwined with normative feminity (Hains, 2012); and so, despite the feminist intent that Joss Whedon claimed informed his relatively progressive *Buffy* series, it too participated in this gender-coding: female Willow served as the series' main representative of witchcraft, while Oz, a boy, was the only major character who suffered from werewolfism.

This gender dichotomy was particularly clear in mainstream Hollywood productions, but less so in texts like the independent Canadian film *Ginger Snaps* (2000) and the international co-production *Blood and Chocolate* (2007), films about teen-girl werewolves. In later years of U.S. texts in the SYM genre, gender restrictions have somewhat loosened, allowing for female werewolves in the MTV series *Teen Wolf* (2011–2017) and the 2023 Paramount+ series *Wolf Pack*, while male witches and fairies abound in *Chilling Adventures of Sabrina* (2018–2020) and *Fate: The Winx Saga* (2021–2022). But problems remain in these texts' representations of gender and sexuality, as the authors whose chapters we feature in Part II of this volume demonstrate.

For example, in "Supernatural Savior or Sacrificial Lamb? The Contradictions and Cost of Young Supernatural Femininity: *Chilling Adventures of Sabrina* in a Post-Buffy Context" (Chapter 6), Lori Bindig Yousman highlights the contradictions of Sabrina's character, interrogating how the series simultaneously celebrates the empowerment (both magical and feminist) of its supernatural teen heroine while simultaneously depicting that very power as the cause of her demise, ultimately revealing the limitations of "girl power" and presenting a more cynical view of the relationship between power and femininity.

In "Youth at the Border: Finding the Monstrous-Feminine in Marvel Comics," Eric Kennedy (Chapter 7) uses Barbara Creed's concept of "the monstrous-feminine" to examine Marvel's portrayal of magically-gifted feminine characters as other, or less than, their male counterparts, while still offering fans an image of how the abject can be embraced and celebrated. The monstrous-feminine likewise informs Erika Thomas' "Saving Herself and Turning Rhetorical Tropes in Disney Films: Subverting the Monstrous Feminine in Supernatural Genre Conventions" (Chapter 8), an analysis of Disney's films *Encanto* (2021) and *Turning Red* (2022). Thomas concludes that these films are altering the features of the "monstrous-feminine" trope by subverting the monster/body horror conventions so that feminine bodies are hopeful, empowered, and inclusive. The final chapter in this section is Hope Russell's "A Zambian Fairytale: Shula And The Magic Of Rungano Nyoni's *I Am Not a Witch*" (Chapter 9). In contrast to Western representations of supernatural youth, as Russell argues, the film employs African narrative traditions to draw a distinction between the genuine magic of its child-heroine and the false conceptions of witchcraft in the oppressive, witch-hunting society she lives in. The chapters in this section reveal the SYM genre's varied efforts to prioritize the power of youthful femininity, even while some texts can perpetuate the very same repressive traditions they seemingly eschew.

Confronting Exclusions in Supernatural Identities

While girls, women, and femininity have been frequently represented as supernatural youth—an improvement over other genres that tend to marginalize female representations—SYM has not been as inclusive of other identities. In Part III of *Supernatural Youth Media*, our contributors confront the genre's exclusion or marginalization of various identities. An intersectional lens makes clear that omissions in the genre reveal underlying biases that, if challenged, would result in more inclusive, richer representations of youth-centric fantasy worlds.

The section begins with "Where Are All of the Black Kids?: A Contemporary Search for Black Youth in the Fantastic Worlds" (Chapter 10), in which Asha Winfield and her collaborators explore Black children's presence in contemporary fantasy media. Noting that Black youth are more often represented in science-fiction than in supernatural texts, the authors examine both genres, illustrating the legacy of historical stereotypes in current representations of Black youth. In Chapter 11, "Queering Teen Supernatural TV Dramas: Fandom's Impact on LGBTQ Youth," Victor Evans explores the representation of LGBTQ characters in supernatural television series, noting the tendency of such programs to marginalize or kill their gay characters. Evans demonstrates that LGBTQ viewers' passionate engagement with beloved characters and storylines have challenged these tropes, demanding that show-runners rethink their approach to LGBTQ representation. In "Welcome to the Witching Hour: *The Craft* as a Neuroqueer Allegory of Legibility" (Chapter 12), Desirée Rowe considers this iconic film's insistence on neurotypical, "legible" self-expression. Noting that the discourse of neuroqueerness celebrates diversity and deviations from an oppressive norm,

Rowe argues that *The Craft* instantiates a rigid and judgmental division between the right and wrong kinds of witch-behavior, celebrating the girl who matches dominant ideologies of morality and normalcy, while shunning as "insane" the one whose self-expression exceeds the boundaries of approved behavior.

As the chapters in this section make clear, SYM's ability to imagine alternate realities has allowed for its increasing celebration of traditionally marginalized identities—but not as equitably or as even-handedly as critics concerned with diversity might wish (a theme that also weaves its way through many of this book's other chapters, as well).

Conclusion

Taken together, the collected essays in this volume reveal consistent themes within SYM, placing young characters at a crossroads of identity formation, and embracing the Other—other realms, other beings, "the dark," the disturbing, and the odd—but with mixed results in championing true inclusivity, a struggle that has produced fluctuating and fascinating storylines in a historical moment characterized by increased attention to intersectionality and the rights of the oppressed.

Thirty years after SYM's emergence in the mid 1990s, the genre's second generation is expanding beyond the first generation's consistent and nearly exclusive focus on youth. Today's fantasy properties can also focus on adult characters, and target a mixed market of youth and adult viewers—as in Netflix's *The Witcher* (2019–), Amazon Prime's *Good Omens* (2019–) or the Disney+ series *Loki* (2021–2023). This might reflect the fact that the genre's original audience, who were tweens and teens in the 1990s, are now mature and drawn to age-appropriate stories in the genre they loved as youths. The sharp division between mysticism and science has also begun to blur in more recent years in such Netflix properties as *Raising Dion* (2019–2022), *Stranger Things* (2016–) and the family film *Jingle Jangle: A Christmas Journey* (2020), all of which include mystical elements in contexts of scientific discovery or technological innovation.

We find it noteworthy that in response to SYM's ongoing popularity, religious conservatives continue to engage in moral panics, condemning networks and streamers for such content—and we wish to highlight that the diversity of SYM, which several of this volume's contributors speak to, may exacerbate the way fundamentalist Christians target them in a 2020s political context. For example, Conservapedia's list of "Worst Liberal TV Shows" includes SYM texts from *Buffy* the Vampire Slayer to Hallmark's *Good Witch* (2015–2021) and WGN's *Salem* (2014–2017), citing such shows' alleged satanism and, in general, complaining about diverse representation, from race to gender identity (Conservapedia, n.d.). (The list, like other conservative outlets, also criticizes Amazon Prime's *Rings of Power* [2022–] for its Black and female representation, which it describes as "a woke utopia that cares only about race and sex, instead of what Tolkien and his son Christopher had set in stone" [n.p.]—inflammatory and problematic rhetoric.) In this vein, in January 2020, fundamentalist conservative group One Million Moms (1MM) petitioned Disney to cancel its tween SYM animated series *Owl House*, citing satanic influences; the organization's outrage increased in August of that year when the show's lead character, 14-year-old Luz Noceda, was revealed to be bisexual and in a romantic relationship with another supernatural teen girl character (Cole, 2020). (Given 1MM's relentless anti-LGBTQ advocacy, readers may be unsurprised to learn that the Southern Poverty Law Center has designated the group's parent organization, the Christian American Family Association, an anti-LGBTQ hate group (Castrodale, 2020).)

In response to these ongoing moral panics, some conservative-run networks and media-related services are newly on offer. These include a youth-oriented streamer from conservative outlet The Daily Wire meant to compete with Disney (Lovato, 2023a) and "Worth it or Woke," a conservative answer to review site Rotten Tomatoes (Lovato, 2023b). As technology evolves, so too do culture wars surrounding youth media, inclusive of the SYM genre. The politically charged desire among some conservatives to have separate media sources in which viewers can avoid, or be cautioned against media that disrupt a conservative Christian worldview, may be an important site for future scholarly inquiry—especially in relation to how such adult-driven conservative separatism may impact younger viewers. As generative artificial intelligence (AI) is now sophisticated enough to revolutionize the media industry by replacing human writers and actors—a major point of contentention in the highly publicized 2023 strikes of the Writer's Guild of America and the Screen Actors Guild—the impulse to hinder young people's access to inclusive, prosocial SYM content and replace it with "anti-woke" or "Christian" content could become more complex, indeed.

An observable difference between the first and second generations of SYM texts is the latter's expansion beyond the folkloric traditions of the British Isles, which dominated the genre in its early years. The traditions of other cultures and countries are evident in series like the Colombian *Siempre Bruja* (2019–2020), the Italian *Luna Nera* (2020), the Jordanian *Jinn* (2020), the Norwegian *Ragnarok* (2020–2023), and the Canadian *Trickster* (2020, based on Native American mythology). Cultural diversity has also become more apparent in American SYM texts, and is poised to grow further: The 2020 US Census found that less than half of the under-18 population identified as white (Frey, 2023), and analysts predict a "minority white" U.S population by 2044 (Colby & Ortman, 2015), at which time "no group will have a majority share of the total and the United States will become a 'plurality' of racial and ethnic groups" (p. 9). The United States' shifting demographics are changing who is on screen and behind the scenes in media at large, and therefore in SYM as well—which matters in both a U.S. and a global context, as U.S.-produced media are a major export. Moving forward, research that accounts for how these changes on and off screen inform one another, like that which the Geena Davis Institute on Gender and Media conducts in other areas (Geena Davis Institute, n.d.), could be insightful indeed.

At the same time, the decline of cable networks and the rise of streamers is increasing fragmentation in the media market, allowing for more niche-targeted entertainment, but also making content less accessible to some sectors of the population, since streamers each require separate monthly subscriptions. Future research might consider what the increasingly fragmented audience that originally gave SYM a leg up (new networks for youth) means for the genre in the future.

Overall, as *Supernatural Youth Media* as a whole suggests, the SYM genre has maintained remarkable staying power. Like many of its immortal or undead characters, the genre continuously resurrects and spreads its influence, while also reflecting and contributing to cultural hopes and anxieties on matters as diverse as youth, social change, inclusivity, and the unknown. As the genre continues to grow and evolve, and as new configurations emerge, scholars of media (and youths' roles in it) must ask how these texts engage with the cultural, technological, and economic contexts of their production and reception. The essays in this collection offer some examples of how such questions can be approached. We hope you'll feel inspired to contribute to this line of inquiry.

References

Aloi, P. (2020, October 28). *The Craft* inspired a generation of teenage witches. Now a sequel is poised to do the same. *Time*. https://time.com/5904701/the-craft-legacy-witches/.

Bauder, D. (2005, May 29). Fans take action over 'Joan' cancellation. *Associated Press News Service*. https://infoweb.newsbank.com/apps/news/document-view?p=AWNB&docref=news/1416D E71181B72A0

Bennett, N., Hays, D., & Sullivan, B. (2022, August 1). 2019 data show Baby Boomers nearly 9 times wealthier than millennials. *U.S. Census Bureau.* https://www.census.gov/library/stories/2022/08/wealth-inequality-by-household-type.html.

Berger, H. A., & Ezzy, D. (2007). *Teenage witches: Magical youth and the search for the self.* Rutgers University Press.

Boyd, R. S. (1994, May 9). Fear of technology phobia of the '90s/Is your VCR flashing 12:00?/Surveys say you're not alone. *Houston Chronicle,* p. 6. https://infoweb.newsbank.com/apps/news/document-view?p=AWNB&docref=news/0ED7B36503468DF4

Castrodale, J. (2020, December 18). Everything 'One Million Moms' wanted to call the manager about in 2020. *Vice.* https://www.vice.com/en/article/bvxdj5/everything-one-million-moms-got-mad-about-in-2020

Clark, L. S. (2003). *From angels to aliens: Teenagers, the media, and the supernatural.* Oxford University Press.

Cohen, R. (1986). History and genre. *New Literary History, 17*(2), 203–218.

Conservapedia. (n.d.). *Essay: Worst liberal TV shows.* https://www.conservapedia.com/Essay:Worst_Liberal_TV_Shows

Colby, S. L., & Ortman, J. M. (2015, March). Projections of the size and composition of the U.S. population: 2014 to 2060. *Census.gov.* https://www.census.gov/content/dam/Census/library/publications/2015/demo/p25-1143.pdf

Cole, M. (2020, August 19). "The Owl House" is worse than 1MM thought. *American Family Association.* https://www.afa.net/the-stand/culture/2020/08/the-owl-house-is-worse-than-1mm-thought/

Ellis, B. (2004). *Lucifer ascending: The occult in folklore and popular culture.* University Press of Kentucky.

Frey, W. H. (2023, August 1). New 2020 census data shows an aging America and wide racial gaps between generations. *Brookings.* https://www.brookings.edu/articles/new-2020-census-data-shows-an-aging-america-and-wide-racial-gaps-between-generations/

Foucault, Michel. (1972). *The archaeology of knowledge and the discourse on language.* Pantheon Books.

Geena Davis Institute. (n.d.). *Research informs and inspires: Key findings/executive summaries.* https://seejane.org/research-informs-empowers/

Geraghty, L., & Janovitch, M. (2008). *The shifting definitions of genre: Essays on labeling films, television shows and media.* McFarland.

Gilbert, J. (1986). *A cycle of outrage: America's reaction to the juvenile delinquent in the 1950s.* Oxford University Press.

Goode, E., & Ben-Yehuda, N. (1994). Moral panics: Culture, politics, and social construction. *Annual Review of Sociology, 20,* 149–171.

Gorelick, V. (2017). Sabrina the teenage witch: Introduction. In G. Gladir, F. Doyle, D. Malmgren, A. Hartley, & J. Edwards (Eds.), *Sabrina the teenage witch: Complete collection* (vol. 1). Archie Comics Publications.

Hains, R. C. (2012). *Growing up with girl power: Girlhood on screen and in everyday life.* Peter Lang.

Hains, R. C. (2014). *The princess problem: Guiding our girls through the princess-obsessed years.* Sourcebooks.

Herring, S. C. (2008). Questioning the generational divide: Technological exoticism and adult constructions of online youth identity. In D. Buckingham (Ed.), *Youth, identity, and digital media* (pp. 72–91). MIT Press. https://doi.org/10.1162/dmal.9780262524834.071.

Hoffower, H. (2022, January 23). Gen Z brought the '90s back because it feels impossible to grow up in today's economy. *Business Insider*. https://www.businessinsider.com/gen-z-nostalgia-y2k-indie-sleaze-old-money-economic-response-2022-1

Hutcheon, L. (2006). *A theory of adaptation*. Routledge.

Janisse, K., & Corupe, P. (Eds.). (2016). *Satanic panic: Pop-cultural paranoia in the 1980s*. FAB Press.

Kern, B. (Writer), & Kretchmer, J. T. (Director). (1998, October 14). I've Got You Under My Skin (Season 1, Episode 2) [TV series episode]. In B. Kern & C. M. Burge (Executive Producers), *Charmed*. Spelling Television.

Levy, S., Hafner, K. with Vistica, Gregory L., & Thomas, R. (1997, June 2). The day the world shuts down—Will power plants shut down and your phone go out? Will your social security checks disappear into cyberspace? Will your bank account vanish? *Newsweek, 129*(22), 52–54, 56–59. https://infoweb.newsbank.com/apps/news/document-view?p=AWNB&docref=news/0EC05F6A9B74979D

Lovato, M. (2023, Oct. 30). The Daily Wire's new streaming service aims to be the anti-Disney. *The Righting*. https://therighting.com/original/the-daily-wires-bentkey-aims-to-be-the-anti-disney/

Lovato, M. (2023, Dec. 11). New film review site wants to be the conservative Rotten Tomatoes. *The Righting*. https://therighting.com/original/worth-it-or-woke-wants-to-be-the-conservative-rotten-tomatoes/

Marvin, C. (2000). *When old technologies were new: Thinking about electric communication in the late nineteenth century*. Oxford.

Meyer, J. (2001, October). Census 200 brief: Age: 2000. *U.S. Census Bureau*. https://www2.census.gov/library/publications/decennial/2000/briefs/c2kbr01-12.pdf

Miller, C. (1984). Genre as social action. *Quarterly Journal of Speech, 70*(1984): 151–167.

Morton, L. P. (2002). Targeting generation Y. *Public Relations Quarterly, 47*(2):46–48.

Nash, I. (2006). *American sweethearts: Teenage girls in twentieth-century popular culture*. Indiana University Press.

One Million Moms. (n.d.). *Disney Channel's controversial Owl House canceled!* https://onemillionmoms.com/successes/disney-channel-s-controversial-series-the-owl-house-canceled/

Paul, P. (2001, September 1). Getting inside Gen Y. *Ad Age*. https://adage.com/article/american-demographics/inside-gen-y/43704

Puhvel, M. (1976). The mystery of the cross-roads. *Folklore, 87*(2): 167–177. https://www.jstor.org/stable/1260026

Quart, A. (2003). *Branded: The buying and selling of teenagers*. Basic Books.

Richardson, J. T., Best, J., & Bromley, D. G. (1991). *The satanism scare*. Aldine De Gruyter.

Rieder, J. (2010). On defining SF, or not: Genre theory, SF, and history. *Science Fiction Studies, 37*(2), 191–209.

Shary, T. (2014). *Generation multiplex: The image of youth in American cinema since 1980.* University of Texas Press.

Turner, V. (1987). Betwixt and between: The liminal period in rites of passage. In L. C. Mahdi, S. Foster, & M. Little (Eds.), *Betwixt and between: Patterns of masculine and feminine initiation* (pp. 3–19). Open Court.

Victor, J. S. (1993). *Satanic panic: The creation of a contemporary legend.* Open Court.

Wittgenstein, L. (1953). *Philosophical Investigations.* Macmillan.

Part I
Adaptation and Interpretation

2

Growing Up in A Winx: Reworking a Children's Text for a Teen Audience

KYRA HUNTING

When *Fate: The Winx Saga* (hereafter *Fate*) (2021–2022) first appeared on my Netflix home page, I did not immediately make the connection with *Winx Club* (2004–2009, 2011–2016, 2019), a colorful animated children's series my undergraduate students had mentioned. Deviating significantly from the *Winx Club*'s aesthetics, *Fate*'s trailer plays to two audiences: fans of *Winx Club* able to make the association based on the name alone, and fans of fantasy or supernatural media, such as *The Chilling Adventures of Sabrina*, whose associations with *Winx Club* may be negative or nonexistent.

While the exploitation of intellectual property (IP) across multiple media texts and platforms is a cornerstone of the American media industry, the adaptation of media developed for children into content for teens or adults—other than as parody—is a relatively nascent phenomenon. In the last few years, as conglomerates and streamers have scrambled to expand their libraries and maximize their IP (Roxborough, 2021), adaptations of children's texts for older audiences have emerged.

We have witnessed the power of childhood nostalgia and recognizability with successful PG-13 films and franchises based on *Teenage Mutant Ninja Turtles* and *Transformers*. These brands packaged themselves in the tried-and-true formula of superhero and action films, featuring characters whose powers stem from science-fiction sources. Rated PG-13 for violence but marketed to families with older children, their franchises boasted pre-existing comic book series targeting older demographics.

More recently, television series for teens and adults based on children's media properties emerged—including some focused on the supernatural. These appear to have been kicked off with *Riverdale* (TV-14, 2017–2023) on the CW, followed by *Titans* (TV-MA, 2018–2023) on DC Universe and HBO Max, and the *Chilling Adventures of Sabrina* (TV-14, 2018–2020) on Netflix. While their previous screen iterations were for children, each series—like the films—belonged to transmedia franchises whose comic book authors had already reworked characters and worlds to tell darker supernatural stories.

Fate, on the other hand, was making a more significant leap: It was TV-MA, not TV-14, making it firmly for older teens and adults. Furthermore, the Winx franchise had no previous offerings targeting older audiences with darker content and themes. In addition to the child-oriented Winx Club series, the franchise had featured three films and two television spin-offs: *PopPixie* (2011), targeted at 4- to 6-year-olds (Getzler, 2011); and *Winx Club WOW: World of Winx* (2016–2017), a sequel distributed on Netflix. Comics, books, and video game also accompanied the series; all featuring supernatural teen girls, fairies and stories appropriate for elementary aged children.

Unlike these spin-offs, *Fate* does not continue the original *Winx Club*: it functions more as a reboot. It shares many of the same main characters—fairies Bloom, Stella, Muse, Aisha and in the second season Flora—while adding an additional fairy to the main group, Terra, and several new adult or male characters. In *Winx Club*, Bloom discovers she is a fairy when she encounters Stella—a light fairy who had come over from her own dimension—and is snuck by Stella into a magic school called Alfea. There she befriends five other fairies, whose magic aligns with a different element of nature, falls in love with a prince named Sky, and, with her friends, battles a stream of villains that threaten their world; frequently a group of teen witches named the Trix. In *Fate*, Bloom is found by Alfea's head mistress and brought to Alfea to learn how to use her magic. As in *Winx Club*, Bloom befriends her suite mates, whose powers largely mirror those in *Winx Club*, and ultimately falls in love with Sky; but instead of navigating schemes with the Trix, they are threatened by powerful creatures called the Burned Ones, whose scratch infects and slowly kills their victims. They are embroiled in a sweeping mystery involving a long past massacre, their teachers, and the fate of Solaria, where Alfea is located. In both series Bloom and her friends are sixteen, but these are—as will be discussed later—two very different sixteens. *Winx Club* has an aspirational depiction of high school role models addressed to children, whereas in *Fate*, the characters are messy, boundary-pushing, conflicted teens, typical of teen drams targeting adolescents.

Like all adaptations or reboots of popular series, questions of fidelity and arguments about comparative quality abound in the audience response to *Fate*. In the majority of texts studied in research on age-shifting adaptations, adult or family franchises are made more accessible for children—an adaptive formulation where significant changes are presumed necessary. In contrast, *Fate* reworks a children's text for a teen or adult audience that, it is presumed, may remember the original.

This chapter explores the challenges that emerge when an adaptation shifts both the core audience demographics and genre of the original text. First, I conceptualize *Fate* through the lens of "media multiplicities" (Klein & Palmer, 2016). *Fate* can be understood, I argue, not only in relationship to its source text *Winx* but also through its relationship to multiple genres including supernatural/fantasy teen dramas. Then I unpack nostalgia's role in age-shifting adaptations and how it shapes and limits the way many *Winx Club* fans responded to *Fate*. Finally, I provide a close analysis of how *Fate* reworks elements of *Winx Club* to respond to the expectations and needs of its new target audience's demographics and its expanded genre influences. I pay particular attention to how *Fate's* approach to the series' coming-of-age narratives impacts gender representation across the two adaptations and their relationship to power.

Fate is an important case study for unpacking the specific challenges of this type of adaptation. It prompts us to look at how the original text's transformation evolved as part of a nexus of influences, including the original intellectual property, genre, and Netflix's teen supernatural/fantasy mystery cycle. Looking at *Fate* as a product of these varied and often conflicting influences allows us to further understand the critical and fan reaction to the series, as well as how this array of constitutive factors shape *Fate* and its departures from *Winx Club*—particularly it constructions of gender and adolescence. This case study demonstrates how nostalgic relationships to *Winx Club* prompted some viewers to expect the original's bright colors, easy magic, and simple morality, while *Fate* instead focused on moral ambiguity, the impact of trauma, and struggles with power's nature. While it was not long-running (cancelled after two seasons), *Fate* is nonetheless an important site of critical analysis: It laid bare the complications that competing norms and demands create when bringing intellectual property into new genres and channel brands and the particular difficulties present in reworking texts designed for children into texts for adults.

Many Media Multiplicities

Fate could potentially be classified as a reboot or an adaptation, albeit a reboot with a different audience and an adaptation within the same medium. But notably, early press coverage of the series eschews this language, describing the series as "inspired by" (Jackson, 2021 ; Petski, 2019) or a "reimagining of" (Ray, 2021) *Winx Club*. The relationship of *Fate* to *Winx Club* is indeed relatively loose, with substantial changes. Critics and audiences varied significantly in how they approached the relationship between the texts. Many fans appeared to expect a "faithful" adaptation of the original series, while other commentators and press coverage accepted a more minimal connection to *Winx Club* and referred to other influences, like the production team, as well. Rather than trying to pin down a stable relationship between the two Winx series, a richer understanding of *Fate* can be achieved by drawing on Amanda Ann Klein and R. Barton Palmer's (2016) notion of media multiplicities. Considering media multiplicities allows us to consider how Netflix's teen series reworks "existing materials, themes, [and] images" (p. 1) to make the Winx brand, developed by Rainbow S.p.A., effective for a young adult audience. It also introduces the concept of "volatilization" arguing that "the volatilization of the original object emerges as an essential element of film's and television's modes of production and exhibition" and that "the essence of the institution, and not just the text, is thus this carefully calculated instability" (Klein and Barton, p. 8). *Fate* exemplifies both instability and multiplicity, which can produce distinctive challenges in texts for children where a sense of stability may be part of the affective experience. Simultaneously, as adolescents and adults try to work through the complexity of feelings and uncertainties in their own lives, instability may offer its own appeal.

Looking at *Fate* as the nexus of a set of multiplicities enriches our understanding of the two texts' relationship and the unique challenges of reworking a children's text or brand for an older audience. In addition to being part of the Winx franchise, *Fate* is a teen drama, part of a cycle of teen mystery series, and a Netflix original series. This positions *Fate* within a history that associates teen television with mystery, crime, and turmoil. Prior to teen television, *Nancy Drew*'s success associated the teen girl with mysteries (Marghitu, 2021, p. 24). Later, series like *Beverly Hills 90210*, *My So-Called Life*, and *Freaks and Geeks* established the teen drama as a space to explore the dangers and emotional turmoil of coming-of-age; and *Buffy the Vampire Slayer* and *Charmed* connected coming-of-age's perils to the supernatural (Clark, 2003, p. 3).

Fate is situated within this network of influences. Its ostensible source text, genre, target demographic, and streaming brand all shape how *Fate* reworks *Winx Club* elements. To unpack this adaptation's complex set of influences, assumptions and responses, I performed a close reading of *Winx Club* and *Fate* and systematically reviewed coverage of *Fate* in television trade press (e.g. *Kidscreen* and *Variety*) and popular press (e.g. *The Guardian* and *Cosmopolitan*). I also reviewed selected coverage of the original *Winx Club*'s release and production history to contextualize the expectations placed on *Fate* by fans and critics familiar with the series.

Even the "origin" text, *Winx Club*, underwent a transformation when first consumed by fans in the United Kingdom and North America. An Italian animated children's series created by Iginio Straffi and produced by Rainbow S.p.A, the series became a global success, broadcast in 150 countries (Sigismondi, 2015, p. 280). In the United States, it originally aired on Fox followed by Nickelodeon, which co-produced later episodes. *Winx Club*'s global success and U.S. presence was unusual for Italian animation, which Elena Di Giovanni (2014) partially attributes to the "neutralization of culture specific elements" in the series (p. 225). She observes that while traces of the Italian origins persevere, the series' translation into English changed the original series, with some of the dialogue's nuance and humor being lost (p. 229). This transformation, as well as its hybrid, globally influenced aesthetic particularly shaped by Japanese animation (Radulovic, 2021), served an industry purpose, facilitating global distribution and economic success.

Winx Club also had a complicated relationship with demographic targeting. Originally targeting a child audience of 4- to 14-year-old girls (Bean, 2021), later seasons of the series and *Pop Pixie* targeted a younger audience, ages 4 to 8 (Dickson, 2016), and ran on Nick Jr. rather than Nickelodeon (Radulovic, 2021). This shift was not always well received, with some fans criticizing *Winx Club*'s later seasons as "shells" of their former selves (Anders, 2016).

The conflict between target demographics' needs and established fans stems from competing brand goals. Franchised television series like Winx function as "brands designed to encourage audience loyalty and engagement with the text" (Johnson, 2012, p. 1). The brand's personality and contours, as a result, need to be maintained and adapted simultaneously to new audience contexts and the needs of the channel brands that host the series. This is particularly thorny for long-running international children's programming, which has to maintain the brand while replacing constantly-aging-out audiences, and adapting to the shifting international platforms that distribute the series. Indeed, *Winx Club* might have aired on pre-school channel Nick Jr. in the United States while airing on a children's television block or older-skewing Cartoon Network in a different country.

These tensions can be seen in Netflix's first foray into the Winx Franchise, *Winx Club WOW: World of Winx*. Netflix launched *Winx Club WOW* in 2016, moving the main characters of *Winx Club* from a magical school called Alfea in a city called Magix to Earth, where they embark on an undercover mission to protect humans from a villain called the Talent Thief. Precipitated by the success of *Winx Club*'s Netflix distribution and Netflix's attempts to expand its library of original kids' shows, the series was "re-conceptualized for a digital audience, meaning more serialization and a target age slightly older (eight to 12)" (Dickson, 2016). Cristiana Buzelli, Vice President of content for Rainbow, said that "serializing the concept for binge-watching and making a show that would please longtime fans of the brand, as well as attract a new audience" were their primary challenges in ensuring "the story meets [Netflix's] requirements for content consumption" (Dickson, 2016).

Buzelli is explicit about Netflix's role in shaping *World of Winx*. In contrast, most coverage of *Fate* privilege its relationship to *Winx Club* or, to a lesser extent, series showrunner Brian Young and star Abigail Cowen, who plays lead fairy Bloom (Jones, 2020). But industrial norms offer an important lens to understand *Fate*. *Fate*'s media multiplicity applies to its relationships with the Winx franchise; the teen drama genre; teen dramas that adapt child-associated content; and—notably—a very specific cycle of Netflix original teen dramas drawing together supernatural and mystery elements. Press coverage of *Fate* regularly and explicitly evokes Brian Young's role as creator and show runner and his history as a writer of CW teen drama *The Vampire Diaries*. In interviews, Young's discussion of the show firmly roots it in the Young Adult (YA) genre and makes the teen drama frame paramount. In an interview about season two, Young explains, "it's kind of an embarrassment of riches just in terms of the amount of mythology that the original source material has. So, for us, it's really about trying to figure out what part of that fits into a YA world that's not necessarily a kid's world . . . .and how we can take some of their mythology and really twist it in an interesting way" (Weintraub, 2022). The connection to Young's other work and *The Vampire Diaries* roots *Fate* in a specific supernatural/fantasy teen drama tradition with specific norms, including alienation from adults, struggles with identity, burdens of global consequence, transgressing social expectations, and the coming-of-age narrative. Many of these attributes can also be understood not just through the lens of the show runner and the genre but the expectations of the distributor, Netflix.

While *Fate* and *The Vampire Diaries* are both supernatural teen dramas, *Fate* can be understood through an even more narrow frame of the supernatural teen mystery as a cycle of programs on Netflix. Similar to the teen crime drama, the supernatural teen mystery's central conflict is uncovering a supernatural perpetrator of violence or destruction that poses an existential threat. As put into practice by "Netflix originals," the supernatural teen drama is often also a boarding school or college drama, as well. I argue that a cycle of programs in this genre began on Netflix with the release of the *Chilling Adventures of Sabrina* in late 2018. Ostensibly a spin-off of the CW's *Riverdale*, *Chilling Adventures of Sabrina* is about a teenage girl who is half-witch and half-mortal. After reaching her 16th birthday, Sabrina finds herself thrust into new challenges due to her burgeoning powers and attends The Academy of Unseen Arts. At this school, she becomes embroiled in a number of magical community conflicts, including the political machinations of Hell.

Both *Fate* and *Winx Club* share parallels with Sabrina, as Bloom discovers her powers at 16 and goes to the boarding school Alfea where she becomes a key player in power struggles between different supernatural groups. However, unlike *Winx Club*, *Fate* shares aesthetic similarities with *Chilling Adventures*, including a darker color palette, a reliance on forest scenes, and a gothic-influenced look. The series are further tied together by the selection of Abigail Cowen, who plays a supporting character in *Chilling Adventures of Sabrina*, to star as Bloom in *Fate*. Other Netflix original series that belong to this cycle include *The Order* (2019 –2020), about a college student who joins a secret society that teaches magic; *Wednesday* (2022-), a spin-off of the *Addams Family* in which Wednesday is sent to Nevermore Academy where she catches a murderer; and arguably *Shadow and Bone*, (2021 –2023) which is not set at a school but still features a powerful young woman whose supernatural powers place her at the center of a war. All these series share with *Fate* key aesthetic and narrative features. Understanding *Fate* as not only an extension of the Winx franchise but as part of this cycle can help scholars and critics better understand its situation within a complex network of media multiplicities. This understanding also helps explain *Fate*'s apparent success on Netflix, with 57 million viewers in the first month (Romano, 2021)—despite negative responses from many *Winx* fans.

Nostalgia's Role in Reception

Press coverage reveals conflicting intentions and expectations for the series. Iginio Straffi constructs the imagined audience for *Fate* as a *Winx Club* audience, saying "after 10 years, I could see that there were new fans and old fans ... and social media was showing us this kind of loyalty. I thought for older fans, who were grown up, we should produce some live-action" (Radulovic, 2021). For Straffi, *Fate* is a culmination of older fans' long-held desire to see the original in a live-action form. In contrast, showrunner Brian Young describes the original as a "rough framework," and is clear about the need to fit *Fate* into a teen drama paradigm, framing the original audience as less central. Young explains, "the fans of *Winx* are super important to us and are key to our success," but also notes that having an entry point for audiences who had never heard of the cartoon was important. He notes, "the big picture thing is how can we take this really great core idea and how can we broaden it out for a wider audience?" (Weintraub, 2022). Both the franchise creator and its showrunner acknowledge Netflix's significant role in shaping the series. Straffi explicitly expressed some regret that Rainbow had limited involvement, and it is probable that Netflix, like Young, targeted an audience much larger than the fan base of the original.

However, many viewers' published responses to the series, both positive and negative, presume that *Fate*'s value intrinsically links to its relationship to *The Winx Club*. A review entitled "I Love My Little Fairy Show," connected the author's viewing of *Fate* to her childhood Saturdays watching *Winx Club* with her sister. While she acknowledges the differences in the two series—describing *Fate*'s aesthetic as autumnal, the series' stance on morality as "gray," and noting that it is, in general, "horny"—she still understands it through the lens of children's viewing. She defends it by noting, "I will never be too old for a little bit of pretending" (Vujić, 2022). In most cases, however, *Winx Club* fans compare *Fate* unfavorably to the original. The Harvard Crimson published a review by a fan of the original with the headline, "*Fate: The Winx Saga* Doesn't Know Why Anyone Liked '*Winx Club*'" (Healy, 2021). Another *Winx Club* fan complained, "the people who grew up watching *Winx Club* wanted a true-to-the-source remake .... I wanted bright colors, the Trix causing mayhem, and pretty fairy transformations complete with shimmering wings" (Stubbs, 2022). Professional reviewers also noted concerns about a presumed conflict between changing the original, described by one reviewer as "a psychedelic Lisa Frank cartoon came to giggling life," in favor of the aesthetics and tropes of teen franchises, compromising the series' fit with viewers (Framke, 2021).

Scholars argue against making fidelity central in the evaluation of adaptation, noting that such judgments are "dogged by value judgments" (Whelehan, 1991, p. 9), but it is valuable to look at expectations around fidelity and how they impact adaptive texts. It is notable that *Transformers* reviews didn't lament the lack of primary colors. This suggests that external factors baked into the experience of viewing the original, like expectations around gender, play a role in *Fate's* reception. Sparkling primary colors have not been a key feature of teen dramas since before *Pretty Little Liars* (2010 –2017) and *The Vampire Diaries* (2009 –2017) topped the teen charts. Yet it is a staple of girls' cartoons, including *Winx's* inspiration *Sailor Moon* (1992 –1997) (Rodulovic, 2021) its contemporary, *Totally Spies* (2001 –2008, 2013 –2014), and the recent *She-Ra and the Princesses of Power* (2018 –2020). In the discourse I examined, fans' responses to *Fate* did not seem to understand the series through norms for teen dramas. Instead, they expected the features of programs geared toward children present in the original to be extrapolated to the teen drama adaptation; nostalgia impacting their acceptance of the new text.

Colleen Kennedy-Karpat (2020) argues that nostalgia and adaptation are often closely interlinked—and that in remakes, which we may consider *Fate*, "nostalgia figures prominently in reception" and can increase negative reactions among viewers (p. 287). She argues that we must consider whose nostalgia is being privileged and what they are nostalgic for. In many cases, she links nostalgic policing to misogyny and racism, as in the negative response to the *Ghostbusters* remake. However, when considering the remaking of a children's program into a teen or young adult program, I argue nostalgia is also a crucial factor in the response to a remake. In this case, the nostalgia is entangled instead with the remembered experience of girlhood. Kennedy-Karpat notes that we can consider adaptations through the lens of the nostalgic text, and Tannock describes nostalgia texts as providing "a relief from or a resource for confronting the sources of the anxieties, fears, and frustrations" (1995, p. 459) heightened, I believe, when the nostalgia is tied into childhood. In the Winx fans' response to *Fate*, we can see how the series may fail, at least for some viewers, as a nostalgic text. Instead of offering a return to the experience of *Winx Club*, and its particular version of girlhood, its use of teen drama tropes and norms focuses *Fate* on the complexity and discomfort of coming-of-age, resisting the possibility of a return to the simplicity of childhood.

From Colorful Play to Embracing the Gray

Before exploring genre-related changes from the original *Winx Club*, it is worth noting that one of *Winx Club* fans' most persistent critiques concerned the whitewashing of *Fate*'s original characters. Commentators decried the decision to cast a white-coded[1] actress to play Musa, who was purportedly based on Lucy Liu, and the creation of a new character Terra, played by a white actress, to represent earth magic instead of including Flora, from the original, who was coded Latina (Oladele, 2021). While the showrunner claimed that adding Flora in the second season was always part of the plan (Weintraub, 2022), in *Fate*'s first season only one of the three non-white characters from *Winx Club* was not replaced or whitewashed: Aisha, a Black water fairy played by Precious Mustapha. The series' problems with racial representation were compounded by having Aisha go against the group in the first season (although she is ultimately correct), which set her apart and made her storylines revolve around other characters rather than her personal growth. In this case, the objection to a lack of fidelity by fans and viewers is not only driven by nostalgia or a commitment to accuracy but is also fundamentally political. In this case, the critique is about both the loss of the perceived diversity in the original text, which was praised for being unusually diverse for its time, and the larger phenomenon of whitewashing characters in Hollywood media adaptations.

But, in other instances, the changes viewers and fans critiqued can be seen as improving other aspects of representation, particularly gender representation. In these cases, an allegiance to how the series originally dealt with these characters and stories can be understood as intersecting with nostalgia's role in adaptations' reception. Among commentators who compared *Fate* unfavorably to *Winx Club*, a common complaint is that the fashion in *Fate* didn't measure up to the original. Unquestionably, style and clothing were a central feature of *Winx Club*. Straffi hired fashion designers to design the *Winx Club* characters' clothes. But the outfits in *Winx Club* relied heavily on crop tops and miniskirts, often together—problematic in a cartoon, and potentially so provocative on live-action actresses that it could have been a source of valid critique about characters' sexualization. Instead, *Fate* puts their cast in casual layers suitable for the school's apparent forest setting, frequently from accessible brands like ASOS or Zara.

Stella's costuming is the exception. As Stella is the only princess in *Fate*, her wardrobe at times features designer clothing. (A notable shift from the original, where every Winx Club member is a princess and Bloom's love interest, Sky, is a prince.) While *Winx Club* was framed by both creators and fans as distinctive for being a girls' action cartoon (Radulovic, 2021), *Winx Club* was also a princess show, with the girls' status legitimized by their Princess designations. Even as *Winx Club* differentiated itself through action, it was simultaneously framed by the "safe" space of the princess genre, a staple of children's programming marketed at girls that connotes desirability, femininity and unthreatening power. It's notable that other attempts to create action-based girls' series continue to rely on this trope, such as *She-Ra Princesses of Power* or *Star Vs. The Forces of Evil*. In *Winx Club*, even Bloom—who in both series is raised on Earth with no knowledge of her fairy origins—is revealed to be a princess. *Fate* shifts this by including girls from a wider variety of backgrounds: some from well-off families, others orphans, and one the child of a teacher at the school. *Fate rejects* the heavily-gendered trope of Princess, giving skill and magical power the more central role. This reflects not only the stronger association of Princess Culture with younger girls over adolescents, but also critiques of Princess Culture in the intervening years (see Orenstein, 2011; Hains, 2014).

The desire for a modern teen supernatural drama to make colorful, glittery, scantily clad girls in wings their heroines can be partially understood as nostalgia, particularly from viewers who praised the original's action heroines as progressive. Why would it be preferable for the Netflix series to "embrace its cheesy, colorful, and fun origins" instead of "looking like another Riverdale or Sabrina" (Larson, 2021)? This critique's persistence suggests a resistance to losing the cheerful appearance of the *Winx Club* world that softened its more dramatic plots and battles to make it comfortable for children. Similarly, a strong gendered critique can be made about the increase in conflict between the main characters in *Fate*, who struggle with one another over conflicting needs, jealousies, and beliefs. The persistent preference for the instant, easy, and conflict-free friendship in *Winx Club* can also be interpreted as a preference for comfort. Both children's and teen media seek to meet their audience's needs. For children, depicting strong, stable friendship bonds with easily resolved conflict meets their need. Teen dramas meet a different need: the need to cope with the complexity of friendships, particularly when teen's maturing goals and value-systems may produce harder-to-overcome conflict. Teen dramas often depict less easy friendships, instead offering friendships built over time and struggle. Some commentators dismissed this possibility, describing the conflict between the girls in *Fate* as a simplistic teen trope while characterizing *Winx Club's* approach to friendship as distinctive—rather than recognizing that it, too, is a function of genre.

Fate also changes the fundamental gender dynamics of *Winx Club*. In *Winx Club*, the fairy school, Alfea, is situated in a city called Magix that is also home to two other schools: the Red Fountain School, housing Specialists, and the Cloud Tower School for Witches. In *Winx Club*, users of magic—both fairies and witches—are exclusively female, while "Specialists," soldiers skilled at using weapons, are male. *Fate* includes only one school, Alfea, where Specialists and fairies both live and learn, and incorporates both male fairies and female Specialists. *Fate* also constructs a formal relationship between fairies and Specialists, creating scenarios in which their skills must be paired to succeed in battle. It also introduces enemies, like the eventual introduction of Blood Witches, where one group is more vulnerable than the other. This creates scenarios that are significant to the series' gender politics—for example, depicting female specialists engaging in physical battle, and linking male fairies' skillsets to traditionally female roles, like nurturing people and plants.

One *Winx Club* element whose absence fans lament is the series' primary antagonists, three young witches called the Trix, whose quest for power and status placed them in regular conflict with the Winx members. The Trix were Winx's mirror images: teens, flirtatious, both the most powerful of their kind and at times doing the bidding of adults—and styled in a goth look that contrasted with the Winx's bright pop aesthetic. Their presence made the *Winx Club* fundamentally a series of conflicts between girls who were different from each other.

While *Fate* does feature conflict between women, including among friends, it eschews an ongoing fight between competing groups of young women as its primary fulcrum. *Fate*'s greatest threats are creatures, lethal zombie-like "Burned Ones" and wormlike scrapers that feed on fairy magic; and adults who will go to any length to achieve what they believe is justice or necessary to protect their own people. Instead of a struggle with malicious girls in pursuit of being the most powerful, the central narrative of *Fate* is about the damage done by war and vengeance. Indeed, even the Burned Ones are revealed to originally be soldiers from a long-ago war. *Fate* nods to the Trix with a frequent enemy, sometimes friend, of the Winx Club, Beatrix. Beatrix causes harm and creates obstacles throughout the series, but she is manipulated by adults, just as Bloom is while searching for answers about her own past, and ultimately chooses to do the right thing for Alfea.

Both series share a focus on the discovery of one's true identity and past and feature a main character, Bloom, whose access to a unique power makes her others' target. But these elements take on a more central and extensive role in *Fate*, and they are shared with other series in the supernatural teen mystery Netflix cycle. Beyond its colorful cartoon aesthetic, *Winx Club* aligns very closely to children's cartoons' attributes, particularly ensemble series. It focuses on literal empowerment, a key feature of Nickelodeon series (Banet Weiser, 2007), giving its main characters extraordinary magical powers. It frames adults as good but essentially hapless, and incorporates features from both popular girls' cartoon series, including a focus on belonging to a nurturing group (Seiter, 1995), and boys' series, including transformations in battle (Hendershot, 1998). *Fate* altered or limited many of these attributes, instead incorporating teen drama elements, like untrustworthy and manipulative adults and a complex relationship to morality. It also incorporated elements of teen supernatural dramas, such as a troubled relationship to power, and specifically the supernatural teen mystery Netflix cycle, in which these attributes combine to create an unfolding narrative where the heroine(s) must discover withheld information to triumph. In the remaining portion of this section, I will explore how *Fate* employs this generic shift from *Winx Club* to explore both relationships and power, the center of both series, as fundamentally troubled and ambivalent things.

Many of *Fate*'s changes from *Winx Club* can be seen as aligning with a consistent teen drama concern about how to adapt to conflicting feelings about adults (who may be at once nurturing and betraying); moral ambiguity around difficult choices; and ambivalence about independence and power that are the source of both desire and fear. Beatrix, introduced as an antagonist for *Fate*'s heroines, becomes an exemplar of this: hedonistic, regularly drinking and smoking with Riven, a cruel specialist, and embroiling a new student, Dane, in both her schemes and love life. She undeniably causes extensive harm, even committing murder. But, unlike the Trix, she is also following the directives of a father who raised her in isolation and a woman whom she has been taught is not only morally right but able to give her answers about her past. This same motivation ultimately leads Bloom to do what Beatrix was attempting and release Rosalind, the ultimate antagonist of the first season. Similarly, while Rosalind—Alfea's former headmaster who commits murder to regain control—is brutal, cruel, and willing to harm people in pursuit of a greater good, she does, ultimately, believe that she is protecting her people. Similarly, the decisions made by good characters, like the original headmistress, to withhold information to protect the students inadvertently places them at more at risk. This construction of adults as potentially untrustworthy and harmful, even when well-meaning, is a staple of teen dramas and is woven throughout the series. Understanding adults as fundamentally flawed, even when loving and good, is part of the coming-of-age story of many teen media texts and is a representation of the greater growth of a character's knowledge about the world. For *Fate*, growing supernatural power is linked to greater knowledge about the complexity of the world, while in *Winx Club* power is a skill that grows with practice.

This intersects with the teen drama's reliance on the coming-of-age narrative as a central theme (Marghitu, 2021). While *Winx Club*'s creator also described the series as a coming-of-age story (Radulovic, 2021), this refers more to the characters simply growing up, rather than the fundamental struggle over identity, power, and morality that is more common to teen dramas' use of the coming-of-age narrative. In *Winx Club*, Bloom's magic comes easily when she encounters Stella in a battle with a minion from the Trix and tries to help, accidentally activating her powers. In *Fate*, Bloom's magic is intrinsically associated with trauma. She is unaware of what is happening to her when she discovers her magic and, in a rage, accidentally sets her house on fire, badly hurting her mother. As a result, she struggles with her magic from the beginning. Other fairies also have complicated relationships to their magic in *Fate*. Stella's mother's approach to teaching her magic pushed Stella until she lost control of her magic, blinding her best friend. Musa is a mind fairy, an empath, in *Fate*, as opposed to a music fairy in *Winx Club*, so her magic forces her to experience everyone else's emotions, even feeling what her mother felt as she died. This results in Musa having a deeply ambivalent relationship to her magic, which causes her suffering. For *Fate* coming-of-age is deeply connected with coming into power, particularly magical power. While *Winx Club* depicts this as relatively easy with challenge and conflict coming from the outside, *Fate* depicts both personal growth and magical power as potentially painful and difficult as well as rewarding.

A similar dynamic can be seen in the series' relatively simple depiction of the friendship group in the series: In *Winx Club*, Bloom quickly becomes a *de facto* leader with little resistance, and she typically shrugs off Tecna's and Stella's occasional awkward or hurtful comments . Some *Winx Club* fans critique the main characters' conflicts in *Fate*, noting they miss what felt like a positive and supportive friend group. However, depicting friendships as forming over time and overcoming conflict to eventually become secure and supportive is more suitable to the context of teen dramas. In many cases, the conflicts stem from trauma, such as Musa avoiding Terra because of her inability to avoid the intensity of Terra's feelings. Dealing with discomfort, fear of vulnerability, and conflicting values and needs is part of a larger coming-of-age arc and, like coming into their magic, is depicted as worthwhile; necessary but difficult.

Ultimately, this is the message of *Fate*. Unlike *Winx Club*, the series is very explicit about the use of magic being linked to emotion. The original headmistress at Alfea, Ms. Dowling, teaches her students that focusing on positive emotions, even in difficult situations, is the key to using magic effectively. Her successor Rosalind, who killed Ms. Dowling to get control of the school, teaches that real power comes from negative emotions. In the second season, Ms. Dowling's spirit returns to tell the Winx girls that accessing both types of emotions is, in fact, what will allow them to access their full power. Indeed, this technique allows them to finally transform, gaining their fairy wings. Like their friendships, the fairy wings have to be earned, rather than simply appear, as in *Winx Club*, and required the acceptance of messiness and internal conflict. While *Winx Club* seems to represent the nostalgic memory of childhood fun and adventure for many viewers, its reinterpretation by *Fate* argues that discomfort is a necessary part of coming-of-age and coming into power—supernatural or otherwise.

Conclusion

Sitting at the intersection of several industrial and genre factors, *Fate* is an interesting case study, with implications that extend beyond studies of supernatural youth media. The reworking of *Winx Club* into *Fate* demonstrates both the potential and perils of trying to rework a children's media text for an older audience. While some frame *Fate* in a simple bilateral relationship with the series that originated the Winx franchise, *Winx Club*, understanding the role that genre and context, in this case the role of Netflix, is essential to understand the influences on both the final text and its reception. Yet, many commentators who were fans of the original series failed to acknowledge how *Fate* might also be understood as a teen drama, except to dismiss it, instead of just an extension of *Winx Club*, including critiques that suggest the desire for cartoon elements in a dark supernatural/fantasy series. The cartoon functioned in a different genre context—fitting into magical girl/female lead action cartoons and weaving in elements of science fiction ranging from technology and space travel. This facilitated a cheerful and playful aesthetic and a narrative driven by external conflict. Conversely, *Fate* aligned more closely with the supernatural mystery version of teen dramas that had become popular on Netflix, restricting itself to a specific lore built on magic and supernatural creatures. Like similar series in the genre, *Fate* rests itself more on questions of morality and personal growth and the discovery of darkness in the surrounding world and the adults that are meant to be relied on.

Fans' critical response to the series can be understood, partially, through the lens of nostalgia's role in adaptation and remakes, an impulse that can limit the understanding of a text. The case study of *Fate* demonstrates the challenges posed in remaking a children's text for an older audience and the necessity of examining these texts as examples of media multiplicities whose genre and industrial context mediate the original text's reworkings. Examining *Fate* using this lens opens up new ways of understanding the text's narrative focus and the competing goals of producers, audiences and genre. In the case of *Fate*'s adaptation, we can see that shifting from one genre to another—from a children's animated series to live-action young adult fantasy—powerfully impacted how the text approaches key themes like power, coming-of-age and friendship. The tensions between genres, producers, and different target audiences also allow us to examine specific textual choices through multiple lenses to understand how they may simultaneously disappoint and fulfill key goals. This can provide a model for approaching future remakes and adaptations that cross genres and target demographics.

Note

1 I have described the actress who plays Muse, Elisha Applebaum, as white-coded here rather than white because some venues have reported that she is, or may be, part Singaporean and predominantly Jewish, and I was unable to verify or deny this claim at the time of this writing. However, she is clearly and consistently read as white and so I have used this phrase to assure I am being accurate.

References

Anders, E. (2016, November). Winx club: World o Wix is finally here. *BSCKids,* https://www.bsckids.com/2016/11/winx-club-world-of-winx-review/

Banet-Weiser, S. (2007). *Kids rule! Nickelodeon and consumer citizenship.* Duke University Press. https://doi.org/10.1215/9780822390299.

Bean, T. (2021, January 23). This new teen fantasy just replaced 'Bridgerton' as the most-watched show on Netflix. *Forbes.* https://www.forbes.com/sites/travisbean/2021/01/23/this-new-teen-fantasy-just-replaced-bridgerton-as-the-most-watched-show-on-netflix/?sh=4d49df7ce0cc

Clark, L. S. (2003). *From angels to aliens: Teenagers, the media, and the supernatural.* Oxford University Press.

Dickson, J. (2016, January 24). Winx Club wows Netflix. *Kidscreen.* https://kidscreen.com/2016/01/24/winx-club-wows-netflix/.

Di Giovanni, E. (2014). The Winx as a challenge to globalization. In F. Zanettin (Ed.), *Comics in translation* (pp. 220–236). Routledge. https://doi.org/10.4324/9781315759685.

Framke, C. (2021, January 22). Netflix's 'Fate: The Winx Saga' stretches fanfic tropes past their limits: TV review. *Variety.* https://variety.com/2021/tv/reviews/fate-the-winx-saga-netflix-review-1234889555/

Getzler, W. (2011, April 12). Nickelodeon plucks PopPixie. *Kidscreen.* https://kidscreen.com/2011/04/12/nickelodeon-plucks-poppixie/

Hains, R. (2014). *The princess problem: Guiding our girls through the princess-obsessed years.* Sourcebooks.

Healy, M. (2021, January 29). 'Fate: The Winx Saga' doesn't know why anyone liked 'Winx Club': Season review. *The Harvard Crimson.* https://www.thecrimson.com/article/2021/1/29/fate-the-winx-saga-season-1-review/

Hendershot, H. (1998). *Saturday morning censors.* Duke University Press.

Jackson, S. (2021, January 20). Fate: The Winx Saga release date, cast, plot, and everything you need to know. *Cosmopolitan.* https://www.cosmopolitan.com/uk/entertainment/a34355958/the-winx-saga-release-date-cast-plot/.

Johnson, C. (2012). *Branding television.* Routledge. https://doi.org/10.4324/9780203597033.

Jones, E. (2020, December 10). 'Boys can be fairies – Its the 21st century': How fate: The Winx Saga finds the reality in fantasy. *The Guardian.* https://www.theguardian.com/tv-and-radio/2020/dec/10/boys-can-be-fairies-its-the-21st-century-how-fate-the-winx-saga-finds-the-reality-in-fantasy

Kennedy-Karpat, C. (2020). Adaptation and nostalgia. *Adaptation, 13*(3), 283–294. https://doi.org/10.1093/adaptation/apaa025

Klein, A., & Palmer, R. (2016). Introduction. In A. A. Klein & R. B. Palmer (Eds.), *Cycles, sequels, spin-offs, remakes and reboots: Multiplicities in film and television* (pp. 1–21). University of Texas Press. https://doi.org/10.1386/ncin_00008_5

Larson, T. (2021, January 26). *The beat comics culture.* https://www.comicsbeat.com/there-is-too-much-wrong-with-fate-the-winx-saga/

Marghitu, S. (2021). *Teen TV.* Routledge. https://doi.org/10.4324/9781315229645

Oladele, B. (2021, January 25). Netflix's "Fate: The Winx Saga" whitewashes original and loses its impact. *Teen Vogue.* https://www.teenvogue.com/story/fate-the-winx-saga-whitewashes-original-loses-impact-op-ed#:~:text=Both%20Bloom%20and%20Stella%20are,is%20thought%20to%20be%20Chinese .

Orenstein, P. (2011). *Cinderella ate my daughter: Dispatches from the front Lines of girlie-girl culture.* Harper Collins.

Petski, D. (2019, September 17). 'Fate: The Winx Saga': Abigail Cowen to lead ensemble cast of Netflix YA series. *Deadline.* https://deadline.com/2019/09/fate-the-winx-saga-abigail-cowebn-lead-ensemble-cast-netflix-ya-series-1202736626/

Radulovic, P. (2021, June 7). No one believed in Winx Club, except for its creator. *Polygon.* https://www.polygon.com/animation-cartoons/22519129/winx-club-creator-interview-netflix.

Ray, A. (2021, January 19). Dive into the magical world of Netflix's *Fate: The Winx Saga* with all-new trailer. *E News.* https://www.eonline.com/news/1228778/dive-into-the-magical-world-of-netflixs-fate-the-winx-saga-with-all-new-trailer

Romano, Nick. (2021, April 21). Outside the wire and fate: The Winx Saga top most watched Netflix movies and TV shows of the year. *Entertainment Weekly.* https://ew.com/movies/outside-the-wire-fate-the-winx-saga-most-watched-netflix-movies-tv-shows/

Roxborough, S . (2021). U.S. streamers bulk up with non-English-language shows. *Hollywood Reporter.* https://www.hollywoodreporter.com/business/business-news/u-s-streamers-non-english-language-shows-4126552/

Seiter, E. (1995). *Sold separately: Children and parents in consumer culture.* Rutgers.

Sigismondi, P. (2015). The Winx Club phenomenon in the global animation landscape. *Journal of Italian Cinema & Media Studies, 3*(3), 271–285. https://doi.org/10.1386/jicms.3.3.271_1

Straffi, I. (2004–2005). *Winx Club.* I. Straffi. Loreto, Italy: Rainbow S.P.A. New York, NY: Nickelodeon.

Stubbs, K. (2022, March 22). Where did 'Fate: The Winx Saga' go wrong? *Pop Tonic.* https://web.archive.org/web/20230127035354/https://poptonic.com/watch/tv/reviewing-fate-the-winx-saga/

Tannock, S. (1995). Nostalgia critique. *Cultural Studies, 9*(3), 453–464. https://doi.org/10.1080/09502389500490511

Vujić, K. (2022, October 28). I love my silly little fairy show. *New York Magazine.* https://www.thecut.com/2022/10/an-ode-to-fate-the-winx-saga.html

Weintraub, S. (2022, October 10). 'Fate: The Winx Saga' show runner Brian Young talks season 2 spoilers, future plans, and adapting the cartoon. *Collider.* https://collider.com/fate-the-winx-saga-season-2-future-plans-season-3-showrunner-brian-young-interview/

Welehan, I. (1999). Adaptation: The contemporary dilemmas. In D. Cartmell & I. Whelehan (Eds.) *Adaptations: From text to screen, screen to text* (3–20). Routledge. https://doi.org/10.4324/9781315006192

Young, B. (2021–2022). *Fate: The Winx Saga.* C. Buzelli & J. Counihan. Los Gatos, CA: Netflix.

3

Sex Magic: Orgasm, Embodiment, and the Erotic Navigation of "the Circumstances" in *The Magicians*

CORY GERATHS

Magic offers an invitation to consumers of popular media. It inspires new ways of thinking and it illuminates new worlds. Two such invitations are useful as a preface for this chapter's exploration of Lev Grossman's *The Magicians* and the Syfy television series of the same name. In the middle of the twentieth century, C.S. Lewis (1997) famously invited his young readers through the wardrobe and into the mystical realm of Narnia, a land teeming with magic where, due to the evil power of the White Witch, it was "always winter and never Christmas" (p. 23). More recently, J.K. Rowling (1997) inspired a generation of readers with her tale of "the boy who lived" who, across thousands of pages and seven books, was introduced to a hidden world fundamentally anchored by magic (p. 18). Lewis's and Rowling's treatments of magic invited readers to follow, and learn from, youth. Both series were principally aimed at younger audiences, though they have received wide attention from adults as well.

Lev Grossman's *The Magicians*, like many contemporary literary treatments of magic, is built upon the work of Lewis and Rowling.[1] Grossman's characters access the magical world of Fillory through furniture (a grandfather clock) and his series introduces magic as an educational pursuit to be studied in an academic setting at Brakebills College for Magical Pedagogy.[2] *The Magicians* features characters beyond the traditional confines of what might be considered "youth."³ The trilogy begins with its characters on the precipice of adulthood, rather than as prepubescent children, and charts their magical journeys across their 20s. The television series jumps straight to the latter by having its characters pursue graduate, rather than undergraduate, studies. Youth, in both Grossman's books and the Syfy adaptation, is consequently something marked less by age and, as this chapter will detail, more by characteristics such as (1) inexperience with magic, (2) reluctance to grow up, (3) a perceived lack of intelligence and maturity as articulated by elder stewards of magic and, of note, (4) the regular embrace of drugs, alcohol, and sex. According to the first three of these standards, *The Magicians*, despite its "aged up" characters, still reflects series like *The Chronicles of Narnia* and *Harry Potter*. Adding the fourth to its universe, however, offers readers and viewers a distinctly embodied take on magical youth. Such a focus on sex and sexuality, which is particularly evident in the Syfy adaptation, allows *The Magicians* to productively expand and rework the contours of who constitutes supernatural youth in media and what they can do within their magical environments. *The Magicians* illustrates the complications inherent in mediated treatments of supernatural youth as embodied, sexual beings who desire. Desire, *The Magicians* shows, is a complex supernatural negotiation of more than simply physicality; it is, for magical youth, a necessary triangulation of physicality, emotional intelligence and, ultimately, raw magical power.

Both Grossman's books and their Syfy adaptation are representative of the genre of the "magic school," and both renegotiate the boundaries of what readers and viewers expect from such a setting and the youth that reside and learn there. Unlike Rowling's Hogwarts, which was, due to the characters' ages, relatively romance- and sex-free, Brakebills is rife with the sort of sexual antics, complex romantic relationships, and desirous bodies that one would more reasonably associate with college and graduate school. Building upon the foundation established in the trilogy's source material, Syfy's *The Magicians* more explicitly positions sex and sexuality as foundational elements both of human existence and, importantly, of magical education. The Syfy adaptation incorporates sex not solely in the sort of salacious way that one might expect of a network eager to increase advertising revenue and boost audience ratings. Rather, Syfy's *The Magicians* embraces sex as both a means for characters to reckon with the metaphysical laws of Grossman's universe as well as an opportunity for viewers to critically reflect on the significance of sex and sexuality within magical contexts. Through the construction of a magical world more robustly anchored in the physicality of magic and the bodies that deploy it, *The Magicians* thus presents a more nuanced and arguably more mature magical ecosystem than those constrained by the limitations of what magic can be for younger audiences.

This chapter focuses on the Syfy adaptation's rhetorical characterization of sex as a conduit for and medium through which magic can be successfully deployed in the face of grave existential and transdimensional danger. Specifically, I focus on "sex magic." Sex is revealed by the television series to be a vital magical tool through which characters in *The Magicians* negotiate what Grossman defines as "the Circumstances." "The Circumstances," as detailed further in this chapter's third section, reveal the unique, and quite severe, complexity of magic in the universe of *The Magicians*. Put briefly, magicians must have a firm grasp of their situational context to even cast magic, let alone successfully deploy its power to their advantage. This contextual focus invites a critical exploration of the ways that the Syfy series utilizes sex as an effective response—sometimes the *only* one—to the prevailing Circumstances that threaten the characters.

I argue that this intersection of sex and magic in the Syfy adaptation of *The Magicians* accomplishes four things for the viewing audience. First, it casts sex as foundational in the development of a magical mythology that embraces, rather than elides, the embodied act of sex. Second, it positions sex as a core mechanism for achieving one's magical *kairos*—the appropriate, timely, and embodied rhetorical response to a situation. Third, it frames sex—and women's orgasms, in particular—as vital to the embodied experience of magic specifically, and to life, more broadly. Finally, and most significantly in the context of this collection, it exemplifies the impact of the sort of "aging up" of supernatural youth in media outlined previously.

This chapter's exploration of *The Magicians* is anchored in the rhetorical concept of *kairos*, specifically, and the disciplines of Communication Studies and Rhetoric, more broadly. Scholars have previously explored the complex and diverse communication in and mediated power of youth fantasy series such as *The Chronicles of Narnia* (see Hill, 2016; Miller, 1991; Munteanu, 2019) and *Harry Potter* (see Camacci, "The Multi-Gaze Perspective of Harry Potter" [2016]; Camacci, "The Face of Evil" [2022]; Hinck, 2020). *The Magicians*, while it has been treated by scholars in other areas of the Humanities, such as Literature (see Vinci, "Posthumanist Magic" [2018]) and Myth and Folklore Studies (see Kramer, 2017), has been comparatively understudied, particularly from the perspective of Rhetoric.

I consider John H. Saunders' 2016 edited collection, *The Rhetorical Power of Children's Literature* as an opportunity for considering *The Magicians* from a rhetorical perspective. Saunders opens by reminding the reader that "[w]e were all children at some point" (p. 1). Grossman's characters, and the audience he cultivates, straddle the lines between youth and adulthood. Saunders' reminder is thus apt. After all, no matter our age in the traditional sense, our youthfulness can and often does remain. Saunders makes this argument as part of his invitation to scholars to take rhetorical analysis of children's literature seriously. Responding to this invitation, I explore how Grossman's trilogy of books and the Syfy television adaptation of the same name complicate our understandings of supernatural youth in media. Looking at *The Magicians* from a rhetorical lens, with a particular focus on the ancient Greek concept of *kairos*, I chart the complex rhetorical intersection of supernatural youth, desire, and embodiment.

Syfy's adaptation of *The Magicians* foregrounds sex as a key tool in the magical arsenal that young stewards of magic are trained to utilize and, in doing so, the television series imbues sex as a core feature of supernatural youth in media. It does so, it is important to note, through a complex and elastic reworking of what constitutes youth. Brakebills students, despite their status as legal adults, lack the sort of adroit dexterity with magic—and, in many cases, the complexities of life—that marks adulthood. *The Magicians*' negotiation of sex, alongside such dangers as drug addiction and sexual assault, thus necessitates additional emotional maturity from its characters than would be found in treatments of children aimed at younger audiences. It necessitates, too, a certain "shamelessness," as detailed in the section below.

Shamelessness and Youth in *The Magicians*

The Magicians trilogy includes *The Magicians* (2009), *The Magician King* (2011), and *The Magician's Land* (2014). The series was written by author and journalist Lev Grossman and has been published in 25 countries ("The Magicians," 2022). The trilogy's opening book was widely regarded for its insertion of classical fantasy themes into more progressive contexts, a theme that is explored more fully below.[4] *Kirkus Reviews* (2010) described *The Magicians* as "fantasy for grown-ups," and Grossman's two sequels received similar praise (para. 3). Yates (2012), reviewing *The Magician King*, casts Grossman as "totally unashamed of his own sense of wonder and fun—unashamed, but not uncritical" (para. 18). Yates' assessment of Grossman's shamelessness is insightful; he describes him as a combination of "[t]he well-read alpha nerd;" "the book critic intent on looking deeper, seeking out the unexamined narrative;" and "[t]he little kid who is straight-up delighted by a man-sized ferret carrying a sword" (para. 18). In summation and inspired by

Grossman's approach, Yates' review offers a provocative summation: "We should all be so shameless" (para. 18).

Grossman is undeterred by what some might perceive as the limits of a more strictly bounded youth fantasy genre in the tradition of Lewis and Rowling: no drugs, no alcohol, and no sex. Because Grossman (2009) positions his characters on the periphery of full adulthood—naïve, inexperienced, and often lost (existentially, romantically, and, as this chapter details, transdimensionally), yet unencumbered by the more rigid limitations of childhood—his books and the mythology they craft are able to invite readers to witness everything from drunken dinner parties to a giant fire monster described by Grossman as "bald [with a blank expression and a] huge, hairless, glowing-red cock and balls [swinging] loose between his thighs like the clapper of a bell" (p. 340). A shameless embrace of the materiality of bodies is a foundational element of Grossman's universe. This shameless quality is a hallmark of Syfy's adaptation as well where, due to the affordances of the televisual medium, it can be rendered directly for audiences. However, the television adaptation must also negotiate shamelessness carefully; for instance, while the scene depicted above does not appear in the Syfy series, the "sex magic" scene analyzed in this chapter's penultimate section does. Shamelessness, both versions of *The Magicians* suggest, is a quality that must be finely calibrated when depicting supernatural youth.

The Syfy series received mixed reviews upon its premiere in 2016. Despite some initial criticisms, however, the adaptation ran for five seasons and received wide acclaim for its middle and later seasons.[5] And, unsurprisingly, reviewers were quick to highlight the "shameless" quality of the adaptation as well—as both a positive and a negative. Schwedel (2016) took the latter tack in her review: "the show is at its worst when straining to be provocative and, in so doing, incorporating various Hollywood clichés" (para. 3). On the other hand, Barr (2016) praised *The Magicians* for this quality. These reviews reveal opposing perspectives on the question of sex and intimacy in mediated rhetorics like those found in *The Magicians* and suggest, as noted in the previous paragraph, the difficulty in depicting shameless youth. For Schwedel, the sex that Quentin and his peers engage in is too rote and blasé. But, importantly, it is there. This visibility is, Nudson (2019) argues, "part of a changing TV landscape [that is] expanding what sex on TV can be" (para. 6). And the fact that sex is being depicted at all in a fantasy series matters, particularly within the subgenre set in so-called "magic schools." In a genre all too often reduced in the popular imagination to a vaguely Hogwartsian setting populated by supernatural, but certainly not sexual, youth, *The Magicians* proves itself to be a pivotal force in the ongoing evolution of the genre of the "magical school" and its negotiation of both shamelessness and sex.

Both *The Magicians* trilogy and television series were marketed as more "adult" instantiations of the archetype of magical youths coming of age.[6] For instance, Quentin Coldwater, the series' protagonist, opens the trilogy's first book at the age of 17 but, due to the text's swift coverage of his formal education, concludes it in his twenties. And, notably, while adults by the legal standards of Earth, Quentin and his Brakebills friends are nevertheless cast as youths by the residents of Fillory. There is a clear Fillorian irreverence for Quentin and those who travel there with him. Quentin is deemed an "Earth child" by Dint, a native Fillorian (Grossman, 2009, p. 335), and he and his friends are called "children of Earth" by the Fillorian ram-god, Ember (p. 346). These references pay homage to Narnian descriptors of the interloping Pevensies offered by Lewis (Kramer, 2017, p. 155).

Quentin functions as something of a synecdoche for both the trilogy's and the Syfy series' rhetorical negotiation of audience. He is an adult but pines for the unrealized dreams of youth that Fillory—and the magic that abounds there—offers. And the target audience for both the books and the television series seems to be those original, primarily millennial youth who grew up with wizard characters like Harry, Ron, and Hermione and who, having crossed the threshold into adulthood themselves, might still desire to embrace the youthful timbre, resonance, and echoes of magic that linger into adulthood. This is evidenced by the marketing of the trilogy's first book by Penguin, which includes a complex milieu of references to Quentin as a "young man," a *New Yorker* affirmation of the text as a "coming-of-age story," and, importantly, a review by George R. R. Martin, author of *Game of Thrones*, declaring that "*The Magicians* is to Harry Potter as a shot of Irish whiskey is to a glass of weak tea" ("The Magicians," 2023). *The Magicians*, then, is cast as a piece of media for adult audiences seeking, as author John Green put it, "a knowing and wonderful take on the wizard school genre," all while sipping a whiskey as they both read and watch Quentin and his friends struggle to learn magic against the frigid backdrops of Antarctica, nurse horrific hangovers spawned by all-night drinking binges, and sleep their way through the struggles of adulthood ("The Magicians," 2023).

A recurring aspect of Quentin's characterization is his love—some might say obsession—with the five books that comprise the *Fillory and Further* series. *Fillory and Further* is a clear parallel to Lewis' *The Chronicles of Narnia*. Quentin both longs for the respite that Fillory offers and possesses something of an encyclopedic knowledge of the series' plot, characters, and other magical intricacies.

Fillory, for Quentin, is an unrealized dream from his childhood that, despite his age, leads him to be "stuck," as it were, in the miasma of youth. Upon graduation from Brakebills and roughly midway through the trilogy's first novel, Quentin and his friends discover that Fillory is real and that the fantasy series he grew up loving is more of a loose ethnography than a purely fictional account.[7] This discovery upends not only the narrative structure of the book and television series but, more broadly, the generic expectations of fantasy itself. Quentin's and his friends' travels to and travails in Fillory further position them as inexperienced practitioners of magic—legal Earth adults yet caught in the Fillorian and supernatural machinations of what they had long considered a fictional children's story.

This point has not been lost on commentators, both popular and academic (see Kramer, 2017; Vitale, 2009; Yates, 2012). Vitale (2009) notes this as a foundational difference between Quentin and a character like Harry Potter: "Quentin differs from Harry Potter in that he reads fantasy novels, and he's enchanted to discover that the magic he's longed for all his life actually exists" (para. 2). Grossman (Vitale, 2009) himself offered such an analysis as well: "If I had grown up the way Harry did [. . .] all I would have done was read fantasy. I would have been consumed by these [. . .] stories about escape and power [. . .] I always wondered why Harry wasn't a fantasy reader" (para. 3). Grossman's reworking of the youth fantasy genre adds important depth to Quentin's character and also invites the reading and viewing audiences to more readily reflect on the respective series' complicated negotiations of the boundaries of and expectations for youth in the supernatural adventures that Quentin and his friends undertake. Circumscribed by the limitations of decorum, emotional intelligence, and other characteristics, children's stories are thematically simpler than those found in both Grossman's trilogy and their Syfy adaptation.[8] The latter two are more layered and more "realistic" in ways that, for all their imaginative prowess, younger children could not comprehend.

Grossman—and those behind the Syfy adaptation—are thus more readily able to incorporate what might be considered more taboo or "off-limits" narrative arcs than authors and producers who are crafting stories more explicitly aimed at children. Both *The Magicians* trilogy and the Syfy adaptation include LGBTQ+ characters (Quentin, himself, as well as Eliot) and explicitly queer themes. They regularly depict characters engaging in sex, both within and outside the boundaries of monogamous relationships. Moreover, characters are uninhibited in their desire to imbibe in numerous alcoholic libations and narcotic substances, including to the point of addiction. Of course, *The Magicians* is not alone in depicting such themes. For example, multiple characters in Rainbow Rowell's novel,

Carry On (and its sequel books *Wayward Son* and *Any Way the Wind Blows*), negotiate sexual identity against the backdrop of both a difficult magical education and a fight against evil. And television audiences have witnessed similar themes—sex, alcohol, and drugs—in quite prolific supernatural series such as *Buffy the Vampire Slayer* and *Chilling Adventures of Sabrina*. These series, like *The Magicians*, prided themselves on offering audiences a darker, more "aged-up" take on supernatural youth. One need look no further than to characters like *Buffy the Vampire Slayer*'s Buffy (White, 2018) losing her virginity to Angel (leading to him becoming a "marauding and sadistic [. . .] vampire," para. 8) and *Chilling Adventures of Sabrina*'s Nicholas Scratch (Mahale, 2020) turning to BDSM upon his return from hell, to find other examples of "aged up" supernatural youth engaging in sex.

The Magicians does not shy away from the realities facing adults stuck longing for youth while attending magical schools. Grossman invites his characters to explore their complex desires for pleasure, pain, and the litany of emotions and experiences that exist in between. Desire, Kramer (2017) argues, is at the heart of *The Magicians* (p. 153). Quentin, for instance, pines after an unrequited love—his friend Julia, who becomes a much more important figure in the series' second book, *The Magician King* (and an important character immediately in the television series)—and faces the stark aftermath of adultery after cheating on his girlfriend, fellow magician, Alice Quinn. He does so in a fashion that reminds readers and viewers at home of his characterization as an immature adult who is prone to the sort of rash decision making and inability to rein in desire expected of teenagers. Sex and desire, characters like Quentin demonstrate, are intimately bound up with the situational and material realities of context. In that spirit, I turn next to a discussion of the rhetorical theory of *kairos* and its significance within the magical ecosystem of both Grossman's books and their Syfy adaptation.

Magical *Kairos* and "The Circumstances"

This section focuses on the complex—and embodied—system of magic developed by Grossman that is introduced for the first time when Quentin and his peers enroll at Brakebills. Magic, they discover there, is more than simply waving a wand or chanting an incantation. It is, instead, an incredibly complicated physical negotiation of what are known as "the Circumstances."[9] Roberts (2018) acknowledges the importance of the body to characters' use of magic in *The*

Magicians. She notes that "[magic] is represented as a meticulous and beautiful choreography of the hands and fingers" (Roberts, 2018, para. 1). It is not only exceedingly complex but something of a "body-language [that is] performed in both language and hand motions" (Roberts, 2018, para. 10).

Grossman frames the use of magic as something akin to the ancient Greek concept of *kairos*, which can be defined as both "due measure, proportion, fitness" and the "exact or critical time, season, [or] opportunity" (Liddell & Scott, 1940). *Kairos* also encompasses both the "right or appropriate body" as well as the "right or appropriate time." Hawhee (2004) invites scholars to "[explore] the commonalities found in the various nuances [of *kairos* and related terms]: namely, an emphasis on immanence, movement, and embodiment" (p. 66). Rhetoricians have also explored the queer dynamics and sexual articulations of *kairos* (see Geraths, 2020; Morris & Sloop, 2006). Building upon such work, this chapter considers *kairos* as a useful theoretical foundation for making sense of Grossman's magical mythology in *The Magicians* and its implications for how the Syfy adaptation negotiates sex as an embodied practice of supernatural youth.

Quentin is introduced to the *kairic* nature of "the Circumstances" early in the series' first novel. He laments that "learning magic [. . .] turned out to about as tedious as it was possible for the study of powerful and mysterious supernatural forces to be" (Grossman, 2009, p. 55). Grossman (2009) invokes the grammatical modification of language as a metaphor for describing the intricate nature of magic in his universe: like verbs, "even the simplest spell had to be modified and tweaked and inflected to agree with the time of day, the phase of the moon, the intention and purpose and *precise circumstances of its casting*" (p. 55, emphasis added). Magic, Quentin is surprised to discover, is far more of an academic pursuit, more akin to learning a new language or mastering advanced calculus than the sort of wand-waving that is all too often foregrounded in the popular imagination. In sum, the Circumstances are revealed to depend on the situational components detailed above as well as "a hundred other factors, all of which [are] tabulated in volumes of tables and charts and diagrams printed in microscopic jewel type on huge yellowing elephant-folio pages" (Grossman, 2009, p. 55). These pages, complete with copious footnotes, lead Quentin to the inevitable, yet significant conclusion: "Magic was a lot wonkier than [he] thought it would be" (Grossman, 2009, p. 55).

Magic, in the world of *The Magicians*, is revealed to be simultaneously academic and archaic, corporeal and circumstantial. Characters study feverishly. They practice hand movements until their bodies ache. They learn centuries-old languages, such as Old Church Slavonic and Old High Dutch (Grossman, 2009,

p. 62). All so that they can correctly cast specific spells in response to particular contexts. Students, Grossman makes clear, must tirelessly complete such work so that they can effectively respond to the contingency of the universe and successfully call magic into action. This is perhaps best illustrated by a scene in Antarctica, at so-called "Brakebills South," where Quentin and his peers are tasked with repeating the Hammer Charm of Legrand (Grossman, 2009, p. 150). In a scene that might make even Erasmus flinch, Quentin was made by his professor to cast the charm thousands of times according to divergent Circumstances.[10]

Quentin's Antarctic teacher, Professor Mayakovsky, mocks Quentin for his elementary and youthful understanding of magic: "You have been studying magic the way a parrot studies Shakespeare. You recite it like you are saying the Pledge of Allegiance. But you do not understand it" (Grossman, 2009, p. 143). Mayakovsky's flippant critique, which calls to mind schoolchildren blithely reciting memorized words before class with a sort of mechanical disinterest, gives way to both confusion from Quentin and further explanation from Mayakovsky. Quentin's professor invokes a gastric metaphor as he continues: "To become a magician you must do something different [. . .] You cannot study magic. You cannot learn it. You must ingest it. Digest it. You must merge *with* it. And it with you" (Grossman, 2009, p. 144, emphasis in original). Mayakovsky is unabashed in his argument that the use of magic requires one's whole spirit, mind and, importantly, body.

Magic, Mayakovsky caustically teaches Quentin, entails an almost natural and unthinking response to the Circumstances: "You need to do more than memorize, Quentin. You must learn the principles of magic with more than your head. You must learn them with your bones, with your blood, your liver, your heart, your *deek* [dick]" (Grossman, 2009, p. 144, emphasis in original). This passage articulates a crucial component of the ecosystem that shapes the use of magic in *The Magicians*. Magic, like the ancient Greek rhetorical concept of *kairos* itself, is foundationally embodied. Mayakovsky's glib tone makes it easy to overlook the importance of this point. The path to achieving one's magical *kairos* can vary dramatically from situation to situation. Contingency reigns. Both Grossman's novels and the Syfy adaptation usually show magicians casting using a combination of exceedingly complex hand movements and carefully worded incantations (often in non-English languages) (see Roberts, 2018). But the Syfy adaptation takes Mayakovsky's directive more literally in the first season episode, "Homecoming."[11] In this episode, so significant and complicated are the so-called "Circumstances" that the series' characters must fully embrace the embodied nature of magic to respond to them—even to the point of utilizing their genitalia, as Quentin and Alice do in the episode from the Syfy adaptation analyzed below.

Sex Magic, Orgasm, and *Kairos*

Sex magic is revealed to be a life-saving tool in the larger magical arsenal available to the supernatural youth of *The Magicians*. It weaves the complicated desires of youth, outlined above, with the physical and contingent nature of magic in Grossman's universe. And, in doing so, the Syfy adaptation's depiction of sex magic renegotiates who can take on the label of "supernatural youth" and, importantly, what sorts of material actions and physical desires they are permitted to enact for audiences. This depiction of sex magic occurs in the first season of the Syfy adaptation of *The Magicians* when Penny, a Brakebills student in Quentin's year, finds himself catastrophically unmoored.

Unlike Quentin, Alice, Eliot, and other primary characters who have been categorized by their elder professors at Brakebills as so-called "physical magicians" (see Grossman, 2009, pp. 95–97), Penny's discipline is much rarer. He is a "traveler." Penny possesses the same power in the television series. He is shown in the Syfy adaptation moving instantaneously between points on campus, between Earth and the astral plane and, importantly, between Earth and a desolate place known as the Neitherlands. The Neitherlands is described in the books as an endless array of fountains and "weathered, ancient [looking]" architecture (Grossman, 2009, p. 258). It is further described in the Syfy adaptation as "the place between all other places" (Myers, 2016). Each fountain is a portal to another realm—Earth, Fillory, and "a million other worlds" (Grossman, 2009, p. 260). It is here, in the Syfy series' ninth and tenth episodes, that Penny finds himself impossibly stuck.

Penny reveals his dire situation to Quentin by "traveling" via the astral plane, where he enters Quentin's dream. Quentin's dream, it turns out, is a sexual fantasy featuring Julia, his unrequited love from high school, and Alice, his current girlfriend. Penny both mocks and applauds Quentin for this "grade A nerd-boy wet dream" before explaining that he is lost (Myers, 2016). Penny, his frustration clear, laments that there are "fountains ... and plazas up the ass" (Myers, 2016). More troublingly, he informs Quentin that he can't easily travel back because "there's three moons here [and his] internal compass is having a grand mal seizure" (Myers, 2016). Quentin makes a similar observation in the trilogy's opening book when he first attempts magic upon arriving in Fillory: "As soon as he started he realized that the Circumstances were scrambled here—different stars, different seas, different everything" (Grossman, 2009, p. 291; also p. 298). Grossman (2009) makes clear that a central aspect of "the Circumstances" is an awareness of one's planetary and astronomical location (pp. 55, 150). Penny's explanation thus makes implicit reference to the previously discussed "Circumstances." Untethered from Earth, Penny runs the risk of death—or worse—were he to utilize magic as a means of traveling home without assistance (Myers, 2016).

The erotic overtones of both Quentin's dream and Penny's sodomitical idiom foreshadow the sexual solution that Alice and Quentin uncover in "Homecoming." Alice is the only character to unearth a realistic path to resolving Penny's plight. She leads Quentin to her family's home in the Chicago suburbs, where they encounter Alice's parents deep in the throes of a Roman orgy (Myers, 2016).[12] They travel to Illinois to learn more about a friend, "Joe," of Alice's parents who is a traveler like Penny, albeit one "from another world, [whose] actual name is impossible to pronounce" (Myers, 2016). "Joe" is revealed to be in a "polyamorous-triad" with Alice's parents and Alice's mother boasts that his "anatomy is adaptable [. . .] like a Swiss Army knife [and] good for every occasion" (Myers, 2016). These details continue to position sex as a core aspect of *The Magicians'* larger magical ecosystem, and Alice's mother's coy reference to "Joe" being sexually "good for every occasion" further previews the *kairic* role that sex will play in saving Penny's life. Sex magic is cast in "Homecoming" as *the* fitting response to the unprecedented Circumstances that Alice, Quentin, and Penny find themselves in.

"Joe," after receiving an explanation from Alice and Quentin about Penny's plight in the Neitherlands, knowingly derides "that place [as] the worst" (Myers, 2016). He offers them a spell that could, if properly cast, help Penny to return to the Earth fountain. "Joe" describes it as "a beacon" that, once cast on Earth, causes the corresponding fountain "for this world [to light] up there [in the Neitherlands]" (Myers, 2016). "Joe" further reveals that the spell is a form of sex magic because, on his world, "all magic is sex magic" (Myers, 2016). He notes that all they will need is "a nice connection between your genitals . . . some blood . . . a globe . . . a few candles bound with twine . . . [and that they] both have to climax at the same time" (Myers, 2016). This final revelation causes consternation on Alice's part, implying that she has been unable to consistently orgasm during previous sexual encounters with Quentin.

Orgasm is ultimately revealed to be the most fraught of "the Circumstances" that Alice and Quentin face as they work to cast the sex magic recommended by "Joe." After a failed first attempt and much dismay on Quentin's part, the couple do successfully cast the beacon, which appears as a towering, phallic beam of light in the Neithelands. Penny spots it as viewing audiences listen to the sounds of Alice and Quentin's joint climax. This final portion of the scene is especially key. Frischherz (2018) invites us to consider "public orgasm rhetoric [and the ways that it] compels us to understand how sound makes public discourses of pleasure possible" (p. 270). This rhetoric, she contends, "allows women to access the structures of feeling so desperately missing in our collective knowledge of women's orgasm" (Frischherz, 2018, p. 270). The climax scene in "Homecoming" emphasizes sex—and orgasm, in particular—as a visual, aural, and ultimately magical response to "the Circumstances." Alice and Quentin's twinned orgasms save Penny and exemplify how sex magic, properly cast, can offer a fitting *kairos* to a complex magical situation, both within the universe of *The Magicians* and for supernatural youth. This response is one that Mayakovsky would likely endorse—it is intricate, intimate, instinctive and, importantly, embodied. The television series' explicit foregrounding of sex magic has larger implications as well for audiences and scholars who continue to negotiate treatments of supernatural youth in media.

The Significance of Sex Magic

The Magicians reveals sex to be a core component of its characters' magical lexicons. Characters, in both Grossman's novels and the adapted television series, regularly utilize their arms, hands, and fingers as the conduits of magic. Quentin and Alice's successful casting of "sex magic" in "Homecoming" adds additional forms of embodiment to what Roberts (2018) artfully dubbed the "meticulous and beautiful choreography" of magic casting in the universe of *The Magicians* (para. 1). Vaginas, clitorises, vulvas, penises, testicles, anuses, nipples, and more, we can presume, might also help magicians to successfully perform this choreography.

Nudson (2019) declares that "*The Magicians* is a sexy show" (para. 1). She further argues that it is important to render sex, particularly from women's perspectives, visible for television audiences.[13] Quentin and Alice's scene anchors sex and sexuality as core components of the magical mythology of the Syfy adaptation of *The Magicians*. In doing so, it also calls on consumers of fantasy texts to see and hear sex. Faris (2019) invites us to consider how "turning toward the materiality of sex provides more radical thinking about how rhetorical action might provide possibilities for new relationalities and ways of being in the world" (p. 142). This argument has significant bearing for depictions of supernatural youth in media. While far from the first instance of magical sex (again, see shows such as *Buffy the Vampire Slayer* and *Chilling Adventures of Sabrina*), *The Magicians* is notable for how it adds to this lineage.

The Magicians locates magic corporeally in the body. And, as exemplified by both Professor Mayakovsky in the trilogy's first novel and "Joe," the alien instructor of sex magic in the Syfy adaptation's first season, *The Magicians* utilizes elder teachers as the arbiters of such knowledge for younger students of magic. Mayakovsky's instruction to Quentin, which urges him to learn magic not just with his brain but with his penis, is telling in this regard. While a disgraced member of the Brakebills faculty (see Grossman, 2009, pp. 134–65, 184–93), Mayakovsky is nevertheless responsible for leading a foundational element of all Brakebills students' training in magic. That he locates magic not just in the mind but in characters' bodies lays a crucial foundation for the television series' incorporation of sex magic in "Homecoming." Furthermore, the suggestion from "Joe" that Alice and Quentin just need a "nice connection between their genitals" seems to owe a debt to the sort of magical instruction outlined by Mayakovsky in the trilogy.

Both Mayakovsky and Quentin's interaction in *The Magicians* and the television adaptation's use of orgasm materially imbue the fantasy genre of "magic schools" with sex. Indeed, as Faris (2019) notes, such material depictions of sex offer an invitation to readers and viewers, albeit a different one than found in texts by fantasy writers like Lewis and Rowling. Lewis famously invited his readers through the wardrobe and into a magical world and Rowling introduced hers to the wonders of Hogwarts. Grossman and those behind the series' Syfy adaptation, writing about and depicting more "aged up" youth for an adult audience familiar with the generic expectations—and limitations—of Lewis, Rowling, and others, renegotiate the "magic schools" fantasy genre as one that can embrace sex and sexuality, and the desires underpinning both, much more explicitly.

After all, much of the success of fantasy series in this genre depends on the creation of vibrant, compelling, and detailed magical environments, including schools and the supernatural curricula they offer. Recognizing this point, Grossman, and those who wrote, directed, and produced the Syfy adaption, render Brakebills as a magical environment that blends elements from the familiar Ivy League ethos of the American northeast with the revered hijinks, mysticism, and awe that readers and viewers have come to expect from other magical schools such as Hogwarts (*Harry Potter*) and Watford (*Carry On*). That *The Magicians* explicitly positions its magic school, Brakebills, as a site of material sex and sexuality, rather than sexuality that is nonexistent or simply implied, is crucial to its function of creating a magical world that relies on older youths.[14]

The Magicians frames sex as not just an important response to the Grossman-specific mythology of "the Circumstances" but, more broadly, expands our understanding of what supernatural youth in media, especially those enrolled in, educated at, or otherwise tethered to magical schools, are permitted to do. That Alice and Quentin's act of sex magic is rhetorically framed as one of heroism rather than one of shame is significant. Mayakovsky and "Joe" are respectively clear that embodiment, desire, and sex can and should be marshalled to respond to unique magical contexts—including those marked by danger, risk, evil, and the very real possibility of death. Magical youth, such as those training at Brakebills, thus expand readers' and viewers' understanding of what constitutes magic, magical education, and their material manifestations in practice. Orgasm, and the bodies that feel and experience it, are positioned as magical resources in the same vein as wands, potions, swords, and other resources made available to supernatural youth. This is, to return a final time to Faris (2019), indeed an exciting way for supernatural youth in media *to be* in the magical worlds printed on audiences' pages and broadcast on their screens (p. 142).

Notes

1   This comparison has been made by Grossman himself. He (2022) describes the trilogy's first book as "a grand, glittering fantasy that reinterprets the grand tradition of C.S. Lewis and J.K. Rowling in a brilliant novel for adults" ("The Magicians"). See, also, Christopher (2016), in which Grossman notes that "[he] always wanted to talk back to C.S. Lewis" (p. 138).

2   Much of the trilogy is set in the world of Fillory, a magical realm rife with talking bears, a crescent moon that is eclipsed each day at noon, and a mysterious horological figure known as the Watcherwoman. Grossman's series begins far from Fillory, however, when a young man, Quentin Coldwater, is granted admittance to Brakebills. Brakebills offers its students an extensive study of the complexities of magical theory, practice, and history (Grossman, 2009, p. 39).

3   For more on Brakebills and treatments of supernatural youth in academic contexts, see Battis (2021). See also Suttie (2016), who utilizes *The Magicians* as a "pedagogical tool" for "recognising the issues inherent in the current North American education system . . ." (p. iv; see, also, pp. 27–35 on the "dominating praxis" of education at Brakebills).

4   Grossman's trilogy has also received criticism. See Agger (2009); Doyle (2014).
5   For an archive of these reviews, see the series' page on Rotten Tomatoes (2022) at https://www.rottentomatoes.com/tv/the_magicians.
6   The Syfy series received a listing of MA; this is a clear difference from adaptations of books like the *Harry Potter* series, which received ratings of PG and PG-13 across the eight films produced. Similarly, Grossman (2022) describes the trilogy's first book as "a . . . novel for adults" ("The Magicians").
7   The television series similarly reveals this twist to audiences in the first season.
8   For more on the rhetorical power of children's literature, see Saunders' (2016) concept of "bedtime rhetoric" (pp. 2–4).
9   This portion of the chapter draws primarily from expositional material provided in Grossman's trilogy, though the importance of "the Circumstances" extends to the television series as well.
10 Erasmus is notorious for having his students engage in the exhaustive practice of *copia*, which required rhetorical composition in a multitude of different styles. For more on *copia*, see Hawhee (2017, pp. 133–159).
11 Like most adaptations, Syfy's *The Magicians* makes a number of changes from the original source material. These changes can be summarized as follows: (1) characters are further "aged up" (they enroll at Brakebills for graduate school) yet, to be clear, retain youthful qualities, as noted previously; (2) character arcs from the first two books are woven into the early seasons of the show; (3) some character names are changed and new characters are developed; (4) action sequences and other plot details are modified or removed to fit the needs of a televisual medium; and (5) new scenes have been created to fill these gaps. This chapter's exploration of "sex magic" in *The Magicians* focuses on a scene that falls within category five above. While added to the Syfy series, this scene draws upon larger themes and mythologies first outlined by Grossman in the trilogy's source material.
12 Alice is from the university town of Urbana, Illinois in the books.
13 Nudson (2019) also calls important attention to the television series' negotiation of sexual assault and rape through the character of Julia. While such a discussion is beyond the scope of this chapter, it is worth noting that both the trilogy's and the Syfy adaptation's negotiation of such themes have received mixed reviews. See Doyle (2014); Vinci, "Mourning the Human" (2017).
14 See Battis (2021), who turns to Brakebills, alongside other "magic schools," in order to "queer the magical academy" (p. 93).

References

Agger, M. (2009, September 8). Abracadabra angst. *The New York Times*. https://www.nytimes.com/2009/09/13/books/review/Agger-t.html.

Barr, M. (2016, January 19). "The Magicians" review: Harry Potter goes to grad school. *Forbes.* https://www.forbes.com/sites/merrillbarr/2016/01/19/the-magicians-review/?sh=e7dc2e63187b#2715e4857a0b53e71812584d.

Battis, J. (2021). *Thinking queerly: Medievalism, wizardry, and neurodiversity in young adult texts.* Medieval Institute Publications.

Camacci, L. R. (2016). The multi-gaze perspective of Harry Potter. In J. H. Saunders (Ed.), *The rhetorical power of children's literature* (pp. 149–172). Lexington Books.

Camacci, L. R. (2022). The face of evil: Physiognomy in Potter. In C. K. Farr (Ed.), *Open at the close: Literary essays on Harry Potter* (pp. 188–200). The University Press of Mississippi.

Christopher, C. (2016). Interview with Lev Grossman. *Manuscripts, 81*(1), 135–43.

Doyle, S. (2014, August 24). Why does the Magicians trilogy keep raping and killing off its best characters? *Salon.* https://www.salon.com/2014/08/24/why_does_the_magicians_trilogy_keep_raping_and_killing_off_its_best_characters/.

Faris, M. J. (2019). Queering networked writing: A sensory autoethnography of desire and sensation on Grindr. In W. P. Banks, M. B. Cox, & C. Dadas (Eds.), *Re/Orienting writing studies: Queer methods, Queer projects* (pp. 127–49). Utah State University Press.

Frischherz, M. (2018). Listening to orgasm: Hearing pleasure sounds in the normative noise. *Argumentation and Advocacy, 54*(4), 270–86.

Geraths, C. (2020). The *coming out* sermon: Brandan Robertson at the National Cathedral. In E. C. Miller & J. J. Edwards (Eds.), *Rhetoric of the protestant sermon in America: Pulpit discourse at the turn of the millennium* (pp. 137–58). Lexington Books.

Grossman, L. (2009). *The Magicians.* Penguin.

Hawhee, D. (2004). *Bodily arts: Rhetoric and athletics in ancient Greece.* University of Texas Press.

Hawhee, D. (2017). *Rhetoric in tooth and claw: Animals, language, sensation.* University of Chicago Press.

Hill, J. D. (2016). "Good readers" in Narnia: C.S. Lewis's rhetoric of invitation. In J. H. Saunders (Ed.), *The rhetorical power of children's literature* (pp. 79–108). Lexington Books.

Hinck, A. (2020). Fan-based social movements: The Harry Potter Alliance and the future of online activism. In N. Crick (Ed.), *The rhetoric of social movements* (pp. 191–206). Routledge.

Kramer, K. (2017). A common language of desire: *The Magicians*, Narnia, and contemporary fantasy. *Mythlore: A Journal of J.R.R. Tolkein, C.S. Lewis, Charles Williams, and Mythopoeic Literature, 35*(2), 153–69.

Lewis, C. S. (1997). *The lion, the witch, and the wardrobe.* Collins.

Liddell, H. G., & Scott, R. (1940). "καιρός." In *A Greek-English Lexicon.* Clarendon Press. Available via Perseus. http://www.perseus.tufts.edu/hopper/text?doc=Perseus%3Atext%3A1999.04.0057%3Aentry%3Dkairo%2Fs1.

Mahale, J. (2020, June 3). Sex, demons, and BDSM: Gavin Leatherwood is Sabrina the Teenage Witch's anti-hero. *Vice.* https://i-d.vice.com/en/article/939gad/sabrina-the-teenage-witch-gavin-leatherwood-interview.

Miller, D. B. (1991). C.S. Lewis: The use of fantasy to communicate reality: A good story is worth a thousand theological words. *The lamp-post of the Southern California C.S. Lewis Society, 15*(2), 3–23.

Morris, C. E. III, & Sloop, J. M. (2006). "What lips these lips have kissed": Refiguring the politics of queer public kissing. *Communication and Critical/Cultural Studies, 3*(1), 1–26.

Munteanu, D. G. (2019). Is Tumblr the new Narnia? A few reflections on C.S. Lewis, Romanticism, and their relevance on Media and Cultural Studies. *Linguaculture, 2*, 179–92.

Myers, H. A. (Writer), & Butler, J. (Director). (2016, March 21). Homecoming (Season 1, Episode 10). In M. Cahill, M. London, J. Williams, S. Smith, J. McNamara, S. Gamble, & H. A. Myers (Executive Producers), *The Magicians*. McNamara Moving Company; Man Sewing Dinosaur; Groundswell Productions; Universal Cable Productions; & Universal Content Productions.

Nudson, R. (2019, April 17). Why sex scenes on *The Magicians* look different than those on the rest of TV. *Paste*. https://www.pastemagazine.com/tv/the-magicians/why-sex-scenes-on-the-magicians-look-different-tha/.

Roberts, I. (2018, May 17). Spell-casting as illusion-dance: The look and laws of physical magic in *The Magicians*. https://ivyroseroberts.wordpress.com/2018/05/27/spell-casting-as-illusion-dance-the-look-and-laws-of-physical-magic-in-the-magicians/.

Rowling, J. K. (1997). *Harry Potter and the philosopher's stone*. Bloomsbury.

Saunders, J. H. (2016). Bedtime rhetoric. In J. H. Saunders (Ed.), *The rhetorical power of children's literature* (pp. 1–8). Lexington Books.

Schwedel, H. (2016, January 25). Sex, drugs, and wizards. *Slate*. https://slate.com/culture/2016/01/syfys-the-magicians-inspired-by-lev-grossmans-book-trilogy-reviewed.html.

Suttie, M. (2016). *The Magicians and North American education: Fantasy fiction as a tool for pedagogical change* [Master's thesis, McMaster University]. https://macsphere.mcmaster.ca/bitstream/11375/20523/2/Suttie_Megan_H_2016September_MA.pdf.

"The Magicians." (2022). *Lev Grossman*. https://levgrossman.com/books/the-magicians-a-novel/.

"The Magicians." (2022). *Rotten Tomatoes*. https://www.rottentomatoes.com/tv/the_magicians.

"The Magicians." (2023). *Penguin*. https://www.penguinrandomhouse.com/books/303321/the-magicians-tv-tie-in-edition-by-lev-grossman/.

"The Magicians: From the Magicians Trilogy Series, Vol. 1." (2010, May 19). *Kirkus Reviews*. https://www.kirkusreviews.com/book-reviews/lev-grossman/the-magicians/.

Vinci, T. M. (2017). Mourning the human: Working through trauma and the posthuman body in Lev Grossman's The Magicians trilogy. *Journal of the Fantastic in the Arts, 28*(3), 368–87.

Vinci, T. M. (2018). Posthumanist magic: Beyond the boundaries of humanist ethics in Lev Grossman's *The Magicians*. In A. Tarr & D. R. White (Eds.), *Posthumanism in young adult fiction: Finding humanity in a posthuman world* (pp. 227–246). University Press of Mississippi.

Vitale, T. (2009, August 11). Morally complex "Magicians" recasts Potter's world. https://www.npr.org/2009/08/11/111751056/morally-complex-magicians-recasts-pottersworld.

White, B. (2018, January 19). Buffy lost her virginity and changed television 20 years ago. *Decider*. https://decider.com/2018/01/19/buffy-lost-her-virginity-and-changed-television-20-years-ago/.

Yates, A. (2012, December 12). Shirking the genre ghetto: On Lev Grossman's *The Magician King* and the fantastical novel in 2012. *The Kenyon Review*. https://kenyonreview.org/kr-online-issue/2013-winter/selections/the-magician-king-by-lev-grossman-738439/.

4

Rewriting the Past and Present: *Ragnarok*, Norse Myth, and Teen Heroes

ILANA NASH AND JANA K. SCHULMAN

When the Danish-Norwegian series *Ragnarok* debuted as a Netflix Original in 2020, it joined a media landscape where the famed epic battle of Norse mythology was already well known from the global success of *Thor: Ragnarok* (2017), the third in Marvel Studio's series of superhero films about the god Thor, which grossed $854 million worldwide (IMDbPro). Netflix's *Ragnarok* distinguishes itself from the Marvel Cinematic Universe's (MCU) version of Norse gods by reimagining the story as a contemporary coming-of-age drama. It offers a new twist, changing the final battle between gods and giants (the original ragnarok) into the planet's destruction by climate change and pollution—an increasingly common theme in Nordic TV series (Souch, 2022). But this seemingly "new" twist is based on Old Norse mythology, in which climate change and disastrous weather events presage ragnarok. Produced by Danish company SAM Productions, written by Danish, Swedish, and Norwegian screenwriters, and filmed in Norway with a Danish and Norwegian cast, *Ragnarok* tells a Scandinavian story from a Scandinavian perspective. Show-creator Adam Price said, "we believe that the Nordics have their own voice when it comes to storytelling" (Netflix, 2018). The series introduced not only a fresh entry in the popular genre of supernatural youth media, but also a fresh interpretation and application of Norse myth, adapting it to fit a modern context while still faithfully following its contents.

Ragnarok begins with awkward teenager Magne Seier, whose name means "great victory" in Norwegian, returning to his former hometown with his brother Laurits and their widowed mother, Turid. The fictional town of Edda is named for Snorri Sturluson's *Prose Edda* and the anonymous *Poetic Edda*, the medieval texts that contain what we know of Norse mythology. Edda is dominated by the wealthy, powerful Jutul family, whose Jutul Industries is the town's largest employer and largest polluter. As we soon learn, the Jutul family—mother Ran, father Vidar, son Fjor and daughter Saxa—are immortal giants who have survived in Edda since the original ragnarok, hiding their identities by passing as human. Their factory's pollution repeats the past's climatic disturbances in a new guise, the second coming of global chaos at the hands of the same perpetrators. Upon arriving in Edda, Magne encounters an old woman, later revealed as a seeress from Norse myth, whose touch initiates him as the god Thor. On his first day at school, Magne befriends Isolde, a classmate who enlightens him about Edda's urgent ecological crises and the Jutuls' culpability. Soon other townspeople begin to embody ancient gods as well, notably Magne's brother Laurits, who becomes Loki; their classmate Iman, who becomes Freya; the town mechanic, Harry, who becomes Tyr; and an elderly man, Wotan, who becomes Odin. The looming conflict between the villainous Jutuls, who poison the planet, and the heroic gods, who strive to save it, is poised to parallel the famed mythological battle.

But *Ragnarok* doesn't hew strictly to ancient texts; rather, it imbricates those texts with the tropes and conventions of more contemporary genres, the superhero adventure and the teenage drama—both of which, like the mythological source material, are simultaneously employed yet altered in *Ragnarok*, persistently confounding viewers' expectations. This convergence of narrative genres evokes familiar patterns only to disrupt what we expect, forcing viewers to imagine beyond our inherited traditions of "how things should be." This chapter offers a textual and thematic reading that analyzes *Ragnarok* in terms of the narrative traditions it borrows from, and challenges. We show that *Ragnarok* argues for how to achieve a better world: do away with traditional boundaries and hierarchies of gender, class, race, and even narrative genres, because such hierarchies create a power imbalance that contributes to chaos and destruction. Using racially and sexually diverse characters, and juggling numerous textual traditions, the show's repeated message is, don't follow "how it is written."

We argue that *Ragnarok*'s first two seasons flirt with teen dramas and superhero adventures, but ultimately use those traditions only to reinforce a greater emphasis on mythology and the message of renewal after destruction, an occasionally forgotten aspect of the original ragnarok. The very playing with genres and audience expectations offers those in Edda and the audience an opportunity to tap into Thor's righteous justice and care for Midgard, the human world. The writers of the series, it seems, drew on Norse mythology to inspire. But in its third and final season, the series practiced what it preached about genre manipulation in a startling way, breaking from how the show was written in prior seasons. This choice alienated many viewers with irresolvable ruptures in the narrative. Nonetheless, the series' finale affirms *Ragnarok's* consistent message of building a better future by focusing on the importance of love and equality.

Adaptations of Norse Myth

Before delving further into *Ragnarok*, we should consider the use of Norse mythology in art and culture. In 1665, a Danish scholar translated the *Poetic Edda* and parts of Snorri Sturluson's *Prose Edda* from Old Norse into Latin, making Norse mythology available to the educated class across Europe. The first vernacular translation of the *Prose Edda* appeared in Danish in the seventeenth century (Hagland, 1994) and in English in 1842 (Dasent). Selections from the *Poetic Edda* were first published in 1797 (Cottle), and the first full English translation of the poem *Völuspá* from which lines are quoted directly in *Ragnarok*, was done in 1823 (Turner). Once translations from Old Norse became available, interest in Norse mythology skyrocketed, as evidenced by its many retellings from the nineteenth century to the present—most recently Neil Gaiman's *Norse Mythology* (2017). The popularity of the Old Norse gods and tales told of them "went viral in the 19th century and have given rise since to [innumerable] stories and fantasies and spin-offs. Everyone has heard of Ragnarok and Valhalla, Thor and Odin, the wolf Fenrir and the Midgard Serpent" (Shippey, 2017).

From the nineteenth century to the present, adaptations of Norse myth have tended to use the source material to serve the creators' visions of an idealized world. Composer Richard Wagner, for example, drew from this mythology and other medieval texts to create *Der Ring des Nibelungenen* (1848–1874), an operatic cycle that celebrates Norse mythology as "the historical heart of [German] national culture" (O'Donoghue, 2007, p. 132). William Morris, translating Old Norse stories in the late nineteenth century, "despaired of the modern world, and ... saw in Norse myth the heroes and values which matched [his] own vision of a better one" (O'Donoghue, 2007, p. 162). More contemporarily, Marvel Comics and the MCU have offered the best-known adaptation of Norse gods. Marvel's *Mighty Thor* comic debuted in 1962, and introduced the young Neil Gaiman to Norse mythology. Today, Marvel's most attention-grabbing adaptation is its *Thor* films, three of which were released before *Ragnarok*'s debut (in 2011, 2013, and 2017). Marvel's presentation of Thor in the superhero genre puts the god in a narrative ethos where heroes and villains are easily distinguishable, and where good prevails—an ideal world indeed.

Ragnarok pursues its own vision of an ideal world, one that averts ecological destruction. This seemingly modern interpretation is grounded in medieval texts. The mythic ragnarok, the "end of the world," is heralded by disastrous climate change. In *Völuspá,* found in the *Edda* and quoted by Snorri, we learn that the seas rise because of the Midgard Serpent's rage. Snorri also explains that ragnarok begins with the *fimbulvetr*, a three-year winter, followed by the world being plunged into darkness and the Midgard Serpent spitting poison into the air and water (*Poetic Edda*, c. 1270/2014, p. 10; Sturluson, c.1220/1996, pp. 52–53). *Ragnarok* hearkens back to these chaotic (un)natural events: in season one, episode one (S1:E1) we hear a radio announcer say, "Wild amounts of water in the river this year, the thaw has started already" (Price & Foldager Sørensen, 2020). Such announcements pepper several episodes and, as Isolde shows on her YouTube channel, fish are dying from pollution in Edda's fjords.

While the original ragnarok and modern climate change may seem synonymous in their movement toward destruction, the myth includes the hopeful promise of rebirth, which *Ragnarok* alludes to when the seeress, Wenche, says, "Many think that ragnarok is the end. They are wrong. It is the beginning" (S1:E6). Price, *Ragnarok*'s creator, sees in the myths a parallel to the modern problem of chaos vs. order, interpreting "chaos" as the destruction of the environment and "order" as a healthy globe; he uses the myths, as others have done, to express hope for a better world.

Ragnarok signals its awareness of prior adaptations with a quiet wink and a nod, not to emulate them, but to highlight its divergence from them. Wagner and his work appear in important characters' names: the elderly man who becomes Odin is named Wotan Wagner, while Magne's best friend and moral guide is Isolde, named by her opera-loving father for the heroine of Wagner's *Tristan and Isolde*. But Wagner, known as a proponent of racial purity, is also popular among white supremacists; as Magne's brother Laurits notes, "Wagner was Hitler's favorite composer" (S1:E1). This line subtly highlights *Ragnarok*'s racially diverse cast and its message of inclusivity as the foundation of a better world. The series offers a more paradoxical response, however, to Marvel's globally popular *Thor* films, echoing some of the MCU's choices while pointedly controverting most others.

Superhero Stories

Ragnarok salutes Marvel's comics and films by positioning Thor as a "superhero" with a clear mission to save the world from evil. Because many people, "not least young people," fear a looming ecological apocalypse, Price says he "figured that people [...] need something to put their faith in. There is a need for a tale of a hero" (Netflix Nordic, 2020b). A familiar trope in many superhero tales is the hero's acquisition of powers from a sudden encounter with a powerful object or figure; in Marvel's *Spider-Man* (2002), for example, Peter Parker becomes the titular hero when bitten by a genetically-altered spider. In *Ragnarok*, Wenche's touch initiates Magne as Thor. Humorously, the only superheroes explicitly named come from one of Marvel's rivals, DC Comics: After Magne's classmate Iman is initiated as Freya, she and Magne jokingly compare themselves to Batman and Robin.

More pointedly, *Ragnarok* copies features of the MCU *Thor* franchise, particularly its repositioning of the god Loki as Thor's brother rather than Odin's blood-brother, as mythology says. In casting these roles, *Ragnarok* follows Marvel's lead: a large blond for Thor (Chris Hemsworth in the MCU, David Stakston in *Ragnarok*), and a skinny brunet for Loki (Tom Hiddleston in the MCU, Jonas Strand Gravli in *Ragnarok*). Both properties expand the myths' portrayal of Loki's ambiguous gender. In Snorri's *Edda*, shape-shifter Loki takes the form of a mare and gives birth to a foal, an eight-legged horse named Sleipnir. Marvel developed Loki's gender fluidity in a 2007 comic-book appearance of "Lady Loki" (*Thor*); in 2014, their comic *Loki: Agent of Asgard* has Odin describing Loki as "both son and daughter" (Ewing), and in 2021 Disney+, Marvel's parent company, announced that Loki is officially gender fluid (Delbel). In *Ragnarok*, Magne's brother Laurits/Loki is both gay and gender fluid, variously identifying as male and female. He "births" a mythical creature (in this case, the Midgard Serpent) as a giant tapeworm, via the equivalent of a C-section, and in one episode Laurits dresses as a woman to impersonate Ran Jutul, the school principal.

But *Ragnarok*'s similarity to Marvel ends with these few, albeit important, details. The superhero genre prioritizes action and spectacle over character; *Ragnarok* reverses those priorities, using sparse special effects and delving deeply into three-dimensional characters to tell a more nuanced story. Where Marvel uses Norse myths only glancingly, as a springboard for action-tales, *Ragnarok* steeps itself in the Old Norse texts. Its focus on a mythical past controverts the superhero genre's typical choice of a futuristic, science-fiction milieu; as Neil Gaiman recounts in his recollection of Marvel comics, Asgard, the home of the gods, was drawn as "a towering science fictional city of imposing buildings and dangerous edifices" (2017, p. 11). Furthermore, superhero movies build towards a climactic battle between heroes and villains, but *Ragnarok* eventually averts a violent ending. *Ragnarok* thus borrows recognizable ideas from the superhero genre only to throw into stark relief its own different priorities. High among them is Price's focus on the "Norse" part of Norse mythology.

Scandinavian Specificity

The biggest difference between this show and the superhero genre is the sheer Scandinavian-ness of *Ragnarok*, which establishes a local specificity for Norse myth: Edda's high school teaches mythology, not as literature, but as history. Magne learns that Edda was the town that longest resisted conversion to Christianity, and that Edda was ragnarok's real location. Viewers receive an education, too; each episode begins with a dictionary-style definition of a word from Norse myth, highlighting the episode's contents. Moreover, Magne's life events parallel the myths he studies at school. For example, he and Laurits visit the Jutul home; suspecting Magne is immortal, the Jutuls get him drunk on mead and test his strength with an arm-wrestling match against Ran. Viewers who don't know that this scene mirrors Snorri's tale of Thor and Utgarda-loki are partially enlightened when the history teacher, Erik, later tells his class, "We have read the story of Thor, who was tested at the giants' house and they made him drink mead" (S1:E4).

Ragnarok's use of language, in particular, shows an extraordinary nod to the medieval sources; although the characters usually speak Norwegian, in key moments the gods and giants speak the "Old Tongue": Old Norse, the linguistic forebear of both modern Norwegian and Icelandic. When giants try to determine Magne's identity, they ask in Icelandic whether he understands the language: "*skilirðu ina fornu tungu?*" (S1:E4) Another use of the Old Tongue is the series' incorporation of lines from *Völuspá*, which tend to be vocally distorted and hard to distinguish; they connect the giants with their past since they occur either at ritual moments or when a Jutul yields to their inner giant. In the first episode, Vidar strips, his eyes glowing yellow, before ripping the heart from a reindeer. Distorted chanting in the background here and Vidar's recitation of those same lines (S1:E6; *Poetic Edda*, p. 11), when he disrobes and his eyes glow, signal the emergence of a giant rage and intent to kill.

Linguistic references to medieval texts differentiate *Ragnarok* from other adaptations and can trigger viewers' curiosity about the source material, potentially drawing a new audience for the original stories. Consider that the mountain where the students take a class trip is named *Ginnungagap*, an Old Norse name referring to the primordial void from which the world is created; the name of the Jutul mansion is Jutulheim, a play on the Norse *Jotunheim*, home of the giants; the Jutuls' dog is named Trym (Norwegian form of Icelandic *Thrymr*), the name of a giant identified in the poem *Thrymskvida* as an opponent of Thor; Trym attacks Magne, who kills the dog by prying apart his jaws, echoing Fenrir's death at ragnarok (Sturluson, c. 1220/1996, p. 54). Other instances echo the myths with humor, as when the mechanic, Harry (Tyr), tells Wotan (Odin, in a mobility scooter), "I'm not pimping your lawnmower thingie with an 8-legged horse in gold," a reference to Sleipnir, Odin's horse (S2:E4).

The Scandinavian past is particularly present in Jutulheim, as the Jutuls are the series' living link to mythological times. Mythology tells us that giants were the original deities, before gods displaced them. Accordingly, Vidar's curio cabinet holds mementos from the Jutuls' glory days of ritual sacrifices, including a mummified head that evokes the Tollund Man, a famous example of the Iron-Age sacrificial victims discovered in Danish peat bogs ("Tollund Man," n.d.). Such regional specificity makes the Nordic past feel real and *au courant* to Magne and to viewers. While Marvel's adaptations of Norse gods pay scant attention to the stories' grounding in Scandinavian culture, this series revels in it. As actor Jonas Strand Gravli said, "It's really nice to take that old Norse mythology and place it in Norway, in the landscape where it belongs" (Netflix Nordic, 2020a).

Because *Ragnarok* interprets Norse myth as local history, Thor and Loki are honored as important local sons by their embodiment in nuanced, three-dimensional people. This attention to the personalities of Norse gods allows us to see how the psyches of Magne and Laurits lead organically into their supernatural identities. Departing both from the mythology and from previous adaptations, *Ragnarok* imagines Norse gods as teenagers whom we watch grow into their mature selves.

Teen Dramas

Netflix and Price intended *Ragnarok* to function partly as a teen drama similar to Netflix's other youth-focused supernatural dramas like *Chilling Adventures of Sabrina* (2018–2020). The series cast several actors—David Stakston (Magne), Herman Tømmeraas (Fjor) and Theresa Frostad Eggesbø (Saxa)—who previously starred in the teen drama *Skam* (2015–2017), produced by Norwegian

Broadcasting Corporation, which broke streaming records in Norway and found fans worldwide (Woldsdal & Michelsen, 2016). These casting choices targeted young viewers who loved *Skam* and signaled *Ragnarok*'s membership in the teen-drama genre that older audiences often also enjoy.

Yet upon the series' debut, some reviewers faulted the show's use of conspicuous teen clichés, outdated musical references from the 1990s–2000s, and the too-familiar premise of a teenager tasked with saving the world (Campbell, 2020; Keller, 2020). The first few episodes are indeed rife with references to the genre of teen media that flourished at the millennium. But some references are far older, representing a longer cultural history surrounding "the teenager." In the first episode, when Isolde's diary falls open to a page revealing her secret crush on Saxa, the soundtrack briefly plays music in the style of 1950s teen love-songs. That episode's title, "New Boy," signals the trope of the teen protagonist as an outsider who moves to a new town and new school, used in *Rebel Without A Cause* (1955) long before resurfacing in TV series like *Beverly Hills 90210* (1990–2000) and *Buffy the Vampire Slayer* (1997–2003). Edda's teenagers hang out at the Edda Grill, where youthful dramas unfold over French fries—a device as old as "The Chok'lit Shoppe" in Archie Comics, which debuted in 1942.

Teen media consumers can recognize other familiar tropes: the hero (Magne), an academic under-achiever, befriends a fellow outsider, smart but shunned for her quirky interests (Isolde, the activist); wealthy, snobbish teens dominate the school (Saxa and Fjor); at Fjor's first appearance, his costume resembles the letterman jackets that signify popular "jocks" in countless American teen tales. As Fjor passes a table where Isolde and Magne sit, he says, "Are you recruiting new members for Greenpeace, or what?," which one reviewer singled out as a "very high-school-TV-show kind of line" (Keller, 2020). The rivalry between supernatural boys (Magne and Fjor) for a human girl (Gry) reminded some reviewers unpleasantly of *Twilight* (2005–2012).

But these familiar tropes quickly shrink in significance; as the conflict between gods and giants becomes the primary narrative, teen-drama conventions appear only to serve the mythological story. For example, the "virginity-loss narrative" and the "mean girl" character were common tropes in Gen X and Millennial teen TV, respectively (Marghitu, 2021, pp. 77, 109). *Ragnarok* employs both in consecutive first-season episodes: Saxa, in typical mean-girl fashion, manipulates Gry into admitting she's a virgin in a private conversation, then leaks that information to other girls, orchestrating Gry's bullying in the presence of their whole social group at the diner. Gry later berates Fjor for not defending her, and soon after, they have sex. In a Gen-X or Millennial teen series, these events would have formed a substantial story arc; in *Ragnarok* they get only a few brief scenes, with limited significance. Saxa lacks the mean girl's usual motivations, which focus on high-school social politics. Rather, Saxa follows giant law: Because Vidar has said the Jutuls must cut human ties, Saxa alienates Gry with brutal efficiency. Gry's experience of first sex is also subordinated to the mythological story. No emotional aftermath follows her intimacy with Fjor; the only significant emergent plot-point is that their coupling allows Gry access to Vidar's private study, where she sees evidence of the Jutuls' immortality. Teenagers' emotions, the crux of the mean-girl and virginity-loss tropes, disappear in the giants' shadow.

Ragnarok follows more closely the time-honored trope of the teen hero who sees a deeper truth beneath society's facade but is treated as a juvenile delinquent by authorities. In teen films, as Driscoll (2011) notes, such boys often suffer a "failure of expert guidance" from a "psychologically trained adviser" (p. 104). In season one, Magne fits this pattern when Edda's police dismiss Isolde's death as an accident; incensed, Magne tells the school psychologist that he, Magne, must pursue justice himself, and that he suspects the Jutuls of killing Isolde for snooping into their secrets. The unethical psychologist repeats this to Principal Jutul, who suspends Magne and requires him to undergo a full psychiatric evaluation. Magne's description of his heroic mission gets him diagnosed as a paranoid schizophrenic, which he and the audience know is unjust. Much later, the series' finale thoroughly undermines this seemingly consistent teen trope by confirming that Magne has, indeed, been living with mental illness.

In typical tales of misunderstood juvenile delinquents, the protagonist's conflict with authorities signals a generational divide. Teen dramas privilege teens and their perspectives, with adults mainly serving the teen story. By contrast, *Ragnarok* gives several adult characters, notably Magne's mother Turid and the Jutul parents, more complexity and screen-time than normal in teen TV. Indeed, the expectation of generational conflict is fundamentally problematized by the Jutul "family," who are unrelated and presumably the same age. They alternate roles as parents/children as centuries pass, using magic to appear younger or older. Thus, irony undercuts every scene of parent-teen conflict among the Jutuls, for whom "parent" and "child" are eternally cyclical and purely performative roles.

Ragnarok gestures at the generation gap by noting young people's prevalence among climate activists: Teenaged Swedish activist Greta Thunberg is mentioned twice, and a youth-organized protest against the Jutuls' factory is central to one episode, while Edda's adults seem apathetic. But the generational divide blurs as more adults become reincarnated gods: In addition to Harry and Wotan, two young-adult men, Kiwi and Jens, later become the gods Heimdall and Baldr.

Moreover, Edda's police chief and officials from Norway's Environmental Agency crack down on Jutul Industries after Magne exposes their leaking toxic-waste barrels. The side of "the good" comprises teens and adults, a reminder that youthful protest alone can't stop climate change, and that generational divisions—like other categorical human divisions—are irrelevant in the face of apocalypse.

Ragnarok thus begins by evoking teen tropes, but quickly destabilizes our expectations. So why raise them at all? Teen TV, like teen film, "works largely by telling us things we already know about characters and situations that we are presumed to instantly recognize" (Driscoll, 2011, p. 83). *Ragnarok*'s inclusion of "clichés" from the genre is, in this sense, normative. But it also signals a critique of genre: As with superhero tales, *Ragnarok* evokes yet subverts teen tropes, interrupting viewers' absorption in the genre-tale with disquieting reminders that genre is a limiting factor. These reminders are clearest when teen drama combines with the tale of gods and giants in the same scene, as when Saxa goes to the Edda Grill to escape Ran and Vidar's arguments. Magne is there, eating a burger. Seeing her, he tenses and prepares for a fight. Saxa dramatically reaches into her purse as though to grab a weapon, then extracts her credit card, waves it at Magne, and laughs, "Gotcha," before sitting down with him. "I thought you wanted to kill me," Magne says. "Not today," she replies, then sighs, "My family is fucked up." "Mine too," says a bemused Magne (S2:E2). While they commiserate about their families, as teens in diners have done for decades, the mythological animosity hovers. Saxa's credit card symbolizes the Jutuls' status as literal "corporate giants," all-powerful and aggressive. To conclude their chat, wealthy Saxa grabs working-class Magne's burger and takes a giant-sized bite. This scene comically confronts viewers with fissures that occur when genres collide, leaving us with a subtle feeling, like Magne's, that we aren't sure what's going on. Again, teen tropes serve a mythological purpose: This détente lays groundwork for Magne's later sexual relationship with Saxa, paralleling Thor's relationship with the giantess Jarnsaxa in mythology.

Ultimately, *Ragnarok*'s references to previous teen media are not the inept fumble that some early reviewers assumed. These references invite viewers to question the concept of genre, which divides by codes of inclusion and exclusion. As the series progresses, it makes increasingly clear a message of erasing divisions between people, and between genres. The critical distance triggered by the show's deliberately unfamiliar handling of familiar tropes underscores the series' thematic message.

Ragnarok follows one element of youth-centered stories more faithfully: the coming-of-age narrative in which youngsters grow into new, mature identities.

The series' final episode underscores this in Principal Jutul's graduation-day speech: "When you started at this school you were big children, but now that you're leaving us, you are adults" (S3:E6). Three of the show's young men—Fjor, Magne, and Laurits—confront critical challenges in choosing their identities, an issue tightly intertwined with the series' consistent theme: blending categories rather than rigidly dividing them.

Fjor, as the Jutul's current "teenage" boy, undergoes an identity crisis worthy of an actual teen when he falls in love with Gry in the first season. He develops concern for Gry's kindly father, a former Jutul employee now dying of cancer from exposure to toxic chemicals. Fjor begins opening his eyes to humans' well-being and feels compelled to reject the giants' self-centered life. When he leaves Jutulheim to live with Gry's family, Vidar argues in bewilderment, "You're still a giant." "Not anymore," says Fjor, and all signs point to his sincerity (S2:E1). He relinquishes interest in Jutul Industries to Saxa, and speaks movingly at the town's anti-Jutul protest.

But at Vidar's funeral, the Christian minister's eulogy about the Jutul legacy of son following father triggers Fjor's memory of Vidar saying "a true son returns to battle" (S2:E4). This phrase echoes in Fjor's mind and causes an epiphany, reversing his character's trajectory: He abandons Gry and seizes control of Jutul Industries, muscling Saxa aside by citing an 1872 corporate bylaw mandating leadership by "the eldest son." As he says to a stunned Saxa, Fjor follows "what is written," a declaration of renewed dedication to outdated, oppressive standards (S2:E5). Fjor's rejection of the promised coming-of-age narrative arc shows that giants are ultimately bound to "the old laws"—a sure sign, in this series, that Fjor must either change with the times or eventually perish. In season three, he finally chooses the former, completing his coming-of-age arc by relinquishing his giant-like lust for absolute power: After Saxa out-bullies him, Fjor gives her the leadership of Jutul Industries, happy to spend more time with his new, human girlfriend—Nora, a Jutul executive whose wisdom he admires.

Magne's and Laurits's coming-of-age trajectories begin with character traits matching what is known about Thor and Loki, showing their transformations as the result of organic growth. Magne demonstrates Thor's care for humans ("Midgard's protector") within two minutes of the first episode by pausing to help Wotan, whose mobility scooter has stalled in the street (Sturluson, c. 1220/1996, p. 55). Wenche then strokes Magne's face, allowing him, like Thor, to predict the weather. Here the series makes its first jab at genre-play, evoking a detail from Marvel's *Spider-Man*: Magne's physical transformation includes not just sudden strength, but also improved vision; his eyeglasses become useless. But unlike Peter

Parker's spider bite, nothing is random about Magne's transformation; Wenche selects him for his moral character. When he later demands why she changed him, she replies, "It's always been within you" (S1:E4).

Magne embodies Thor almost immediately because of his innate kindness and hatred of injustice. But becoming the god who represents law and order takes time. Magne has simplistic notions of good and evil as pure opposites, a moral code he must violate at a critical moment, sparking an identity crisis. To save Laurits from imminent murder, Magne physically fights Vidar, killing him in the heat of the moment—a moral rubicon for Magne. Horrified, he renounces his supernatural identity, praying to both pagan and Christian gods to remove his powers (S2:E4). His prayers are granted, but with costs: the Jutuls' villainy continues unchecked, and Magne, again a bespectacled teenager, is powerless. Turning to Wotan for counsel, Magne learns that simplistic moral binaries are useless; betrayal and killing are necessary means to Thor's goal of defeating giants. Wotan confirms that Magne, as Thor, must inhabit the grey zone between black and white absolutes of good and evil: "That's who you are," says Wotan, addressing the episode's title: "Know Yourself" (S2:E5). Magne becomes Thor again, implied to be his real self.

But season three proves that Magne's maturity isn't accomplished yet. Possessed by the martial spirit of Mjolnir, Thor's hammer, Magne goes to the opposite extreme of becoming a bully, humiliating the Jutuls and alienating his family, his girlfriend, Signy, and his fellow gods. Mythology provides the corrective Magne needs: it tells us that Thor should not bully giants but fight for order to protect both gods and humanity. For giants, Thor may be an agent of death, but for humans, he is their protector and was worshipped for his power to affect the weather and thus agriculture, an agent of life. Thor's father Odin, as Wotan, gives Magne a father-son talk about tempering power with responsibility to others. Magne takes this lesson to heart when the gods finally face the Jutuls for their climactic battle. Seeing how unfairly outnumbered the giants now are, and knowing that nothing but death can follow, Magne suddenly commands everyone to drop their weapons. They make peace through agreements; the Jutuls agree to stop production of toxic materials, and no one need die. Magne has found the balance between power and wisdom. His girlfriend, Signy, demands that he make a better effort to treat her as a respected partner, and Magne learns this lesson, too. Human love, he finds, is a mightier force than brute power.

Like Magne's, the series builds Laurits' character from the beginning with an eye towards his future supernatural identity: Loki, the hybrid half-giant, half-god. *Ragnarok* describes Loki as "unsteady, unreliable, teasing and ambiguous"

(S2:E2). Laurits doesn't seamlessly fit in to any social or family grouping. When his mother demands he discard the ever-growing, toothy tapeworm he keeps in his bedroom, Laurits defends this disturbing choice of pet by citing his non-traditional identity: "I don't like bunnies or cute little puppies ... I wear different clothes, listen to different music. [. . .] I don't believe in races, sexual identity, and normality" (S2:E5). Laurits, in fact, rejects strict categories of any kind—moral, gendered, or supernatural—and his loyalties shift mercurially. He feels familial affection for Turid and Magne, but repeatedly insults them with cruel "jokes." Even when defending his family, Laurits doesn't admit loving motives. After overhearing Ran insulting Magne, Laurits dresses as Ran at a town celebration to mimic her with a blistering speech about the Jutuls' disregard for others. But when schoolmates later praise Laurits' performance, he disavows any principled motivation: "I just wanted to piss on the tallest tree, and in this town, that happens to be the Jutuls" (S2:E1). Like Loki, Laurits disrupts for the sake of disruption. But pain underlies his mischief; he speaks to Turid of feeling like a "freak," unable to find a love-partner and alienated within his own family, as he is nothing like Magne or their deceased father. Turid then reveals a secret: she conceived Laurits in a one-night stand with Vidar. Thus, viewers understand that Laurits is half-giant.

Now that he's a Jutul, Laurits no longer feels like pissing on the family "tree." Thrilled to discover a new father and a sense of belonging, he undergoes Vidar's initiation to activate his immortality as a giant—an identity Laurits enthusiastically embraces, not realizing this will put him at odds with his brother, Magne. Like Loki, Laurits attempts to play both sides; but when he goes to Wotan's sanatorium to join the gods, Wotan, with the supernatural sight of Odin, sees Laurits/Loki's true character: "You're a traitor. It's not your fault, but that is what you are" (S2:E3). Hurt at being rejected again, Laurits injects himself with a stolen sample of Wotan's blood, knowing that Loki was Odin's blood brother. Divine blood finalizes Laurits' transformation to Loki, but his heartbreaks aren't finished; after Vidar's death, Laurits learns that his father had planned to kill him. As the other Jutuls now attempt to do so, Laurits saves himself by offering them the Midgard Serpent as a weapon against Magne. Laurits' evolution from snarky brother to traitorous Loki is made to look like the predictable result of lifelong pain.

To the humans around Laurits, who see none of his mythological identity-drama, Laurits represents Loki's ambiguity in the more visible way of gender fluidity. In addition to being gay, Laurits styles himself often in gender-neutral or sometimes feminine attire, donning his mother's blouse for a school dance, and increasingly wearing eye makeup as the series progresses. He dresses in the traditional women's national costume on Norway's Constitution Day (May 17) to mock Ran. In the third season, when visiting the Midgard Serpent now growing in Edda's fjord, Laurits says, "It's just me. Mommy" (S3:E1). Finding a loving boyfriend, Jens, becomes the crux of Laurits' transformation to a more consistent, happier person. His role as "double agent" between the gods and giants only ends when Fjor threatens Jens' life; this shifts Laurits' allegiances firmly to the gods' side, especially when Jens is initiated as a god, himself. As with Magne and Fjor, love ultimately leads Laurits to finding his true self—an identity that remains hybrid, but more peaceful and positive, as his mother happily notes. By giving him this developmental arc in the coming-of-age frame, *Ragnarok* alters the myths in which Loki fights on the giants' side. The series rewrites history to make human love the desired outcome.

Gender Identities

Ragnarok champions a message of dismantling antiquated social divisions and the hierarchies they cause. Just as the series asks viewers to consider the commingling of genres, it also questions old-fashioned ideas about gender identity, a significant site of progressive change examined in the series. Consistently problematizing the traditional, dichotomously opposed portrayal of men as strong leaders and women as subordinate nurturers, *Ragnarok* criticizes hypermasculinity and gender-rigidity while identifying better alternatives: acceptance of LGBTQ people, a nurturing form of masculinity and fatherhood, and significant, strong female characters.

Ragnarok seems at first to make a callous statement about LGBTQs by killing Isolde shortly after identifying her as a lesbian; this choice echoes the widely vilified #BuryYourGays trope, the tendency among TV series to kill gay characters (Waggoner, 2018). But Isolde remains present and important after death, appearing in Magne's dreams and visions to guide him on his quest. Her disembodied voice delivers voice-over narration throughout season three, and the series finale shows her appearing to Magne in the last moment, assuring him, "I'll always be with you" (S3:E6). But the show's greatest support of LGBTQ identity is in Laurits, whose gay orientation is mentioned throughout the series and is fulfilled in the third season, when his transformative relationship with Jens becomes a vital component in saving the world.

Ragnarok consistently disapproves of homophobes, sexists, racists, and other supporters of traditional patriarchal values. When Magne and Gry choose environmentalism as their topic for a class project, their elderly, white, male teacher warns, "Just be careful that your entire project doesn't end up about how it's only old white men who are destroying the world and causing all the ice to melt." Magne replies, "But isn't it true?" (S1:E2). Yes, it is: as the oldest white men in town, and the alternating leaders of Jutul Industries, Fjor and Vidar *have* caused the ice to melt from Edda's glacier. They also embody the retrograde masculinity that Kara M. Kvaran (2017) noted in her study of superhero films, "characterized by a belief that violence is manly and danger exciting, paired with a callous attitude toward women and the derision of anything considered feminine" (p. 226). That includes the environment, for the Jutul men. Taking a rather ecofeminist stance, *Ragnarok* presents climate change as the byproduct of a male-driven, capitalist ideology that violates nature to pursue profit; meanwhile, the series' beacon of environmentalism is a teen girl, Isolde. Vidar kills her, Fjor urinates on her memorial, and both poison the landscape that she loved. *Ragnarok* is not coy in blaming toxic masculinity for the world's looming destruction.

Moreover, the hero's journey in *Ragnarok* is not initiated by a real or symbolic father-son relationship, as it was in Marvel's *Thor* (2011) and other superhero films (Kvaran, p. 219). Rather, two women initiate the journey: Isolde, named for the healer in *Tristan and Isolde*, who teaches Magne environmental activism, and Wenche, who awakens him as Thor. Both continue after death to guide Magne in his dreams. Interestingly, the planet (*iord*) they seek to save is a feminine noun in Old Norse, and Thor's mother is the personified earth (Iord), suggesting that the motivating force behind Magne's quest is fundamentally feminine.

In *Ragnarok*, female characters have more interiority and importance than in a typical hero or superhero tale, where women are often portrayed as clueless nurturers (Kvaran). Turid, for example, while superficially (and at times, comically) resembling a cliché of the clueless nurturer, embodies a more realistic range of motherly emotions, including anger at her sons when they deserve it, and depression when they speak cruelly to her. The series' writers show more respect to Turid than her teenage sons do, highlighting her wisdom and warmth especially in season three. Similarly, Magne's and Fjor's love-interests—Gry, Signy, and Nora—display integrity, emotional maturity, and wisdom.

Among the giants, the women are as strong and brutal as the men. But Vidar, as the *pater familias*, has unparalleled freedom to rule with iron fists. In one episode, when Ran tries to stop Vidar from acting rashly, he backhands her across the face. In the English dub track Ran responds, "After 3,000 years you still think hitting someone makes you a man" (S1:E5). Violence and domination characterize Vidar's familial roles, a fact *Ragnarok* highlights by juxtaposing Vidar with other fathers, who model care and compassion. One episode emphasizes this contrast. Mourning his daughter Isolde's death, Erik puts aside his own grief to comfort the heartbroken Magne, hugging the boy as Magne cries; meanwhile, at Jutulheim, Vidar exercises authority and control, offering his hound a piece of meat but withholding it until Trym obeys orders. Ran enters, showing Vidar evidence that Fjor threatened the family's public image by desecrating Isolde's memorial. "I'll handle it," says Vidar. The "handling" is literal, as we soon see in his vicious beating of Fjor (S1:E2).

Even in a happier context, when offering gifts to his newly discovered son, Laurits, Vidar can only think of the most obvious clichés of powerful masculinity: a fast motorbike and meals of red meat. Despite his enjoyment in having a biological son, Vidar plans filicide when he later learns of Laurits' treachery. Not even paternity can change a giant's fundamentally brutal nature. *Ragnarok* implies a further critique of Jutul-style fatherhood in Wotan who, as Odin, is the "All-father" of the gods; Wotan variously offers younger gods wise counsel and patience, without force or cruelty. Thus, the series rewrites the mythological Odin to make him a more modern, kinder father-figure than the old ways would suggest.

The only Jutul to embrace progressive gender ideas is Saxa, whose giant-like lust for power makes her eager to run Jutul Industries. The company's board members have always been old, white men; as Saxa says, "I think we should do something about that. The world doesn't look like that anymore[. . . .] And those of us who have lived through 1,000 years of women's oppression are ready to show that it can be done so much better" (S2:E4). Though the series agrees with Saxa, as evidenced by her superior handling of the company's public-relations crisis, giants' traditions trump feminism. Ran fails to support Saxa's ambitions, begging Fjor to return and take control. When Fjor does so, he becomes even more of a traditionalist than Vidar was. Vidar, Ran, and Fjor are happy with old-style patriarchy and its specified gender roles.

Changing Times

A lack of stability, identity, and moral degeneration, according to Snorri, demarcate the coming of ragnarok: "Then brothers will kill each other out of greed and no one will show mercy to father or son in killing. [. . .] The whole earth and mountains will shake so much that [. . .] all fetters and bonds will snap and break" (Sturluson, c. 1220/1996, p. 53). Everything changes in the lead up to the final battle between giants and gods.

In *Ragnarok*, identity categories that have historically comforted those in power blur. For the Jutuls, eroding boundaries can only be disturbing: their fortunes fall because of leaking waste-barrels, and the Jutuls themselves, who have stayed perfectly static for millennia, are flummoxed to find their own boundaries becoming permeable, as they start turning a little human. The starkest example is Vidar's mysterious impregnation of Turid; giants are normally barren, one of the series' several indicators that "the old ways" are fruitless. Despite centuries of sexual dalliances with humans, the giants have never invested emotions in these couplings. Yet Ran finds herself having emotions—something all Jutuls note is not their strong-point—when she learns Vidar fathered a child with Turid. To Ran's consternation, something foreign slides out of her eye: a tear. Meanwhile, Vidar is turning "soft" in his habits of eating junk food on the couch while watching TV, and Fjor has fallen in love for the first time ever. In addition, the giants, because of their corporate greed and resultant pollution, are losing status with the populace—it's been a long time since humans worshipped them—and because of failure to adapt with changing times, they are rupturing from within. Watching Fjor speak against his family at the anti-Jutul protest, Vidar worriedly asks, "What's happening to us?" (S2:E3)

While the Jutuls find change terrifying, the series argues that changes are good and necessary, especially when they erase boundaries that categorize people hierarchically. This emphasis may be a reminder that ragnarok, the destruction of the world, is followed by rebirth. We see evidence of such positive changes when we examine how the series positions modern Norway and its people. One example is the references to Wagner, named in the first episode as Hitler's favorite composer as a comment on white supremacy. In the series' world, there is not, nor should there be, any racial purity: the teens' friend-group includes Oscar, who is Black, and Iman, a Sri Lankan adopted into Norway. Iman's transformation into Freya makes a powerful point: If the gods themselves don't discriminate by race, neither should humans. Furthermore, a Black woman—Yngvild, Oscar's mother—is Edda's police chief. Other forms of "purity" are equally destabilized: LGBTQ romance is embraced by the series' writers and main characters, while neurological and physical disabilities are included in the series' collection of heroes. Magne copes with dyslexia and anger-management issues by using audio books and fidget-toys. Wotan needs a mobility scooter. The series shows its audience a Norway containing a motley crew of people, young and old, light and dark-skinned, gay and straight, abled and disabled, allowing for and accepting diversity; the pristine and perfect giants do not represent all of Norway.

An awareness of a diverse population, together with pride in Edda and its past, replaces the twisted patriotism of white supremacists and xenophobes with a modern patriotism that embraces diversity and a care for the environment. This combination of regional pride and patriotism appears vividly in S1:E6, "Yes, We Love This Country." The episode's title is the name of Norway's national anthem, sung on May 17, a day marked by parades, speeches, and the wearing of national costumes (Visit Norway, n.d.). At Edda's celebration, Laurits dresses in traditional female costume to deliver his speech about the Jutuls' disregard for people and the planet. Being anti-corporate, anti-capitalist, anti-racist, is the right way to be patriotic. The best way to "love this country," *Ragnarok* suggests, is to stop poisoning it with industrial waste and social hatreds.

Ragnarok concludes the first two seasons with an idealistic message about environmentalism, equality, and diversity that changes somewhat in the third season. Idealism continues in the expression of the importance of love: love for one's fellow, one's home, one's planet. Season three's finale depicts the former giants and gods—together with Signy and Nora—sitting around a table, happy. This loving and lovely ending is foreshadowed by Iman's speech in S3:E3 that summarizes the show's most consistent theme—the importance of love—and does so in the words of the only reincarnated goddess in the entire show, bringing us back to the instantiation of Magne's quest by women. In some ways, the show has come full circle.

In other ways, however, it has not. In the first two seasons, *Ragnarok* relied heavily on Norse mythology, toying with the genres of superhero stories and teen dramas to disrupt viewers' expectations. In the third season, the show introduced another twist, the psychological genre. The series certainly had played with ideas of changing how "it was written," but the third season deviated sharply from its *own* established narrative when it revealed that every mythological element of the tale was all in Magne's head, a childish fantasy exacerbated by paranoid schizophrenia—justifying the season-one diagnosis that viewers had been led to believe was wrong.

In making everything mythological a delusion, the writers trivialized what they previously spoke so positively about: belief in gods, faith, the supernatural. Taking to various online forums, angry viewers demonstrated what Linda Hutcheon (2013) observed in *A Theory of Adaptation*: loyal fans dislike it when content creators make changes to an original's fidelity (p. 190). As one incensed fan wrote, "We were betrayed this season" (Sean C., 2023). Even worse, by suggesting that Magne throws away his fantasy when he discards his Thor comics, that he steps into mature sanity when he graduates from high school and is "cured" by Signy's love, *Ragnarok* implies that Magne is also cured of schizophrenia. Mental illness does not work like that.

Ultimately, *Ragnarok*'s trivializing messages about schizophrenia and faith made it difficult for many viewers to accept the ending. The show promised us mythology but then dismissed it as a fantasy. As Sean C. (2023) further mused, "This show could have rectified and added to what people know about this mythology." After all, *Ragnarok* had no qualms in rewriting what is written, as its messages about the need to dissolve hierarchies, to heal the planet, to seek equality, to reimagine patriotism and to embrace the power of love reveal.

References

Campbell, K. (2020, February 10). Netflix's Ragnarok: Season 1 review [Review of the TV series *Ragnarok*, by A. Price, Creator]. *IGN*. https://www.ign.com/articles/netflixs-ragnarok-season-1-review

Cottle, A. S. (1797). *Icelandic poetry or the Edda of Saemund*. N. Briggs.

Dasent, G. (1842). *The Prose Edda or Younger Edda*. Nordstedt and Sons.

Delbel, J. (2021, June 6). Disney confirms gender fluidity of Tom Hiddleston's Loki. *The Direct*. https://thedirect.com/article/loki-tom-hiddleston-disney-gender-fluid

Driscoll, C. (2011). *Teen film: A critical introduction*. Berg.

Ewing, A. (2014–2015). *Loki: Agent of Asgard*, #11. Marvel Comics.

Gaiman, N. (2017). *Norse mythology*. Norton.

Hagland, J. R. (1994). The reception of Old Norse literature in late eighteenth-century Norway. In A. Wawn (Ed.), *Northern antiquity: The post-medieval reception of edda and saga*, (pp. 27–40). Hisarlik Press.

Hutcheon, L. (2013). *A theory of adaptation* (2nd ed.). Routledge.

IMDbPro. *Thor: Ragnarok*. https://www.boxofficemojo.com/release/rl2959312385/?ref_=bo_fr_table_2.

Keller, J. (2020, January 31). Stream it or skip it: 'Ragnarok' on Netflix, A Danish drama about another end-of-world battle, and a teen that could stop it [Review of the TV series *Ragnarok*, by A. Price, Creator]. *Decider*. https://decider.com/2020/01/31/ragnarok-netflix-stream-it-or-skip-it/.

Kvaran, K. M. (2017). Super daddy issues: Parental figures, masculinity, and superhero films. *The Journal of Popular Culture, 50*(2), 218–238. https://doi.org/10.1111/gpcu.12531.

Marghitu, S. (2021). *Teen TV*. Routledge. https://doi.org/10.4324/9781315229645

Netflix. (2018, November 7). From the creator of Borgen and Ride upon a storm comes Ragnarok a new Norwegian Netflix original series [Press release]. https://about.netflix.com/en/news/from-the-creator-of-borgen-and-ride-upon-the-storm-comes-ragnarok-a-new-norwegian-netflix-original-series

Netflix Nordic. (2020a). *The making of Ragnarok: Ep 1*. [Video]. YouTube. https://www.youtube.com/watch?v=sIKNvE6g4qg&t=88s.

Netflix Nordic. (2020b). *The making of Ragnarok: Ep 6*. [Video]. YouTube. https://www.youtube.com/watch?v=5OrMr_QmMCI.

O'Donoghue, H. (2007). *From Asgard to Valhalla: The remarkable history of the Norse myths*.Tauris.

Price, A., & Foldager Sørensen, M. L. (Executive Producers). (2020–2023). *Ragnarok* [TV series]. SAM Productions; Netflix.

Sean C. (2023, September 11). Ragnarok: Season 3 Reviews. *Rotten Tomatoes*. https://www.rottentomatoes.com/tv/ragnarok/s03/reviews?type=user

Shippey, T. (2017, February 3). Neil Gaiman on the Old Norse myths; The stories of Thor and Loki and Freya, which went viral in the 19th century, remain funny and irreverent. [Review of the book *Norse Mythology*, by Neil Gaiman]. *Wall Street Journal (Online)*.

Souch, I. (2022, Fall). Troubling the water: Hydro-imaginaries in Nordic television drama. *Academic Quarter*, *25*, 51–63. https://doi.org/10.54337/academicquarter.vi25.7635.

Sturluson, S. (ca. 1220/1996). *The Prose Edda* (A. Faulkes, Trans.). Dent.

The Poetic Edda (c. 1270). (C. Larrington, Trans., rev. ed.). (2014). Oxford.

Thor vol 3 #5. (2007, December 28). *Thor: Special delivery*. Writer: J.M. Straczynski. Art: Olivier Coipel. Marvel Comics.

"Tollund Man and Elling Woman." (n.d.). *Museum Silkeborg*. https://www.museumsilkeborg.dk/tollund-man-and-elling-woman.

Turner, S. (1823). *The history of the Anglo-Saxons* (4th ed.). Longman.

Visit Norway. (n.d.) *Innovation Norway*. https://www.visitnorway.com/typically-norwegian/norways-national-day/.

Waggoner, E. B. (2018). Bury your gays and social media fan response: Television, LGBTQ representation, and communitarian ethics. *Journal of Homosexuality, 65*(13), 1877–1891. https://doi.org/10.1080/00918369.2017.1391015.

Woldsdal, N., & Michelsen. I. (2016, December 21). Skam slå alle rekorder. *NRK*. https://web.archive.org/web/20170211130806/https://www.nrk.no/kultur/skam-slar-alle-rekorder-1.13282929

5

Mystical and the Mundane in Netflix's *The Irregulars:* Exploring Supernatural Narrative Engagement and Reception

GWENDELYN S. NISBETT AND NEWLY PAUL

A hallmark of supernatural teen media is the focus on that which makes the supernatural strange and otherworldly juxtaposed with the banality of everyday struggles. Characters regularly battle demons and nightmares by calling upon magic and mystical powers, battling personal demons all the while. These shows and movies often find success because they adeptly weave a supernatural storyline with a typical teen storyline revolving around relationships, mental health, identity, belonging, and friendship. By getting swept up in the compelling narratives of these shows, viewers can escape their troubles while learning to handle real-world problems by watching these characters navigate similar issues (Green & Brock, 2000). They may even carry the stories with them, mull them over, and call upon them in negotiating everyday problems (Slater et al., 2018).

A great tradition of successful supernatural teen television shows mixes the magical with the mundane to transfix viewers by both the human storylines and the fantastical rush of the faerie tale (e.g., *Buffy the Vampire Slayer*). For this chapter, we explore a newer transmedia text: Netflix's *The Irregulars*, which ran for one season in 2021 and was then canceled. The show exists in two worlds, flirting with the supernatural while firmly planted in the corporeal issues of friendship, belonging, grief, and mental well-being. The show follows a group of teens (some with supernatural abilities) as they explore paranormal mysteries in

Victorian London, interwoven within the Sherlock Holmes narrative universe—juxtaposing esoteric supernatural themes and the Holmes' canon's empirical tradition. *The Irregulars* is interesting to analyze because it appeals to both a younger audience (with its focus on adolescent struggles) and adults (with its placement within the Holmes narrative tradition). Because these audiences are often drawn to a show's different aspects, this chapter explores audience responses to the characters and supernatural storylines.

In analyzing *The Irregulars*, we explore the notion that mixing the mystical with the mundane can help viewers think about societal problems. In particular, we explore the show's approach to issues common among young people, including mental health and wellbeing, belonging, and exploring identity. We also consider the show's exploration of heavier concepts such as grief, suicide, and drug addiction. Oddly enough, the showrunners appear to have made an effort to select a diverse cast, but do not really address issues of race within the wider storylines about gender. They do address class issues, which is not surprising considering the show's British origins. In using a diverse cast, the show joins a host of others such as *Gossip Girl*, *The Rutherford Falls* and *The Wonder Years*, signaling a growing trend of the diversification of writers and casts. But by skirting racial issues in the storylines, the show signals that its focus is firmly on escapism and that it envisions a world where characters see race as a part of their identity without necessarily focusing on interracial tensions in the plotline. By adopting this approach, the show joins others such as *Bridgerton* that sacrifice perceived historical accuracy for escapism (Tillet, 2021). While this approach could be problematic in that it whitewashes diverse characters' experiences, it could also be seen as a way to expand possibilities for actors of color who tend to be cast negatively in primetime shows (Mastro & Greenberg, 2000). Read in the context of increased social awareness of mental health and wellbeing, it is possible that *The Irregulars'* narratives can increase audience understanding and acceptance of these issues. Therefore, we also examine whether these narratives work with different audiences.

A good narrative aids the audience above and beyond fulfilling immediate entertainment desires. Our project is grounded in Entertainment-Education (E-E) research, which explores how entertainment can help audiences negotiate social topics. E-E research focuses on the potential for viewers to learn about social issues through identifying with characters and deeply engaging with narratives (Singhal et al., 2004; Singhal & Rogers, 2002). This chapter utilizes the E-E concepts of narrative transportation (Green & Brock, 2000) and the extended transportation imagery model (Van Laer et al., 2014) to explore how the show's narratives about struggle and acceptance can demystify mental health issues, reduce stigma, and inspire information seeking. Narrative transportation concerns the ability of people to become highly engaged with a narrative, and through the process of being transported by the story, they can learn from the content (Slater & Rouner, 2002). Specifically, enjoyment of a great story can reduce resistance to messages within a narrative intended to educate. Thus, entertainment can successfully help people to negotiate issues like mental health because people drop their defenses and allow the content to soak in (Moyer-Gusé & Nabi, 2010).

The chapter utilizes a qualitative approach to examine how the show's themes interplay with narrative engagement surrounding social issues and the characters' journey for belonging. Following previous studies (see for example, Champlin & Paul, 2020), we evaluate the show for themes and elements that cause narrative transportation, namely, the use of identifiable characters, imaginable plotlines, and verisimilitude. Thus, our project demonstrates the mechanisms by which showrunners play the role of "storyteller" while presenting their content to audiences.

The chapter first presents an overview of the show with focus on modern themes intermixing with supernatural storylines, presenting narrative transportation and engagement as an analytical framework for the study. We then offer details on our methods for analyzing the text of the show and the reaction from different audience platforms, followed by our examination of the show in terms of the narrative engagement elements of identifiable characters, imaginable plotlines, and verisimilitude. Finally, we discuss audience reception and the importance of audience engagement.

The Irregulars

The Irregulars began as a graphic novel that subsequently developed as a Netflix show, upon which this chapter focuses. As mentioned earlier, *The Irregulars* offers a supernatural take on the detective trope. It depicts a rag-tag team of Victorian London teens that investigates mysterious, supernatural cases as "irregular" associates of Sherlock Holmes and John Watson, both of whom have been dabbling with magic and parallel dimensions while attempting to deal with personal demons.

The ensemble of characters has very modern problems. Among the Irregulars, Bea, their leader, is bright, strong, and logic-driven; she is dealing with poverty and parental abandonment. Her younger sister, Jessie, has supernatural powers that allows her to see and visit other realities and dimensions, but the series presents her as emotionally and physically fragile. (We find out later that Bea and Jessie are half-sisters, and that Holmes is Jessie's biological father and had been Bea's adoptive father when she was a toddler.) Thus, though Jessie and Bea are inseparable sisters, they are quite different from one another. Bea and Jessie are friends with the pugnacious Billy, who has a crush on Bea and a hang-up about his working-class status. Spike functions as a comic-relief character. Leopold is a posh yet sickly prince, who hides his royal identity from his friends for most of the season. While the show's storytelling emphasizes the teens, these characters float in the orbits of Holmes (a drugged-out mess) and Watson (who has a jealousy-driven evil streak and is the mastermind behind the supernatural happenings). Taken together, the cast offers some diversity in representation: Thaddea Graham, who portrays Bea, is Chinese-Northern Irish. British actors McKell David (Spike) and Royce Pierreson (Watson) identify as having a mixed ethnicity, while a recurring supernatural villain called "The Linen Man" (played by American actor Clarke Peters) is Black. The rest of the ensemble lead characters—Holmes, Jessie, Leopold, Billy—feature cast members who appear to be British and white.

The primary supernatural teen in the show is Jessie, played by teen actor Darci Shaw. Jessie is clairvoyant and possesses the ability to understand the supernatural occurrences plaguing London. Jessie possesses psychic powers and often has nightmares that foreshadow events that occur later in the show. As Battis (2011) points out, supernatural literature positions marginalized youth as heroic and magic as a weapon for "outcast and exiled children" (p. 7). We see this clearly in Jessie's characterization, as other characters like Bea and Watson increasingly seek her powers to resolve cases that involve supernatural activities.

Narrative Engagement

The transportation-imagery model (Green & Brock, 2000) explains how narratives in television shows, movies, advertisements, newspapers, songs, and other media content influence people (Brechman & Purvis, 2015; Wang & Tang, 2021) and transport them into the world described by the narrative and the characters that inhabit them. The transportation-imagery model has five assumptions (Green & Brock, 2002). First, narrative transportation applies to stories with a discernible beginning, middle and end. Second, transportation occurs when readers become absorbed in the fictional world and accept the narrative as real.

Third, people who can evoke powerful mental images are more likely to be transported than others. Fourth, the text should have qualities such as suspense and drama that keep people engaged. Lastly, the medium of the message matters. Narratives presented on film are "concrete, complete and fast-flowing" (p. 330) and tend to limit imagination. Print narratives, on the other hand, allow more freedom to the reader to read at their own pace, which facilitates transportation.

An extension of this model, called the Extended Transportation-Imagery Model or ETIM, maps the primary antecedents and consequences of narrative transportation and explains the qualities necessary in a storyteller and a story receiver for transportation to occur (Van Laer et al., 2014). According to ETIM, these three qualities are identifiable characters, imaginable plot, and verisimilitude. Characters should be clearly identified from the beginning of the story such that audiences can identify with them and develop empathy for them. The idea of imaginable plot implies that the occurrences described in the narrative should resemble real-world experiences such that people are able to imagine the elements of the narrative without any difficulty. Verisimilitude is the possibility of a story occurring in real life. It applies more strongly to fiction than non-fiction narratives. When people believe there is a chance that a given narrative might occur in the real world, they are more likely to suspend disbelief. This raises an interesting question with supernatural storylines, as they are not literally possible, but can nevertheless function as metaphors and fables about real-life issues.

RQ1: Are these elements reflected in the text?

The ETIM states six important antecedents that should be present in a story receiver for transportation to occur: familiarity, attention, transportability, and age, education and gender of the audience. People who are culturally familiar with the topic of the narrative are likely to experience stronger transportation effects than others. Related to this, when audiences feel motivated to pay attention to the story and sympathize with the characters, they are more likely to be transported than others. Lastly, audience demographics play a role in the effectiveness of a narrative. Broadly speaking, younger people, women, and those with higher education levels have a higher likelihood of being transported. To better understand *The Irregulars'* impact on audiences, we will analyze reviews and social media posts about the show to address the following research question:

RQ2: How do different audience members react to the show?

Though studies have not yet examined the adaptation of Sherlock Holmes stories in the supernatural genre, we drew broadly from the literature on modern-day adaptations of Sherlock Holmes and broadly, detective story formats. As Bassnett (2017) observes, the detective story format falls into two broad categories—one that is escapist and one that uses plotlines, characterizations, settings and language to comment on society. Sherlock Holmes stories, often set against the backdrop of English mansions, are thought of as escapist, but their modern-day adaptations such as the BBC drama *Sherlock* have clear political undertones. As Rixon (2014) argues, *Sherlock* offers a glimpse into modern British identity. This version is exclusionary, however, because it portrays Holmes as a modern, technology savvy detective who solves cases against the backdrop of modern-day London, portrayed as a shiny city filled with brilliant skyscrapers, minus a homeless population or public housing. In presenting a sanitized version of the detective and London, the show ignores the "multicultural vision of the city" (p. 171). Few scholarly works have examined the portrayal of the Baker Street Irregulars in particular, but Cheetham's (2012) analysis finds that while this group of children were decidedly depicted as working-class in the original series, subsequent adaptations showed them as belonging to a higher class and living in safer environments. Contrary to this, our analysis, as explained below, finds that in *The Irregulars'* supernatural genre, the Baker Street Irregulars fall back to their original depictions.

Studying Storytelling and Audience Reactions

We watched all eight episodes of *The Irregulars,* ranging in duration from 49 to 58 minutes. We used a coding guide adapted from previous works such as Champlin and Paul (2020) and Kreuter et al. (2007) and qualitative thematic analysis to analyze the show's use of story factors and storyteller antecedents in the show's narratives. In this section, we explore three findings regarding the show's creators' use of storyteller antecedents: identifiable characters; an imaginable plot; and verisimilitude, with attention to how these features persuade audiences and spark their attention. We offer themes and examples from the show to illustrate our arguments.

To gauge the show's impact, we chose to include an analysis of audience reviews and social media posts in response to the show's supernatural storylines, diverse casts, and take on modern issues. To incorporate audience reception and get a snapshot of how audience members perceived the show, we sampled posts from IMDb and Tumblr. IMDb posts consist of short text reviews, while

Tumblr users post in a variety of formats. IMDb provided us with reviews from a wider, more general audience, while Tumblr offered us perspectives from more niche audiences, including people posting about fandoms and pop culture (Tiffany, 2022).

These differences are rooted in the platforms themselves. IMDb has been a mainstay for technical information on films and shows, attracts a variety of age groups (Statista, 2022), has more male users than Tumblr (Reynolds, 2017), and attracts audiences with passing or general interests in information about a show/film. In recent years, IMDb has also seen an uptick in "review bombing" from people in opposition to progressive texts or from super fans unhappy with the adaptation of a familiar canon (Sanders, 2022). In contrast, Tumblr brands itself as a platform for "fandom, art, chaos" and greets app downloaders with the phrase "welcome back to weird." Tumblr draws users that are heavily invested in shows/films and the fandoms that accompany them. Users skew younger (Statista, 2022) and more female than the wider IMDb audience. Users post fan art, fan fiction, screen grabs, gifs, and discuss theories about a show/film. While our data from these sites do not constitute a generalizable picture of audience reception, their inherent differences do give us an idea of the complexities of different types of viewers, reflected by IMDb's more general audience and Tumblr's supernatural fandom audience.

In taking a sample of posts from IMDb, we gathered reviews from the date that the show was released (March 2021) through until Fall 2022, gathering 589 reviews. For our Tumblr sample, we searched for keywords "the Irregulars" and "Netflix Irregulars" posted from the beginning of the show until Fall 2022, yielding approximately 100 posts. We read all comments from the IMDb show page and all Tumblr posts using the above hashtags for our analysis. Each researcher then coded the posts using a textual analysis approach (Hesse-Biber, 2017), which included reading each post and making note of the contents and the tone. We noted themes that emerged from the data were noted, then met to discuss the themes, which we subsequently reduced to two main themes for each platform.

Story Factors and Storyteller Antecedents in *The Irregulars*

Identifiable Characters

The concept of identifiable characters refers to those characters that the audience can easily connect with and see the world from a similar perspective (Van Laer et al., 2014). *The Irregulars* features two key characters—Watson and Holmes—who are identifiable to many audience members, given the long history of Sherlock Holmes media. Audience data suggest that the "irregular" main characters were also identifiable as complex people inhabiting many of the characteristics and issues in modern society (e.g., diversity, economic strife, etc.).

Similar to other modern versions of Holmes such as the BBC's *Sherlock* and the U.S. television series *Elementary*, we found that this show incorporates Watson and Holmes as identifiable characters. Already well-established icons in popular culture, *The Irregulars* repurposes Watson and Holmes for a modern audience, reimagining them in a supernatural/paranormal context. While popular culture traditionally depicts Dr. Watson as a friend and confidante of Holmes—a constant companion with an agreeable, if bumbling persona—*The Irregulars* overturns this characterization. Instead, it recasts Dr. Watson as a negative, egoistic character who is tired of living in Holmes' shadow and driven to evil acts to prove his intelligence. Adding further complexity, *The Irregulars* ultimately reveals that Watson is in love with Holmes, and that he was jealous of Holmes' partner, Alice, and her emotional connection with Holmes.

Holmes himself appears halfway into the season. Though traditionally Holmes is portrayed as an aloof genius, *The Irregulars* portrays Holmes as an ambivalent character, addicted to opium, prone to outbursts; an unsuitable parent who abandoned Bea and Jessie after their mother's death; and devoid of his characteristic wit, charm, and deductive powers. Bea aptly describes him as a "broken old man who is trapped in his memories" (Ep. 5, 50:11).

The show also reimagines the Baker Street Irregulars. In Conan Doyle's books, the group were teen boys who lived on the streets and assisted Holmes in gathering information discreetly. In the show, the irregulars are teenagers of various races and genders, who are hired by Watson to help solve cases, one of whom has supernatural powers that become more important as the series progresses. The show's violation of the canon is likely aimed to increase the audience's attention and cognitive involvement (Kreuter et al., 2007).

The Irregulars attempts to make these main characters identifiable by giving them backstories, which helps audiences understand the reasons behind their actions and emotions—including those rooted in or manifesting as supernatural. For example, Bea and Jessie suffer from lack of parental love, having lost their mother, Alice, in their childhood to supernatural acts, after which Jessie's father, Sherlock, abandoned them. Throughout the series, Bea is shown to have used her ordeals to become mentally tough and mature beyond her age—no-nonsense and serious. She rarely displays emotions and is overly protective of clairvoyant Jessie, who is presented as child-like. For example, for Bea's birthday, Jessie presents her sister with an imaginary gift and good cheer, to which Bea scoffs lightly and worries herself with real-world problems like rent and food (Episode 1). The backstory helps us understand these character dynamics better.

Perhaps due to the show's young adult target audience, the teen characters use contemporary language and show more fortitude, courage, and wisdom than the adults who constantly underestimate them. We found that the teen characters are multi-faceted and display a wide range and intensity of emotions, which further aids their identification with the audience, whether in the supernatural or non-supernatural contexts of the show. For example, Billy is filled with anger about his past and the cruelties he endured as a child, but he demonstrates tenderness toward Bea, his love interest, and protectiveness toward his friend Spike. Similarly, Bea is resolute and fierce with most people she interacts with but displays her softer side to her sister and friends.

Imaginable Plot

Imaginable plots within the context of the analysis refers traditionally to a plot having enough of a real-world touchstone that audiences can both follow and relate to the story (Van Laer et al., 2013). Moreover, imaginable plots can refer to stories and character relationships that logically progress in a recognizable narrative format. Imaginable plots are important to examine in the supernatural youth genre, as viewers who are fans of supernatural shows may be more likely to understand supernatural story arcs and plot points and find the plots more imaginable than audiences who have less experience with the genre.

In our analysis of *The Irregulars*, we noted that although the show's plotline uses supernatural elements, all episodes feature a number of unifying strands that are likely familiar to average teen and young adult audiences. Regardless of their supernatural plot points, the episodes' storylines touch upon the characters' difficult childhoods, strained parental relationships, grieving for lost loved ones, budding teen romances, strong friendships, and romantic and professional rivalries—all relevant real-world touchdowns.

Many narrative arcs use specific elements that viewers are likely to find familiar. For example, the show traces Jessie's transformation from an under-confident teenager to one responsible for saving the world. Jessie is shown to possess the ability to read minds and foretell the future, but she is plagued with self-doubt and considers herself a freak because of her abilities. The show demonstrates her struggle to conquer her insecurities, master her skill, and use it to defeat the enemy. Our analysis suggests that audiences may appreciate that the story is a metaphor for growing up as an outsider, not fitting in, and finding the people who appreciate and know you.

Similarly, the series depicts Leo's transformation from rebellious teen to confident person comfortable in his own skin. For example, despite his chronic illnesses and the combative disapproval of royal footman Daimler, he joins the irregulars' raucous adventures. Since audiences are familiar with storylines showing protagonists facing problems, working hard to find solutions, and getting rewarded in the end, our analysis suggests that each episode's narrative—as well as the show's overall storyline—are likely to be imaginable and familiar to many audience members.

We also found that many episodes include suspense, conflict, and dramatic tension, which aim to increase audience members' emotional and cognitive involvement. For example, in episode 7, when the Linen Man traps Jessie in an unending stream of nightmares, audiences are left in a state of suspense because it is unclear how she will get out of this state. The show attempts to inject reality into the narratives by referencing real-world events, such as the great plague of London that killed thousands of people, and social issues, such as class-based discrimination, economic deprivation faced by working class people, and sexual assault. These ongoing social issues likely speak to a broad swath of audiences—another example of a real-world touchdown predictive of audience members following and relating to the story.

Verisimilitude

The concept of verisimilitude refers to the possibility that events occurring in the show could also occur in real life (Van Laer et al., 2014). Entertainment shows can achieve this effect in various ways, including realistic character responses to situations, use of recognizable imagery, and cultural appropriateness or use of familiar "visual and linguistic conventions" (Kreuter et al., 2007, p. 230).

In our analysis, we found several instances where characters behave in real-world ways. For example, when Holmes loses his partner and love Alice to "the Rip" (a portal to purgatory), he falls into deep depression and takes to addiction to deal with his pain. Similarly, faced with the choice of rejoining her family at the cost of destroying earth or staying apart forever, Alice–Bea and Jessie's mother–demonstrates a selfish desire to re-join her family. In contrast, Bea and

Jessie make difficult decisions that demonstrate emotional maturity. They choose friendship, life, and joy instead of destruction, underscoring the show's message that regardless of one's past negative emotional experiences, it is possible to hope for brighter future outcomes and make choices accordingly. All these examples fit within the concept of verisimilitude.

We observed other realistic character responses, including the desire for revenge and the desire to become all-powerful and play God. For example, *The Irregulars* featured a character who wanted to resurrect her dead husband wanted to play God by stealing organs from others (Episode 6); depicted Holmes as wanting to become a genius by demonstrating documented contact with the dead (Episode 5); and showed the Linen Man as seeking to destroy the world so he could rule over humans by controlling their thoughts and actions (Episode 7–8). The show portrays these characters' narcissism and larger-than-life desires as products of their emotionally stunted minds. In contrast, we noted that *The Irregulars* depicts Jessie, who possesses mind-control powers, using her gifts for the greater good. In this sense, the show subverts existing narratives about the undeveloped minds of young people. By showing teens as having firmer moral compasses than adults, the show comments on young minds' power, optimism, and resilience.

In terms of familiar imagery, we observed that the show uses several types associated with death, all drawn from popular culture and likely to be familiar to diverse audiences. These include axe-wielding executioners in black masks, the repeated use of nightmares and dreams to portend the future, and ravens as harbingers of impending death. Ominous music, gray colors and dark backdrops are common in dramatic scenes, while warmly lit scenes signal the change in content. The show itself is set in Victorian England, and scenes featuring architecture, clothing, and elements of social life from that era add historical authenticity that could be perceived as contributing to realism. Unlike many other shows, however, *The Irregulars* does not romanticize the era, but sticks to depicting life through the lens of the four orphans.

Despite these factors, we observed that the show falters in some ways in the use of verisimilitude in its narratives. While the show's themes touch on several contemporary issues, the narratives steer clear of incorporating racial issues in a meaningful way into the story arc, even though these issues were globally at the forefront at the time the show was released on Netflix in March 2021. We posit that these would have been of interest to the young adult audience at whom this show was aimed.

Audience Reception of *The Irregulars*: Negotiating Narrative Canon and Versimilitude

Above and beyond producing entertaining content, shows like *The Irregulars* have the potential to address societal issues while creating a fanciful world in which audiences can lose themselves. Indeed, entertainment researchers argue that getting caught up in a narrative can influence audiences about important issues, ranging from diverse representation, civic engagement, and health issues (Brechman & Purvis, 2015; Wang & Tang, 2021). While it is informative that our textual analysis signaled that *The Irregulars* features identifiable characters, an imaginable plot, and versimilitude that might sweep audience members up in a story where they can negotiate difficult concepts like identity, grief, isolation, abandonment, and hopelessness, we wished to triangulate: To what extent does *The Irregulars* actually work as a transportative narrative for audiences—and for which audiences? *The Irregulars* focuses so deeply on characters who are battling with personal demons that we wonder if integrating these issues into the storyline is enough to prompt audience members to interpret them with compassion rather than derision, and if so, to what extent.

To address this question, we examined audience responses from IMDb and the social media platform Tumblr, as detailed earlier in our "Analyzing *The Irregulars*" section. As we will explain in the sections below, in our samples, those who liked the show tended to indicate that they were drawn in by the interesting take on the characters and storylines. In contrast, those critical of the show were overwhelmingly focused on issues of identifiable characters, imaginable plotlines, and verisimilitude. Our analysis found two overarching themes that affected the transportability of the narrative: narrative canon and verisimilitude. Diversity was a subtheme for both the main themes.

Narrative Canon

Identifiable characters can help viewers increase narrative transportation. In pop culture fandoms, fans emphasize the importance that any transmedia text should stay in canon, meaning main characters and timelines must not veer away from the socially-agreed-upon set facts of those characters and timelines. Texts that stray too far from ascribed character traits are in danger of fan rejection as being outside of the canon. A theme that emerged in both the IMDb sample and Tumblr sample pertained to narrative canon.

While some comments sampled indicated that Netflix's version of *The Irregulars* appears to do a good job of staying true to the graphic novels (as one IMDb viewer noted, "It's based on a graphic novel and I think they've [done] a fabulous job"), some IMDb posters expressed concern about straying from Conan Doyle's canon. Using Sherlock Holmes characters polarized some IMDb viewers, who suggested it lacked the narrative gravitas to engage fans enough to pull them away from their concerns about the Holmes canon.

For example, *The Irregulars'* detractors found the departure from normal character traits (e.g., a humble Watson, a charismatic Holmes) too distracting or disingenuous. Those wanting to see a Holmes detective story true to canon expressed displeasure at the textual treatment of the show. One viewer noted, "I do think an injustice was done by using known Doyle characters in a disparate manner to the existing character traits"—and some commenters seemed to find Sherlock's drug addiction and supernatural plotline alienating, rather than inspiring much compassion or interest.

Among the comments drawn from IMDb, many commenters mentioned that they believed staying with a Holmes canon would have improved *The Irregulars'* season arc and plotlines. One noted, "Frankly, most of the show doesn't really make sense, and I only saw the whole thing because I had a hope that Sherlock would do his Sherlock thing, and outsmart everyone in a fascinating matter, but instead it's down to the 2 completely average teenage girls to do so"—a rather sexist take on a show led by strong women characters.

The overall tenor of the backlash against *The Irregulars'* divergence from narrative cannon frustrated some fans in our sample. Examples of comments reflecting this frustration include:

- "It is a pity, people who dropped in negative reviews, either think Sherlock was a real person, or that this series is about the real history; and worst, cannot obviously see beyond race … It is a bold and fresh interpretation of the fictitious world Sir Conan Doyle once created." (IMDb)
- "Is *The Irregulars* perfect? No, it's not. What is it with this black-or-white attitude these days?" (Tumblr)

Another Tumblr post referenced the racism in complaints over accuracy. Its author noted: "I saw a comment being like 'so your problem really is "inaccuracy," as if there's anything that can be accurate about supernatural, or the diversity of the cast?' and honestly, I think all those bad reviews don't have much to do with the plot or the accuracy."

Overall, the Tumblr posters we sampled were also quite interested in the established characters from the Sherlock Holmes narrative tradition. As opposed to concerns over breaking from established canon, Tumblr posters seemed to regard canon as an evolving and malleable thing. Many referenced other modern Sherlock shows including BBC's *Sherlock* and Netflix's *Enola Holmes* as other favorite shows, and they appreciated the supernatural nature aspect of *The Irregulars*. As one Tumblr poster noted, "I do not mind that it has a supernatural take." Our data suggest that among such viewers, the expanded notion of what could be "real" in a Holmes universe also allowed for other things to also be acceptable—namely, diversity.

One notable example that emerged often on Tumblr was the notion that Watson was a gay character in *The Irregulars*, and that the show established him as a gay character in canon. While the depiction was up for debate within the comments analyzed, many LQBTQ+ posters liked that the canon could be expanded and updated. One poster noted, "We have [a] TV adaptation in which Watson canonically, clearly (and not as a joke) expresses his (romantic) love for Holmes and it feels kinda historical for the Holmesian fandom."

Another interesting example of divergence in canon that we observed Tumblr posters seemed to like was the foregrounding of strong people of color as the characters driving the show. As one Tumblr poster noted:

- "I love that Bea, played by Thaddea Graham, a Chinese-Irish actress, is seen as the leader of the group. And while all of the Irregulars are main [sic], we have a WOC as a center focus!"

This was echoed minimally by some fans on IMDb, where one poster commented:

- "This is based on a graphic novel based on a fictional world. It's full of supernatural stuff. Literal fiction. Also, it's quite obviously geared toward a young audience. This 'woke' show is quite entertaining if you stop pretending that it's canon to the original Sherlock Holmes mysteries[.]"

Differences in Verisimilitude

Verisimilitude, or the plausibility of events happening in real life, helps audience members make connections between characters' lives and their own lives. While entertainment researchers often cite the ability of a narrative to influence audiences, this works best on stories that transport an audience into the narrative.

In our study, we found a noticeable split between viewers that indicated they were fans of the supernatural genre (mostly posting on Tumblr) and those that indicated they were not. In the comments we sampled, self-identified supernatural fans seemed much more willing to roll with the historical setting interspersed with more modern elements like the dialogue, social commentary, and music. As one IMDb viewer noted, the show "has all the ingredients of teen drama with adventure, paranormal, romance and angst," but added, "if you're searching for historical accuracy this is not your series and if you're a Holmes purist it's definitely not for you." While this comment in some ways resonated with our findings, we also observed that many Tumblr posters were also fans of BBC's *Sherlock* and Netflix's *Enola Holmes* and are quite steeped in the Sherlock Holmes canon and narrative tradition.

Imaginable plotlines allow people to engage with the story without constantly questioning where and why a story arc existed. In general, we observed that IMDb commenters in our sample who panned the show indicated that the modern casting and dialogue were too incongruous with the Victorian setting. As one IMDb commenter mentioned, "A bunch of teens/young adults in a drama set in Victorian London, but they talk like modern kids with modern slang and current-day expressions. It just doesn't work at all, it's bizarre[.]" Though another called out review bombing as the reason for poor reviews, saying "This has been review bombed by those who didn't give it a chance and brought their own biased presumptions against 'woke' cinema."

This also pertained to the diversity of the casting and representation within the show. Representations of diversity were a subtheme of the verisimilitude of the show because IMDb commenters in our sample repeatedly made reference to "accurate" casting, while Tumblr posters in our sample often expressed interest in cast diversity. Some IMDb commenters called out the show over the racial diversity of the cast not being historically accurate, while other IMDb viewers called out fellow reviewers for having a hang up about the diverse casting in a period drama. One commented: "If you want a show that portrays the horrors of history, watch something else. Clearly that's not what a comic book ghost fighting TV series is about. Women and people of all races can be cast in supernatural comic alternative history shows without portraying historical atrocities. It's 2021."

As these comments suggest, in general, Tumblr posters did not seem to dwell on historical accuracy. Rather, they focused on the importance of diversity and representation, and in signaling an understanding that the show is a fanciful supernatural take on a classic set of characters, some expressed appreciation that the showrunners leaned into the diverse casting:

- "this genre I'm seeing more of lately that combines multiracial period drama and supernatural/fantasy elements looks pretty damn cool actually."
- "shows taking place in a historical time period are not obligated to be accurate because people of marginalized communities deserve to see ourselves represented without our identities being the crux of our trauma."

At the same time, many Tumblr posters commented that while they loved the diversity, they felt frustrated by the show's failure to address diversity in its narratives, criticizing a lack of nuance in the show's presentation of diversity. One Tumblr poster quipped, "[N]etflix fantasy shows are like we are going to make a diverse world where there's racism but there's not but there is but it's inconsistent but it's not but it is but it's colourblind casting but it's not." This is likely in reference to race not being a major theme within the context of the show, even though the cast was diverse. This may also reflect broader cultural issues about creating more inclusive storylines that go beyond token diverse casting.

Conclusion

Modern society is decidedly a stressful place. As of this writing, people are grappling with the aftermath of a deadly pandemic, climate change, and political upheaval, all at once. Not surprisingly, depression and mental health issues have been on the rise—and more than ever, people have been turning to the mental escape provided by a bingeworthy show with a storyline viewers can get wrapped up in (Nisbett et al., 2022). Supernatural shows may serve as a particularly good escape, given their mystical and fanciful storylines.

Based on the transportation-imagery model (Green & Brock, 2002), we know the importance of getting absorbed into a great story, where it is important to suspend disbelief and accept that the premise and plot of the show could be real. Perhaps the mark of a great supernatural story is that we dismiss the implausible and start believing it could be real. When transportation into the narrative is really strong, people get attached to characters and the situations they are going through. With this comes the potential to suspend our own prejudgments, biases, and viewpoints, and see life from someone else's perspective. Indeed, narrative transportation research has linked media consumption with things like reducing stigma and bias against people with mental health diagnoses (Wong et al., 2017). Moreover, people potentially call upon and reflect on really great narratives even after they finish viewing a media text (see Slater et al.'s (2018) retrospective imaginative involvement). Given the potential increased importance of pop culture narratives, we argue that supernatural shows are a crucial way for viewers to ponder and negotiate the very real problems in their lives.

Does the show work? *The Irregulars'* cancellation is still mysterious, as Netflix was not forthcoming about the reason (even though the ratings and overall reviews were decent) (Otterson, 2021). Utilizing a textual analysis of the show in combination with viewer responses sheds some light on how a text can impact different audiences. Our data suggests that for the more general IMDb viewers and for viewers who were not fans of the supernatural genre, the show did not really work. Many were hung up on preconceived expectations about historical accuracy and an antiquated notion of the Holmes canon, with racism and objections to the diverse cast peppering the IMDb reviews.

On the flip side, Tumblr posters generally really liked the show for its willingness to break with canon and historically white casting. The data suggest that the supernatural genre of the show paved the way for Tumblr commenters to accept things outside of preexisting canon, breaking the confines of being true to the original characters and setting. The Tumblr posts in particular showed us how certain themes within the media text (e.g. diversity, LGBTQ+ identities, etc.) spoke to certain audiences who in turn contributed fandom content (fan art, theories, head cannon, fan fiction, etc.). It is interesting to see viewers develop fandom communities based on the way they connect with the characters and content.

Narrative transportation is conceptually newer, but brings with it many avenues in which to explore the power of narrative further. Future research could further explore combining diverse representation and audience transportation. Our analysis suggests the show's portrayal of a diverse cast was a glaring issue. Even though the casting is fairly diverse, the show failed to address race in conjunction with other character traits or plotlines. In its silence on matters of race, racism, and racial bias, the show missed a chance to connect further with different audiences. Future research should look at the impact of narrative genre differences and dive into the themes found in this chapter—that people can view the supernatural as having verisimilitude.

This study's primary limitation is understanding nuances of how audience members reacted to the show. The data present a snapshot in time of IMDb audience reviews and Tumblr posts. We argue that making the effort to track viewer responses to a given text is worthwhile to better understanding media impact. Future research could delve deeper into the link between a fandom audience and identification with supernatural shows. Moreover, a more varied set of audience reactions (either from interviews or surveys) could provide interesting insight into the impacts of shows like *The Irregulars*.

References

Bassnett, S. (2017). Detective fiction in translation: Shifting patterns of reception. In L. Nilsson, D. Damrosch, & T. D'haen (Eds.), *Crime fiction as world literature* (pp. 143–56). Bloomsbury. https://doi.org/10.3366/ccs.2023.0468.

Battis, J. (2011). Supernatural youth: the rise of the teen hero in literature and popular culture. Lexington Books. https://hdl.loc.gov/loc.gdc/cip.2021678604

Brechman, J. M., & Purvis, S. C. (2015). Narrative, transportation and advertising. *International Journal of Advertising*, 34(2), 366–381. https://doi.org/10.1080/02650487.2014.994803.

Champlin, S., & Paul, N. (2020). Long-format commercials in a world of short attention spans? How advertisers create engagement through storytelling. In S. Schartel-Dunn & G. S. Nisbett (Eds.), *Implications and innovations of persuasive narrative*. Peter Lang. https://doi.org/10.3726/b17049.

Cheetham, D. (2012). Middle-class Victorian street Arabs: Modern re-creations of the Baker street irregulars. *International Research in Children's Literature*, 5(1), 36–50. https://doi.org/10.3366/ircl.2012.0042

Green, M. C., & Brock, T. C. (2000). The role of transportation in the persuasiveness of public narratives. *Journal of Personality and Social Psychology*, 79(5), 701–21. https://doi.org/10.1037/0022-3514.79.5.701

Green, M. C., & Brock, T. C. (2002). In the mind's eye: Transportation-imagery model of narrative persuasion. In *Narrative impact* (pp. 315–341). Psychology Press. https://doi.org/10.4324/9781410606648-22

Hesse-Biber, S. N. (2017). *The Practice of Qualitative Research* (3rd ed.). Sage.

Kreuter, M. W., Green, M. C., Cappella, J. N., Slater, M. D., Wise, M. E., Storey, D., & Woolley, S. (2007). Narrative communication in cancer prevention and control: A framework to guide research and application. *Annals of Behavioral Medicine*, 33(3), 221–235. https://doi.org/10.1007/BF02879904

Mastro, D. E., & Greenberg, B. S. (2000). The portrayal of racial minorities on prime- time television. *Journal of Broadcasting & Electronic Media*, 44, 690–703. https://doi.org/10.1207/s15506878jobem4404_10

Moyer-Gusé, E., & Nabi, R. L. (2010). Explaining the effects of narrative in an entertainment television program: Overcoming resistance to persuasion. *Human Communication Research*, 36, 26–52. https://doi.org/10.1111/j.1468-2958.2009.01367.x

Nisbett, G. S., Schartel Dunn, S., & Paul, N. (2022). The escapism and social bond of pandemic binge watching. In D. Macey, M. Napierski-Prancl, & D. Staton (Eds.), *Persevering during the Pandemic*. Lexington.

Otterson, J. (2021, May 4). "The Irregulars" Canceled at Netflix after one season. *Variety*. https://variety.com/2021/tv/news/the-irregulars-canceled-netflix-1234966411/

Reynolds, M. (2017, October 24). You should ignore film ratings on IMDb and Rotten Tomatoes. *WIRED UK*. https://www.wired.co.uk/article/which-film-ranking-site-should-i-trust-rotten-tomatoes-imdb-metacritic#:~:text=This%20all%20sounds%20very%20egalitarian,are%20aimed%20more%20towards%20men.&text=Rotten%20Tomatoes%20gives%20films%20a,reviews%20of%20professional%20film%20critics

Rixon, P. (2014). Sherlock: Critical reception by the media. In L. E. Stein & K. Busse (Eds.), *Sherlock and transmedia fandom: Essays on the BBC series* (pp. 165–178). McFarland.

Sanders, G. (2022, December 30). Review bombing: The toxic tactic that doesn't work – It's full of stars – Medium. *Medium*. https://medium.com/itsfullofstars/review-bombing-the-toxic-tactic-that-doesnt-work-4c75fd269004.

Singhal, A., Cody, M., Rogers, E. M., & Sabido, M. (2004). Entertainment-education and social change: history, research, and practice. Lawrence Erlbaum Associates.

Singhal, A., & Rogers, E.M. (2002), A Theoretical Agenda for Entertainment—Education. *Communication Theory*, 12: 117–135. https://doi.org/10.1111/j.1468-2885.2002.tb00262.x

Slater, M. D., Ewoldsen, D. R., & Woods, K. W. (2018). Extending conceptualization and measurement of narrative engagement after-the-fact: Parasocial relationship and retrospective imaginative involvement. *Media Psychology*, 21(3), 329–351. https://doi.org/10.1080/15213269.2017.1328313

Slater, M. D., & Rouner, D. (2002). Entertainment-education and elaboration likelihood: Understanding the processing of narrative persuasion. *Communication Theory*, 12, 173–191. https://doi.org/10.1111/j.1468-2885.2002.tb00265.x

Statista. (2022, March 14). ***IMDb TV audience in the U.S. 2020, by generation***. *Statista*. Retrieved September 19, 2024, from https://www.statista.com/statistics/1128393/imbd-tv-us-audience-generation/

Tiffany, K. (2022, February 1). How the Snowflakes Won. *The Atlantic*. https://www.theatlantic.com/technology/archive/2022/02/tumblr-internet-legacy-survival/621419/.

Tillet, S. (2021, April 2). 'Bridgerton' takes on race. But its core is escapism. *The New York Times*. https://www.nytimes.com/2021/01/05/arts/television/bridgerton-race-netflix.html

Tumblr usage penetration in the United States 2020, by age group. (2022, April 28). Statista. https://www.statista.com/statistics/202359/tumblr-users-demographics/.

Van Laer, T., De Ruyter, K., Visconti, L. M., & Wetzels, M. (2014). The extended transportation-imagery model: A meta-analysis of the antecedents and consequences of consumers' narrative transportation. *Journal of Consumer Research*, 40(5), 797–817. https://doi.org/10.1086/673383.

Wang, S. T., & Tang, Y. C. (2021). How narrative transportation in movies affects audiences' positive word-of-mouth: The mediating role of emotion. *Plos One*, 16(11). https://doi.org/10.1371/0259420.

Wong, N. C., Lookadoo, K. L., & Nisbett, G. S. (2017). "I'm Demi and I have bipolar disorder": Effect of parasocial contact on reducing stigma toward people with bipolar disorder. *Communication Studies*, 68(3), 314–333. https://doi.org/10.1080/10510974.2017.1331928

Part II
Intersecting Magic and Femininity

6

Supernatural Savior or Sacrificial Lamb? The Contradictions and Cost of Young Supernatural Femininity: *Chilling Adventures of Sabrina* in a Post-Buffy Context

LORI BINDIG YOUSMAN

Teen television offers an ideal site to explore young femininity in popular culture. Over the years, studios and networks have successfully marketed the genre, which focuses on teen characters and storylines, to young women, particularly 12-to-34-year-old female viewers who have been difficult to reach though other programming (Murphy, 2014, p. 18). By featuring young women more centrally and seriously than other genres, teen TV has significantly shaped the portrayal of young femininity (Nash, 2006). This chapter explores how one teen television program, *Chilling Adventures of Sabrina* (Netflix 2018–2020), frames young femininity in seemingly contradictory ways: by simultaneously celebrating the empowerment (both magical and feminist) of its young supernatural protagonist, while at the same time depicting that very power as the cause of her demise. Debuting on the heels of the #MeToo movement, the young heroine of *Chilling Adventures of Sabrina* was heralded as "Resistance Sabrina" (Sheffield, 2018); yet, as this chapter shows, Sabrina's feminist potential is never fully realized. Certainly, supernatural youth narratives of the past have offered new perspectives on power and young femininity—most notably *Buffy the Vampire Slayer* (The WB/UPN, 1997–2003). In fact, Buffy's feminist potential has been the site of much scholarly debate (Byers, 2003; Crosby, 2004; Hohenstein, 2019; MacDonald, 2004;

Magoulick, 2006; Pender, 2016; Vint, 2002). Although critics and scholars have explicitly likened Sabrina to Buffy and the two series may share some similarities (Ballard, 2018; Henesy, 2020), *Chilling Adventures of Sabrina* undermines its heroine in ways *Buffy the Vampire Slayer* never did. Thus, this chapter considers how, like the supernatural heroines that came before her, Sabrina suggests what is, and is not, possible for young women within a given cultural moment.

Femininity in Contemporary Teen TV

While its roots can be traced back to 1949, contemporary teen television emerged in the 1990s as fledgling cable networks attempted to gain a foothold in the market by catering to young audiences (Osgerby, 2004). Osgerby (2004) noted that in teen programming from the 1950s and 1960s, young women were idealized if they were beautiful, nice, self-sacrificing, and focused heterosexual romance. This depiction of femininity was sustained throughout the 1980s and 1990s, as young women continued to be portrayed as "dependent, passive, nurturing types, uninterested in competition, achievement, or success, who should conform to the wishes of men in their lives" (Douglas, 1995, p. 17). As a result, these popular media "... have been profoundly engaged in the policing of difference and the construction and validation of hegemonic femininities, in the correcting of 'aberrant' femininity" (Moseley, 2002, p. 405). Contemporary teen television continued to perpetuate portrayals of traditional femininity while also expanding representations to reflect changing cultural mores. Accordingly, as the new millennium approached, popular media responded to "girl power" rhetoric, which emerged out of post-feminist discourse and reframed young femininity as empowered, assertive, and dynamic (Gonick, 2006).

On the surface, teen TV's embrace of girl power appeared to be a positive step forward because it challenged the long-standing stereotype of passive femininity. However, a deeper look reveals the problematic nature of girl power, which erroneously suggests that gender equity has been achieved and young women are now dominant (Taft, 2004). Predicated on the false notion that gender barriers have been eradicated, girl power claimed that now young women could "have it all." Rather than promoting actual political engagement, girl power ignored structural obstacles in favor of focusing on the behaviors of individual young women. Girl power promised young women "power through and control over one's own identity invention and re-invention" (Hopkins, 1999, p. 95), but essentially operated as a marketing strategy—selling young women a host of products (from clothes and cosmetics to movies and television shows), which could be consumed to symbolically demonstrate their own so-called "empowerment." Yet, as Hains (2009) astutely noted, "Once feminism has been co-opted and used not to empower people, but rather to sell anything and everything, it is inflated rhetoric—empty, meaningless, useless in effecting or inspiring change" (p. 109). In other words, "girl power" offers a diluted message of empowerment that does nothing to actually challenge the status quo (Hains, 2009). Therefore, instead of broadening conceptions of femininity, girl power simply offered a different variation; one that still posed "a limited range of acceptable physical behaviors and appearances for girls" and "problematically targets slender, white, middle-class girls above all others" (Hains, 2012, p. xi). As a result, girl power helped maintain teen television's construction of young femininity as primarily cis, white, middle to upper-class, heterosexual young women that conform to Western beauty standards and whose stories ultimately conclude with marriage and motherhood (Bindig Yousman, 2022). That said, in recent years, media have responded to the #MeToo movement through meaningful engagement with feminism by addressing issues of politics, identity, and power through popular culture texts (Henesy, 2020).

While often associated with "teen soaps" like *Beverly Hills, 90210, Dawson's Creek, The O.C., One Tree Hill,* and *Gossip Girl,* teen programming also features stories about supernatural youth as exemplified by series like *Buffy the Vampire Slayer, Charmed* (The WB, 1998–2006), and *The Vampire Diaries* (The CW, 2009–2017). In supernatural teen television, the metaphor of "high school as hell" takes on new meaning with monsters and demons representing the challenges of burgeoning adulthood (Magee, 2014). Thus, supernatural youth still grapple with the trials and tribulations of adolescence, but they must do so while battling dark forces and negotiating magical powers. The occult elements, such as the mystical birthrights that empower young heroines, fundamentally impact gender representations in these programs because the departure from "realist believability" frees young women from the constraints of traditional femininity (Driscoll & Heatwole, 2018, pp. 121–122). As a result, supernatural teen television has the potential to showcase "free-thinking, independent-minded young women" who are not only capable of, but fully responsible for, saving the world (Murphy, 2009, p. 67).

Undoubtedly, one of the most iconic characters in supernatural teen television is the titular character from *Buffy the Vampire Slayer*. First appearing in a 1992 film and then later reimagined for television, Buffy Summers was created by Joss Whedon.[1] He has characterized his intent as an attempt to subvert gender expectations, explaining, for example, in a Season 1 DVD bonus feature:

> I saw so many horror movies where there was that blonde girl who would always get herself killed.... The idea of Buffy came from just the very simple thought of a beautiful blonde girl walks into an alley, a monster attacks her, and she's not only ready for him—she trounces him. (Saltzman, 2019, p. 87).

While Buffy, played by actress Sarah Michelle Geller, was the embodiment of the stereotypical petite blonde cheerleader, she was far from a passive girl relegated to the sidelines. Rather, Buffy was the "Chosen One" of her generation, destined to fulfill a prophecy that foretold, "She alone will stand against the vampires, the demons, and the forces of darkness. She is the Slayer."[2] Dressed in the latest fashions and armed with supernatural strength, skills, and quips as biting as her vampiric adversaries, Buffy is a wise-cracking warrior ready to battle the evil surrounding the town of Sunnydale.

Although she was known to "save the world ... a lot,"[3] Buffy is presented as a reluctant hero. Even with her sass and superpowers, she is burdened by her prophecy and longs to be "just a girl."[4] From the first episode, Buffy establishes her desire to "Be like everybody else."[5] When her mentor, Giles, speaks to her of duty, Buffy responds with "I don't care" and "I've been there and done that. I'm moving on." Yet, her words ring false; she has clearly already accepted her role as Slayer as evidenced by the stakes she perpetually carries and the way she immediately launches into action when trouble arises. Throughout the series, there are moments where Buffy seemingly attempts to deny or escape her destiny, but she always acquiesces—reconciling her own desires with the world's expectations. Kramer (2017) explained that it is Buffy's knowledge and ethical awareness that "prevents her, even when it becomes a possibility, from truly desiring to give up her abilities" (p. 22). Therefore, "although Buffy struggles with her fate ... Buffy (almost) always knows who she is and what she must do," making her a "complex individual with strong moral authority" (Early, 2001, pp. 19, 23).

While Buffy's heroism transgresses traditional stereotypes of a damsel in distress, the series does adhere to some conventions of teen television. Henesy (2020) suggested that although Buffy was a strong female character, as in other shows of the era (such as *Charmed* and *Sabrina the Teenage Witch*) she did not explicitly identify as a feminist and reflected post-feminist tropes of "being clever and witty but in a feminine way" (p. 4). In addition to her appearance and demeanor, Buffy also conformed to traditional femininity through her focus on romantic relationships with male love interests. However, Buffy's storyline significantly deviates from other young women in teen TV by ending without her having attained "heteronormative bliss" (Driscoll, 2002, p. 233). Rather, Buffy prioritizes her duty to save the world over love and romance. Far from relegating her to a life of isolation and loneliness, as is often the case for exceptional women (Pender, 2016), Buffy has an array of meaningful relationships and is characterized as a loyal friend, devoted sister, and brave leader of empowered women.

Given Buffy's significance, much debate has taken place over what, if any, type of feminism, she promotes. Scholars and critics alike have made claims that Buffy has reflected second and third wave feminist agendas as well as post-feminist sensibilities. For example, some have critiqued Buffy's feminist potential due to her sexualized, hyperfeminine appearance and heterosexual relationships (MacDonald, 2004; Magoulick, 2006) while others celebrated her intellect, strength, and independence (Hohenstein, 2019; Vint, 2002) as well as her demonstration of sisterhood (Byers, 2003; Crosby, 2004). Pender (2016) has suggested that the numerous binary analyses predicated on how much Buffy conforms to or contradicts traditional femininity, ultimately reduces the possibilities of the character's political potential. Rather than trying to place her squarely within a particular category, Pender (2016) posited that it is more useful to consider the ways in which Buffy has impacted the "mythology of the American teen girl" through her "reconciling [of] the heroic and the feminine" (p. 51). Thus, Buffy serves as a vital touchstone in the construction of young femininity and as an ideal point of comparison with the way subsequent supernatural heroines, like Sabrina, are portrayed in teen television.

Casting a Spell: Sabrina Through the Years

Just as Buffy predated her television series, Sabrina Spellman, the protagonist of *Chilling Adventures of Sabrina*, predates the Netflix series—but by decades, rather than just a few years. First introduced in the 1962 comic book series *Archie's Mad House*, Sabrina appeared in other Archie comics throughout the 1960s—eventually receiving her own comic in 1971. Additionally, a 1969 animated television special (*Archie and His New Pals*) featured Sabrina, which led to later appearances in other cartoons (*The Archie Comedy Hour* and *The New Archie and Sabrina Hour*). In 1970, Sabrina's own animated series, *Sabrina the Teenage Witch*, aired on CBS until 1974 (Woolery, 1983).

After a nearly twenty-year hiatus, Sabrina reemerged on television in 1996 in the form of actress Melissa Joan Hart, who starred first in the live-action Showtime movie, *Sabrina the Teenage Witch*, and then in a half-hour primetime sitcom of the same name (Gerston, 1996). The series was comprised of seven seasons totaling 163 episodes, with the first four seasons airing on ABC and the final three airing on The WB. The series proved quite popular with audiences—the first season brought in more that 17 million viewers and consistently rated highest in ABC's Friday night lineup for four years (Fuller, 2018). Attempting to capitalize on the sitcom's popularity, ABC greenlit several short-lived animated spin-off series that focused on a younger version of Hart's Sabrina (12–14 years old respectively): *Sabrina: The Animated Series* (1999), *Sabrina: Friends Forever* (2002), and *Sabrina's Secret Life* (2003–2004). The sitcom also generated ancillary media including books, a soundtrack, TV movies, video games, and DVDs.[6] Though limited, much of the previous Sabrina scholarship focused on the post-feminist sensibility and privileging of white, middle-class femininity in *Sabrina the Teenage Witch* (Moseley, 2002; Murphy, 2009; Projansky & Vande Berg, 2000).

In 2013, Sabrina returned to her roots—albeit with a very different tone—when Roberto Aguirre-Sacasa reintroduced the character in the comic, *Afterlife with Archie*, which shifts from wholesome teen hijinks to supernatural horror. Building on *Afterlife with Archie*, Aguirre-Sacasa gave Sabrina her own horror comic, *Chilling Adventures of Sabrina* in 2014. Around the same time, Aguirre-Sacasa, who had been named the chief creative officer of Archie comics, created *Riverdale*, a teen television series based on Archie characters, for The CW. With *Riverdale*'s success, Aguirre-Sacasa started developing *Chilling Adventures of Sabrina* as a companion series for the network, but the show eventually found a home on Netflix. The streaming series was comprised of 36 episodes, which ran over four seasons (or "Parts," as Netflix named them) from 2018–2020 and featured Kiernan Shipka in the role of Sabrina. After Netflix cancelled *Chilling Adventures of Sabrina*, Aguirre-Sacasa announced that Sabrina's story would continue in two different comic books[7] (taking a "multiverse approach") (Cordero, 2021). In the meantime, Aguirre-Sacasa revived Shipka's Sabrina by incorporating her into the sixth season of *Riverdale*. Beyond advancing the plot, Sabrina's cross-over appearances in *Riverdale* also provided an opportunity to address the *Chilling Adventures of Sabrina* finale, which had left many fans unhappy (Opie, 2021). Recent Sabrina scholarship has interrogated feminist issues, intersectionality, and evolving gender representations in *Chilling Adventures of Sabrina* (Corcoran, 2022; Henesy, 2020; Mathis et al., 2023).

Given Sabrina's many iterations, her origin story has varied over the years, as have her magical talents and her friends' knowledge of her powers. Originally, the comic book depicted Sabrina as a "mischievous teenager who enjoys playing tricks on her classmates," who could not fall in love without losing her powers (Fuller,

2018). However, Archie Comics quickly rewrote the character so she could engage in typical high school romances, eventually leading to a long-standing relationship with her mortal boyfriend. The early versions of Sabrina are lighthearted and focus on the young witch secretly using her powers to solve problems. Similarly, in the 1990s sitcom, "Sabrina is a good-natured, loveable, bumbling girl-next-door"—her spells constantly go awry, but fail to have any lasting impact (Ho, 2021, p. 2). As such, her laughable mistakes serve as life lessons for the character and her audience, reinforcing that Sabrina is a "normal girl" (Gerston, 1996).

In contrast, the protagonist of *Chilling Adventures of Sabrina* is anything but a "normal girl." The occult series trades humor for horror as Sabrina attempts to navigate the "witch world of her family and the human world of her friends,"[8] and it depicts her as an unambiguously powerful young woman. As Ho (2021) noted, from the start, "Sabrina comes fully formed and possesses a strong sense of self-identity: assertive, loyal, ambitious, intelligent" (p. 2). Unlike Buffy, who reluctantly accepts her birthright, Sabrina enthusiastically embraces hers—both in terms of her supernatural capabilities and her potential political power. The half-witch, half-mortal sixteen-year-old girl is explicit about her desires from the outset; she openly acknowledges, "I want freedom and power."[9] Sabrina's proclamation stands out in a media culture that often frames ambitious women as abhorrent, power-hungry and ultimately punished for failing to conform to stereotypical femininity (Chesney-Lind & Eliason, 2006). As a result, *Chilling Adventures of Sabrina* seemingly offers a unique approach to young femininity since it "is rare to see on the small screen a confident and ambitious woman, and rarer still to witness a girl with the same qualities" (Ho, 2021, p. 1).

Chilling Adventures of Sabrina is also distinctive in that Sabrina explicitly and unabashedly identifies as a feminist. With storylines speaking directly to the issues raised the aftermath of the 2016 U.S. presidential election and by the #MeToo movement, critics have described *Chilling Adventures of Sabrina* "a darker show, for darker times" (Sheffield, 2018, n.p.) and Shipka has noted that her character ". . . is totally the Sabrina for 2018, in so many ways. She's a woke witch" (Yang, 2018, n.p). As such, throughout the series Sabrina and her friends advocate for equity and fairness while fighting against the patriarchy in both the witch and human worlds (Henesy, 2020). For example, while in high school Sabrina demands justice for sexual assault, forms a women's empowerment group, and confronts gender discrimination. Throughout the series she also seeks out positions of power like "Top Boy," student council co-president, and Queen of Hell. Likewise, Sabrina regularly questions authority (particularly Father Blackwood and the Dark Lord) and challenges tradition in both realms.

Despite her (generally) good intentions and immense magical abilities, "Sabrina is a headstrong character who seeks to solve all of Greendale's problems on her own" (Comeforo, 2020, p. 233). Unfortunately, for Sabrina and the mortal and witch worlds, this means that there are times when her powers yield horrifying consequences that are not easily remedied.

A Tale of Two Saviors

As supernatural youth narratives, *Chilling Adventures of Sabrina* and *Buffy the Vampire Slayer* have "shared generic codes and conventions, such as characterization, setting, and narrative" (Henesy, 2020, p. 7). Given that they are petite, conventionally attractive young women, Buffy and Sabrina's foes—often older men in positions of power—regularly underestimate them. Therefore, Buffy and Sabrina can both be read as gothic heroines, using their agency to challenge patriarchal forces and structures all while attempting to establish their sense of self (Gilliland, 2018). As heirs to supernatural birthrights, Buffy and Sabrina must balance everyday adolescence with their duty to fulfill their extraordinary prophecies. Although both young women have a close-knit group of friends and loved ones, their magical powers' magnitude set them apart from others.

Buffy and Sabrina are also distinguished from other supernatural heroines—such as the sisters from *Charmed* or Sabrina from *Sabrina the Teenage Witch*—because their series use religious allusions to frame them as supernatural saviors. Ranging from subtle visuals to episode titles, supporting characters, and explicit dialogue, both series contain numerous Christian references. Likewise, both young protagonists embody the Christ-like qualities of befriending outcasts and championing the weak. Most notably, like Christ, Buffy and Sabrina's birthrights enable them to occupy a liminal space between the human and supernatural world. Their powers have the potential to deliver humanity from evil, but they must also accept the ever-present possibility of martyrdom. Thus, the Christian themes of sacrifice and resurrection are present in both series. That said, the circumstances surrounding Buffy and Sabrina's resurrections differ significantly and offer contrasting versions of what it means to be a young female savior.

Over the course of seven seasons, Buffy dies and is resurrected twice. Buffy's first death and resurrection occur in the Season 1 finale, "Prophecy Girl," when a prophecy predicts her impending death at the hands of a vampire known as The Master. Although Buffy initially lashes out when she learns of her fate—claiming to "quit" and "resign" as Slayer—she willingly resumes her role when she learns that Giles is planning to battle The Master in her place. As they fight in his subterranean lair, The Master captures Buffy and she falls face first into a pool of water and drowns. When Buffy's friends discover her lifeless body, Xander performs CPR, and revives her. Despite returning from the dead, Buffy says that she feels "strong" and "different" and insists on confronting The Master once more, this time killing him. At the end of the episode Giles reaffirms Buffy's Christ-like abilities, stating that even death wouldn't stop her from saving the world.

Buffy the Vampire Slayer revisits death in the Season 5 finale, "The Gift," when Buffy is faced with sacrificing her younger sister, Dawn, in a ritual to prevent Hell from being unleashed on Earth. Although Giles explains that if Dawn lives, "then every living creature in this and every other dimension imaginable will suffer unbearable torment and death," Buffy refuses to accept Dawn's destiny. Buffy realizes that since they are sisters and share the same blood, she can take Dawn's place; her gift to Dawn (and the world) is sacrificing herself. After ensuring that Dawn is safe, Buffy embraces her sister for the last time, and leaps to her death. As she disappears, the audience hears Buffy's voice telling Dawn, "I love you. I will always love you. But this is the work that I have to do. Tell Giles . . . tell Giles I figured it out. And, and I'm okay . . . ," and the episode closes with a close-up of Buffy's tombstone. However, in the Season 6 premiere, "Bargaining," Buffy's friends are unable to accept her death, so Willow uses magic to raise Buffy from the dead. Although Buffy's second resurrection is traumatic—wrenching her from a peaceful afterlife—Buffy does not blame her friends for her anguish. Instead, Buffy thanks them for bringing her back, sacrificing her own truth to protect their feelings, and relegating herself to resuming her role as the Slayer and the burdens associated with it.

In contrast, Sabrina's death and resurrection over the course of two episodes, "Chapter 17: The Missionaries" and "Chapter 18: The Miracles of Sabrina Spellman," favor power over sacrifice. In Chapter 17, Sabrina confronts witch-hunting angels, who are holding her classmates from the Academy of the Unseen Arts captive. Although she is shot with an arrow and a crown of thorns is placed on her head to prevent her from spellcasting, Sabrina defiantly declares, "I choose death over your False God." In response, the witch hunters continue to shoot her with arrows "like Saint Sebastian," and Sabrina falls to the ground, blood spilling from her motionless body. As the angels begin killing other students, Sabrina miraculously rises from the dead. Floating in the air, with white eyes, and flames shooting out of her hands, Sabrina announces in a deep and otherworldly voice that she is the "the Dark Lord's sword" and proceeds to vengefully burn the angels with her hellfire. She then resurrects two of her classmates that were slayed by the angels by simply saying "arise sister" and "arise brother" before collapsing. Chapter 18 begins just moments after, with Sabrina's friend Harvey carrying an unresponsive Sabrina to be treated by her Aunt Hilda, who is also caring for her wounded cousin Ambrose. Harvey and the two resurrected students recount what happened to Hilda, noting that, "She died and brought herself back to life" and "Sabrina was like unto a god." The "miracle" repeats itself moments later when Hilda's spells are unable to cure Ambrose; Sabrina suddenly arises of her own volition, lays her hands on her cousin, and he is healed.

Taken together, Buffy and Sabrina's deaths and resurrections clearly imply both young women are supernatural saviors. While these deaths and resurrections demonstrate the agency and empowerment of both heroines, they point to differing conceptions of young femininity. Buffy's deaths and subsequent resurrections epitomize her selflessness. Because the prophecies foretell her death, Buffy does not expect to survive or anticipate being brought back to life. She enters these situations with the knowledge that she will die, but she does so willingly, putting her loved ones before herself. Conversely, Sabrina knowingly enters a dangerous situation to save others, but it is not presented as a sacrifice. Rather, Sabrina is confident in her power; she assumes she will persevere and does not anticipate death. Although Sabrina does end up dying for her beliefs, her ability to revive herself reifies, rather than undermines, her strong sense of self and faith in her magic. Buffy's deaths and resurrections are made in service to others—her self-sacrifice is "properly feminine" (Kramer, 2017, p. 17)—whereas Sabrina's death and resurrection focus on her audacity and innate power, which the series associates with formidable male figures like Christ, Saint Sebastian, and the Dark Lord.

Sabrina and Sacrifice

As Golden (1998) noted, stories about women often revolve around sacrifice and tend to celebrate women who put others before themselves. As mentioned above, Buffy's sacrifices are rooted in her sense of duty and love, which conform to these gendered cultural expectations. Although her death and resurrection are not necessarily framed as such, there are other instances throughout the series where Sabrina engages in sacrifice. However, unlike Buffy, Sabrina is depicted as having multiple motivations for her sacrifices—some of which are less than selfless—making Sabrina a complex and complicated supernatural heroine.

Supernatural Savior or Sacrificial Lamb? | 115

The most traditional depiction of sacrifice in *Chilling Adventures of Sabrina* occurs in "Chapter 19: The Mandrake." In this episode, after discovering a prophecy that says she will bring about the end of days, Sabrina bravely accepts that her only recourse is to relinquish her powers and become fully mortal. Although her family and friends tell her this equates to "witch suicide," Sabrina states, "I couldn't let my legacy be the destruction of the world." Sabrina's willingness to sacrifice her powers (and in turn, her witch identity) appears truly altruistic because she is privileging the greater good over her own self-interest. However, given that Sabrina's powers are restored in the very next episode, it seems as if she is being rewarded for putting others before herself, undercutting the selflessness of the act. That said, Sabrina has no way of knowing that she would ever regain her abilities, making her decision more akin to Buffy's noble and "feminine" self-sacrifice.

In contrast, at other times in *Chilling Adventures of Sabrina*, the young heroine frames her actions as a sacrifice when, in reality, she is simply justifying her pursuit of power. In "Chapter 24: The Hare Moon," Sabrina's Aunt Zelda is upset when she learns that Sabrina has secretly become Queen of Hell. Sabrina claims that she had "no choice" and "did it to save the realms." Yet, Zelda does not accept Sabrina's rationale and instead rebukes, "You did it because you wanted to! You did it because you like power!" While Zelda acknowledges that Sabrina's desire for power is "healthy ... up to a point," she also admonishes her niece when she says, "You have a savior complex. You always have." Nevertheless, Sabrina's desire to continue as Queen of Hell is so strong that in "Chapter 27: The Judas Kiss" she considers partaking in "The Judas Challenge," which would allow her to secure her position by betraying her friends. Although Sabrina cannot bring herself to hurt Harvey and Roz, her single-minded focus on being queen still results in her being framed as a "betrayer." In fact, Caliban, Zelda, and Nick all critique Sabrina for choosing "a throne in Hell over her coven and her family."[10] Sabrina does eventually acknowledge the allure of power to her boyfriend in "Chapter 28: Sabrina is Legend" when she says, "You were right, Nick—I let everything in Hell pull me away from what really matters—my family, my friends, everything I love, but not anymore." Despite this realization, Sabrina nevertheless creates a catastrophic time paradox, which allows an alternate version of herself, Sabrina Morningstar, to rule Hell while she returns to Greendale to "be a teenager," just so she can experience both worlds.

Sacrifice also underscores "Chapter 33: Deus Ex Machina," when Sabrina Spellman and Sabrina Morningstar discover that the time paradox allowing them to co-exist has generated a parallel cosmos, which is on a collision course with Earth. To avert deadly impact, one of the Sabrinas must travel to an alternate universe as "an offering or a sacrifice." As their friends and family debate which Sabrina should go, Sabrina Morningstar says, "We are both equally responsible for this" and Sabrina Spellman concurs. While it is true that Sabrina Morningstar has been complicit with Sabrina Spellman's desire to spend time together, it is Sabrina Spellman who has been explicitly warned multiple times that the pair interacting "could precipitate a cataclysm ... that could snuff out both timelines completely." Furthermore, when a game of "rock, paper, scissors" determines that Sabrina Morningstar must go, Sabrina Spellman does not try to intervene, despite having more culpability in their dual existence. Although the Dark Lord objects to the outcome, Sabrina Morningstar replies, "You always said you wanted me to bring honor to the House of Morningstar. What kind of queen would I be if I let my subjects die?" Thus, Sabrina Morningstar is willing to sacrifice her husband, throne, and life in Hell out of a sense of honor and duty. Though clearly distressed over her separation from Sabrina Morningstar, Sabrina Spellman fails to fully register the scale of the sacrifice. Instead of employing her incredible powers to intercede, she simply opts to wish that "Sabrina be safe. That we all be safe" when she sees a falling star in the night sky.

In addition to her exile to the alternate universe, Sabrina Morningstar's principles result in the ultimate sacrifice—her life—in "Chapter 35: The Endless," when she attempts to warn Sabrina Spellman of the encroaching Void. Afterward, in "Chapter 36: At the Mountains of Madness," Sabrina Spellman acknowledges her doppelgänger's selflessness, "Thanks to Sabrina Morningstar. She gave up her life for us, and now my soul is in her body. How many sacrifices does she have to make for us? For me?" When juxtaposing the two Sabrinas, Sabrina Morningstar's actions conform to past depictions of feminine sacrifice while Sabrina Spellman's self-preservation is a radical departure. In fact, only when she is confronted with the loss of Sabrina Morningstar—and her role in it—does Sabrina Spellman begin to take a different approach.

In the series finale, Chapter 36, Sabrina twice feels she must sacrifice herself in an attempt to save the world. Determined to thwart impending doom, Sabrina travels to the Void, in hopes of trapping it inside Pandora's Box even though she may be trapped along with it. When Sabrina explains this decision to her cat Salem, who is her familiar, her motivation becomes apparent: "It has to be me, Salem. It's my life weighted against billions. And even though people say it's not my fault, I feel like it is." Although a sense of duty may be a contributing factor, Sabrina clearly believes that she must make this sacrifice to assuage her sense of guilt. Fortunately for Sabrina, she escapes before being engulfed by the Void, allowing her to atone for her past actions without suffering deadly consequences. However, while on her mission, Sabrina unknowingly assumes the Void's properties; unintentionally making objects and people disappear. When Sabrina realizes what is happening, she vows, "I won't hurt anyone again." To protect others from her uncontrollable powers, Sabrina banishes herself to the Mountains of Madness where she plans to drain the Void from her body. Sabrina understands that while this bloodletting will rescue those that have disappeared, it will also result in her own painful death. Both literally and figuratively draining, during Sabrina's last moments she says a series of goodbyes to her loved ones and the life she knew, indicating that she has made peace with her fate. Hilda reaffirms the intention of Sabrina's sacrifice when she exclaims, "She knew! She knew what she had to do to save everyone," presenting Sabrina as self-sacrificing savior.

All's Well That Ends Well?

Just as Buffy and Sabrina's sacrifices and resurrections differ, so do their final outcomes. In "Chosen," the series finale of *Buffy the Vampire Slayer,* Willow uses magic to share Buffy's power with an army of potential slayers, allowing them to defeat The First Evil and destroy the Hellmouth. Beyond the slayers in Sunnydale, Willow's spell also awakens potential slayers across the world, creating a community of newly empowered women. When the series ends, Buffy is shown surrounded by her loved ones, smiling because she is no longer the "one and only Chosen," the lone person responsible for the fate of humanity, and instead, is part of a powerful collective that changed the world. Kramer (2017) aptly encapsulated the underlying message of the finale when she stated, "*Buffy the Vampire Slayer* is about the joy of female power: having it, enjoying it, and sharing it" (p. 29).

While Buffy ends on an optimistic note, *Chilling Adventures of Sabrina* closes much more ambivalently. Following Sabrina's death in the Mountains of Madness, her aunts host a funeral in Greendale with Zelda eulogizing Sabrina Spellman and Morningstar as a crowd mourns at their graves. Sabrina is also memorialized through a life-size statue in the center of the Academy's foyer, literally placed on a pedestal and standing in a spotlight, functioning similarly to a crucifix by honoring the supernatural savior and all her potential while serving as a perpetual reminder of her sacrifice. Although Sabrina is treated with reverence by those who survived her, the series ending is nevertheless problematic. As

Gennis (2020) explained, "... by killing both Sabrinas, the show let her off the hook completely, allowing her to die a hero rather than live and grapple with her mistakes. Through her death, all of Sabrina's texture and flaws were flattened and forgotten until she became nothing more than a saint-like figure who martyred herself for the greater good" (n.p.). Therefore, the series ultimately frames Sabrina as a sacrificial lamb, instead of a complicated young woman attempting to navigate the rewards and responsibilities of her awesome powers.

To be fair, the show's creator had not originally slated Chapter 36 to be the series finale. In fact, the final scene was supposed to show Zelda summoning a god from the underworld to help bring Sabrina back to life, but upon cancellation, Netflix asked Aguirre-Sacasa to cut the scene, to avoid giving "fans false hope that the story would continue" (Cordero, 2021). Consequently, *Chilling Adventures of Sabrina* ends with Sabrina in the afterlife. Although Sabrina expects to be alone, her boyfriend Nick drowns himself so he can join her. He explains, "What's important is that we're together here forever and ever" to which Sabrina replies, "That is a plus." As a result, the series closes with a blissful Sabrina and Nick embracing in the Sweet Here After. By reuniting Sabrina and Nick, the series erases the significance of Sabrina's powers as well as her sacrifice, and instead conjures the specter of post-feminist "girl power" by reducing her to a stereotypical teen television ending.[11] Moreover, *Chilling Adventures of Sabrina* takes the resolution one step further by privileging heterosexual romance not just in life, but also in death—making it, quite literally, the end-all and be-all of her existence. As discussed earlier, following the finale of *Chilling Adventures of Sabrina,* the young heroine does make cross-over appearances in the sixth season of *Riverdale*, which addresses her death by quickly offering that Sabrina is alive because Nick traded his life for her (Nelson, 2022). While this "explanation" provides new possibilities for the character in another series, *Chilling Adventures of Sabrina* nevertheless functions as a closed text, which, in its conclusion, does sentence its supernatural savior to death.

Discussion

Chilling Adventures of Sabrina offers contradictory messages about the construction of young femininity in contemporary teen television. It portrays Sabrina as a powerful young woman who openly embraces her magical abilities and expresses her desires. She seeks positions of authority while at the same time advocating for social justice, reflecting a genuine engagement with feminism. Unlike past representations, Sabrina does not view her birthright as a burden—she is a supernatural savior who revels in her power (Ho, 2021). As such, Sabrina's empowerment appears to eschew the post-feminist girl power that plagues much of contemporary teen television representations. At the same time, *Chilling Adventures of Sabrina* also capitulates to many problematic tropes as reflected by the young heroine's arrogance in her powers as well as her self-indulgent behaviors. Sabrina believes that she can, and should, "have it all," and is ultimately punished for her audacity. However, the series cleverly repackages Sabrina's death as duty and sacrifice, masking the regressive underpinnings of these acts. In turn, Sabrina is seemingly redeemed of her past transgressions and rewarded with everlasting heterosexual romance, aligning with the ideals of traditional femininity. Unlike the ending of *Buffy the Vampire Slayer*, which celebrates and promotes the collective empowerment of young women, Sabrina's incredible powers and feminist potential die with her in the series finale.

With the decades that passed since *Buffy the Vampire Slayer* and the recent strides made by the #MeToo movement, *Chilling Adventures of Sabrina* was poised to be a true celebration of female resistance. However, rather than making good on its initial promise, the show's disappointing failure to support female power undercuts the feminist integrity of its protagonist. Therefore, Sabrina's demise suggests that despite some progress, contemporary media representations continue to conform to sexist norms that punish ambitious young women—and with the successful containment of empowered femininity, the patriarchal status quo remains intact.

Overall, like supernatural youth narratives of the past, *Chilling Adventures of Sabrina* offers new perspectives on young femininity, particularly what it means to be a young woman grappling with power. As Henesy (2020) rightfully acknowledged, *Chilling Adventures of Sabrina* "has reimagined the magical heroine as a gothic teenage feminist icon" (p. 13). However, when placed within a broader context of supernatural youth media, the series offers a markedly different and deeply troubling outcome for Sabrina—one that suggests being a powerful young woman is ultimately untenable. Perhaps then the true value of Sabrina is how she embodies the "paradoxical space" of feminine adolescence where "Adolescent girls, wavering at the brink of adulthood, are told that they can do and be anything they want, and yet they feel compelled to fit into archaic images of womanhood and femininity" (Byers, 2002, p. 173). Thus, despite her depiction as a supernatural savior, Sabrina is a sacrificial lamb that ultimately serves to reinforce gender stereotypes about young women and their social roles.

Notes

1. Although Whedon was once celebrated as a "man on the front lines of feminism," reports of his "toxic" behavior on *Buffy the Vampire Slayer* and other projects have compromised his reputation as a feminist auteur (Shapiro, 2022). In this context, Whedon's claims of a "feminist agenda" appear to be an appropriation of feminist discourse rather than an authentic ideological stance (Flint, 2022).
2. As noted in the show's opening sequence.
3. This phrase appears on Buffy's tombstone in the Season 5 finale, "The Gift."
4. This phrase is used in the 1992 film and again at the start of the Season 5 finale.
5. Buffy says this to Darla in the pilot episode, "Welcome to the Hellmouth."
6. Ancillary media included books like *Sabrina's Guide to the Universe* and *Salem's Tails* (a companion series); the CD *Sabrina the Teenage Witch: The Album*; video games like *Sabrina the Teenage Witch: Spellbound, Sabrina the Teenage Witch: Brat Attack* and *Sabrina the Teenage Witch: Bundle of Magic*; the televised specials *Sabrina Goes to Rome* and *Sabrina Down Under*; and the complete series on DVD.
7. Although the two new comics were slated to appear by late 2022, *The Occult World of Sabrina* has not yet been released.
8. Sabrina states this in the pilot episode, "Chapter 1: October Country."
9. Sabrina declares this in "Chapter 2: The Dark Baptism."
10. Caliban, Zelda, and Nick repeatedly condemn Sabrina's actions in Chapter 27.
11. It should be noted that the marketing rationale that essentially drove Netflix's request to change the series' ending also aligns with the commercial interests of post-feminist "girl power."

References

Ballard, K. (2018, October 24). The Chilling Adventures of Sabrina showrunner talks channelling The Exorcist, why it's not Buffy, and our fascination with witches. *Gameradar+*. chilling-adventures-of-sabrina-showrunner-talks-channelling-the-exorcist-why-its-not-buffy-and-our-fascination-with-witches/.

Bindig Yousman, L. (2022). Same girl, different show: Representations of young femininity in teen TV. In A. Damico (Ed.), *Women in media* (pp. 144–148). ABC-CLIO/Greenwood.

Byers, M. (2003). Buffy the Vampire Slayer: The next generation of television. In R. Dicker & A. Piepmeier (Eds.), *Catching a wave: Reclaiming feminism for the 21st century* (pp. 71–187). Northeastern University Press.

Chesney-Lind, M., & Eliason, M. (2006). From invisible to incorrigible: The demonization of marginalized women and girls. *Crime Media Culture, 2*(1), 29–47. https://doi.org/10.1177/1741659006061709.

Comeforo, K. (2020). Archie Comics publications & Warner Bros. Television (Producers). The Chilling Adventures of Sabrina. *Women's Studies in Communication, 43*(3), 322–324. https://doi.org/10.1080/07491409.2020.1803654.

Corcoran, M. (2022). The monstrous girl: Teen witches, power and fourth-wave feminism. In H. Gavin (Ed.), *Women and the abuse of power* (pp. 41–78). Emerald Publishing. https://doi.org/10.1108/9781800433342.

Cordero, R. (2021, July 21). How Roberto Aguirre-Sacasa will expand on Netflix's "Chilling Adventures of Sabrina" in new comic books. *Deadline*. https://deadline.com/2021/07/roberto-aguirre-sacasa-will-expand-netflix-chilling-adventures-of-sabrina-new-comic-books-1234796705/

Crosby, S. (2004). The cruelest season: Female heroes snapped into sacrificial heroines. In S. A. Inness (Ed.), *Action chicks* (pp. 153–178). Palgrave Macmillian.

Driscoll, C. (2002). *Girls*. Columbia University Press.

Driscoll, C., & Heatwole, A. (2018). *The hunger games*. Routledge.

Douglas, S. (1995). *Where the girls are*. Three Rivers Press.

Early, F. (2001). Staking her claim: Buffy the Vampire Slayer as transgressive woman warrior. *Journal of Popular Culture, 35*(3), 11–27.

Flint, H. (2022, March 10). How tainted is Buffy the Vampire Slayer, 25 years on? *BBC*. https://www.bbc.com/culture/article/20220310-buffy-the-vampire-slayer-at-25-how-tainted-is-it

Fuller, D. (2018, October 25). Excited for the 'Sabrina' Reboot? Here's how the teenage witch (and her cat) have evolved. *New York Times*. https://www.nytimes.com/2018/10/25/arts/television/chilling-adentures-sabrina-teenage-witch-history.html

Gennis, S. (2020, December 31). Good riddance to Sabrina Spellman, TV's most entitled character. *Bustle*. https://www.bustle.com/entertainment/good-riddance-to-sabrina-spellman-caos-season-4

Gerston, J. (1996, October 6). A 'normal kid' with magical powers. *New York Times*. https://www.nytimes.com/1996/10/06/tv/a-normal-kid-with-magical-powers.html

Gilliland, E. (2018). Double trouble: Gothic shadows and self-discovery in Buffy the Vampire Slayer. *Slayage: The Journal of Whedon Studies, 16*(47), 1–26.

Golden, S. (1998). *Slaying the Mermaid*. Harmony Books.

Gonick, M. (2006). Between "girl power" and "reviving Ophelia": Constituting the neoliberal girl subject. *NWSA Journal, 18*(2), 1–23. https://www.jstor.org/stable/4317205

Hains, R. (2009). Power feminism, mediated: Girl power and the commercial politics of change. *Women Studies in Communication, 32*(1), 89–113. https://doi.org/10.1080/07491409.2009.10162382.

Hains, R. (2012). *Growing Up with Girl Power*. Peter Lang. https://doi.org/10.3726/b15101

Henesy, M. (2020). "Leaving my girlhood behind": Woke witches and feminist liminality in Chilling Adventures of Sabrina. *Feminist Media Studies*. https://doi.org/10.1080/14680777.2020.1791929

Ho, A. K. H. (2021). *The new witches*. McFarland.

Hohenstein, S. (2019). *Girl warriors*. McFarland.

Hopkins, S. (1999). "The art of 'girl power': Femininity, feminism and youth culture in the 1990s." In Rob White (Ed.), *Australian youth subcultures: On the margins and in the mainstream*. Australian Clearinghouse for Youth Studies.

Kramer, K. (2017). "How do you like my darkness now?": Women, violence, and the good 'bad girl' in Buffy the Vampire Slayer. In J. A. Chappell & M. Young (Eds.), *Bad girls and transgressive women in popular television, fiction, and film* (pp. 1–31). Palgrave Macmillan. https://doi.org/10.1007/978-3-319-47259-1.

Magee, S. (2014). "High school is hell": The TV legacy of Beverly Hills, 90210 and Buffy the Vampire Slayer. *Journal of Popular Culture, 47*(4), 877–894. https://onlinelibrary.wiley.com/doi/10.1111/jpcu.12165

MacDonald, D. C. (2004). Iconic eye candy: Buffy the Vampire Slayer and designer peer pressure for teens. In R. Schubart & A. Gjelsvik (Eds.), *Femme fatalities* (pp. 111–125). Nordicom.

Magoulick, M. (2006). Frustrating female heroism: Mixed messages in Xena, Nikita, and Buffy. *Journal of Popular Culture, 39*(5), 729–755. https://onlinelibrary.wiley.com/doi/10.1111/j.1540-5931.2006.00326.x

Mathis, C., Graves, S. A., & Tyndall, M. (2023). *Netflix's chilling adventures of Sabrina*. Lexington Books.

Moseley, R. (2002). Glamorous witchcraft: Gender and magic in teen film and television. *Screen, 43*(4), 403–422. https://doi.org/10.1093/screen/43.4.403.

Murphy, B. (2009). *The suburban gothic in American popular culture*. Palgrave Macmillan. https://doi.org/10.1057/9780230244757

Murphy, C. (2014). Secrets and lies: Gender and generation in the ABC Family brand. In B. Kaklamaniduou & M. Tally (Eds.), *The millennials on film and television* (pp. 15–30). McFarland.

Nash, I. (2006). *American sweethearts*. Indiana University Press.

Nelson, E. (2022, July 11). 'Riverdale' finally answers the biggest question about Sabrina Spellman and 'Chilling Adventures'. *Showbiz Cheat Sheet*. https://www.cheatsheet.com/entertainment/riverdale-explains-sabrina-spellman-alive-chilling-adventures.html/

Opie, D. (2021, December 8). Riverdale's Sabrina crossover tackles the spin-off's controversial ending. *DigitalSpy*. https://www.digitalspy.com/tv/ustv/a38460462/riverdale-sabrina-crossover-explained/

Osgerby, B. (2004). "'So who's got time for adults!': Femininity, consumption and the development of teen TV—From *Gidget* to *Buffy*." In G. Davis & K. Dickinson (Eds.), *Teen TV* (pp. 71–86). British Film Institute.

Pender, P. (2016). *I'm Buffy and you're history: Buffy the vampire slayer and contemporary feminism*. I.B.Tauris.

Projansky, S., & Vande Berg, L. R. (2000). Sabrina, the teenage . . . ? Girls, witches, mortals, and the limitations of prime-time feminism. In E. R. Helford (Ed.), *Fantasy Girls* (pp. 13–40). Roman & Littlefield.

Saltzman, S. (2019). Girl power and depression in *Buffy the Vampire Slayer*. In J. M. Still & Z. T. Wilkinson (Eds.), *Buffy to Batgirl* (pp. 85–98). McFarland.

Shapiro, L. (2022, January 17). The undoing of Joss Whedon. *Vulture*. https://www.vulture.com/article/joss-whedon-allegations.html

Sheffield, R. (2018, October 24). 'Chilling Adventures of Sabrina' review: The witch is back!. *Rolling Stone*. https://www.rollingstone.com/tv-movies/tv-movie-reviews/chilling-adventures-of-sabrina-review-745479/

Taft, J. K. (2004). Girl power politics: Pop-culture barriers and organizational resistance. In A. Harris (Ed.), *All about the girl: Culture, power, and identity* (pp. 69–78). Routledge.

Vint, S. (2002). "Killing us softly"? A feminist search for the "real" Buffy. *Slayage: The Online International Journal of Buffy Studies, 5*.

Woolery, G. (1983). *Children's television: The first thirty-five years 1946–1981: Part 1: Animated cartoon series*. Scarecrow Press.

Yang, R. (2018, October 20). 'Chilling Adventures of Sabrina' stars on the Netflix show's feminist themes. *Variety*. https://variety.com/2018/tv/news/chilling-adventures-of-sabrina-woke-witc-premiere-1202987527/

7

Youth at the Border: Finding the Monstrous-Feminine in Marvel Comics

ERIC M. KENNEDY JR.

The superhero narrative, at its core, centers heroes who are white, male, heterosexual, and cisgender (Goodrum et al., 2018, p. 9), and Marvel Comics has reflected this since its inception: Captain America, Thor, Iron Man, The Hulk, Spider-Man, and Wolverine remain some of the most prominent characters on the page and screen today. While superhero comics have seen great strides with regards to diversity and representation in recent years, thanks to the success of characters such as Marvel's Pakistani-American Ms. Marvel, out gay X-Man Iceman, and Afro-Latino Spider-Man Miles Morales (Donohoo, 2023; Gramuglia, 2019; Standlee, 2015), the genre is still far from achieving gender parity. As Carolyn Cocca (2016) points out in her introduction to *Superwomen: Gender, Power, and Representation*, the mere presence of "popular, strong, complex female superheroes" is not enough to create a level playing field. Female heroes remain underserved and, despite having incredible powers and engaging backstories[1], their stories often sexualize them and situate them in heteronormative narratives that situate them as *less than* or *other* compared to their male counterparts (p. 7).

This chapter expands upon the work of Goodrum et al., Cocca, and others by explicating one of the ways that white, male, heterosexual identities are privileged in Marvel Comics, while female and feminized male identities are sidelined. I argue that the feminine, when combined with youth and magic, is treated by authors and character as especially dangerous within the Marvel Universe. Using Barbara Creed's theories of the "monstrous-feminine," this chapter reveals how the narrative of Marvel Comics casts youth, magic, and femininity as a threatening mixture in a fictive universe that privileges science (fiction) and mature masculinity. Although Creed's theory concerned horror films, superhero stories are also fertile sites for applying the theory, because like horror stories, they put their heroes in states of prolonged threat from dangerous Others, and in Marvel's comics, the youth-fem-magic nexus is marked as especially dangerous. This trend applies both to young female characters, and to a young gay male character.

Examining the Monstrous-Feminine

In this chapter, I examine three of Marvel's most prominent female teenaged magic-users: Magik of the New Mutants; Nico Minoru of the Runaways; and Pixie of the New X-Men. To add complexity to conversations about the monstrous-feminine, I also examine a fourth teenaged magic-user from the Marvel franchise: Wiccan of the Young Avengers, a gay male who is often feminized in his narratives. I discuss each, in turn, with reference to their comic book iterations and, where relevant, their filmic iterations, in terms of how they are constructed as monstrous-feminine.

These characters are not the only young magic-users in the Marvel Universe,[2] but they have the most extensive publication histories and backstories compared to their lesser-known peers such as Cullen Bloodstone (Hallum & Walker 2012) or Zoe Laveau (Young & Ramos 2020). Each character is central to the plot of the books that feature them, elevating them beyond "background characters" or "extras" to full-fledged ensemble cast members, if not outright stars. Three have appeared in film or television adaptations: Magik in *The New Mutants* (2020); Nico Minoru in *Runaways* (2017–2019); and a child-aged Wiccan in *WandaVision* (2021) and *Doctor Strange in the Multiverse of Madness* (2022). This chapter briefly addresses Magik and Nico's live-action counterparts, although Wiccan's filmic iteration is not addressed because his powers are featured only briefly. By analyzing each character in turn, I identify an emergent pattern wherein Creed's theories of the monstrous-feminine and Kristeva's theories of the abject can be applied to Marvel Comics' female and feminized magic-users, who have access to magical powers that threaten the symbolic order.

The order of the Marvel Universe, like our own,[3] is deeply gendered, privileging the traditionally masculine realms of science and technology over feminine spirituality, mysticism, and magic. This is evident in the origins of mainstay heroes such as Tony Stark (Iron Man), Bruce Banner (The Hulk), Reed Richards (Mister Fantastic), and Peter Parker (Spider-Man), which reflect traditional associations between masculinity and science. The presence of magical, feminine power presents a threat to the primacy of science and technology in the genre (Clover, 2015, p. 98). While prominent adult male magic-users such as Doctor Strange and Brother Voodoo practice the mystic arts without interference from the larger superhero community, young, feminine (and feminized) magic-users present a perceived threat to their teammates and authority figures in the superhero community who believe that their abilities must be curbed, surveilled, or exterminated to maintain order.

Representing Women: Comics and Superhero Narratives

The representation of women in comics and superhero narratives has been a subject of considerable scrutiny, reflecting broader societal discourses on gender, identity, and empowerment. Scholars and fans have pointed to both quantitative and qualitative differences in how female heroes are represented. In "Analyzing the Gender Representation of 34,476 Comic Book Characters," Amanda Shendruk examines the portrayal of male and female genders by analyzing naming conventions, superpower types, and team compositions. Shendruk shows that female characters more frequently possess non-physical, cognitive abilities such as empathy, telepathy, psychic powers, and precognition. In contrast, male characters are more likely to have enhanced physical powers, energy manipulation, and gadget-related abilities. This disparity is further illustrated by the limited number of physical abilities dominated by female characters, such as pheromone control, sonic scream, and prehensile hair, which are often tied to gender stereotypes. She found that, while 8% of male and female characters have gendered superhero names, female characters are more than twice as likely than male characters to have a name that could be considered "diminutive," such as those including the terms "girl," "miss," or "princess" (as opposed to "woman," "Ms.," or "Queen"). These kind of names may convey a sense of weakness or diminished agency, especially when compared to the more authoritative names of male characters (Shendruk, 2017).

In *Superwomen: Gender, Power, and Representation* (2016), Carolyn Cocca delves into the systemic and economic factors influencing diversity in comic creation and character development, arguing that affirmative action and capitalism play pivotal roles in driving changes, with an emphasis on the profit motive as an incentive for diversification. She argues that increasing diversity "requires being conscious of historic vectors of discrimination such as gender, race, ethnicity, religion, sexuality, and disability in hiring creators, and a similar consciousness in creating and fleshing out character" (2016, p. 217). Comic fans play an important role in increasing this consciousness, identifying problematic representations, advocating for change, and leveraging social media to push for increased diversity in comic narratives. This reflects an evolving landscape where audience engagement influences industry practices (Cocca, 2016, p. 222).

Marvel Comics has responded to fan feedback by rehabilitating existing characters and introducing new characters. Giancola and Coleman discuss Marvel's 2014 introduction of an alternate version of the long-dead Gwen Stacy as the costumed hero called Spider-Gwen. While the original Gwen Stacy was characterized as a flirtatious "party girl" and defined primarily by her tragic death, Spider-Gwen is not confined to such reductive terms. Instead, this version of Gwen Stacy as a skilled detective, musician, and hero, defying limitations imposed by genre expectations (Giancola & Coleman, 2018, p. 275). An example of a new character is Kamala Khan, the current Ms. Marvel, who was created by editor Sana Amanat and writer G. Willow Wilson in 2014. Kamala is a young Muslim Pakistani-American who, inspired by her idol Captain Marvel, becomes a superhero after she develops body-morphing powers. Her characterization has been praised by fans and critics. Gibson writes, "Kamala is marginalized as a child and as a girl; however, her powers mean that she is constantly engaging as a 'knowing' person acting within an adult world" (Gibson, 2018, p. 38). Kamala actively pushes back against the societal and genre rules that would limit her, acting not just as a solo hero, but as a member of several teams where she is able to demonstrate her ability to lead.

Filmic adaptations of comic books display many of the same trends as their source material. Kara Kvaran's (2017) analysis of comics-based superhero films reveals a significant reliance on male role models and father figures while sidelining or obscuring their female counterparts. This trend reinforces the notion that only male characters can be inspirational or worthy of emulation, fortifying patriarchal ideals that link masculinity to validation from other men (p. 217). Notably, renowned actresses in these films, like Emma Stone, Natalie Portman, and Maggie Gyllenhaal, receive minimal screen time, underscoring the inessential nature of their characters (p. 220). Despite assertions of gender neutrality within the film industry, superhero films perpetuate an insecure hypermasculinity entrenched in homosocial interactions, where men seek validation from one another, relegating women to accessory roles. This cinematic portrayal reflects a cultural bias favoring masculine narratives, ultimately reinforcing gender imbalances and the marginalization of female characters within the superhero genre (Kvaran, 2017, p. 234).

Robinson, Gonzales, and Edwards highlight pivotal moments in the Marvel Cinematic Universe (MCU) related to female representation. They identify the release of the Netflix series *Jessica Jones* in 2015 as a significant milestone as the first MCU project centered on a woman (excluding the 2005 Twentieth Century Fox film *Elektra*) (Robinson et al., 2023, p. 256). Despite these supposed gains, the quality of female representation has been questioned by fans and critics. For example, 2015's *Avengers: Age of Ultron* was met with backlash from fans when Black Widow, a hero played by Scarlett Johansson, seemed to imply that her inability to have children made her feel like a "monster" (Goodrum et al., 2018, p. 9).

It is the idea of female monstrosity in superhero comics that I explore to in this chapter. Earlier scholarship has applied the concept of the monstrous-feminine to individual comic book characters or books, such as Esther De Dauw's discussion of The Scarlet Witch's fatherless birth (2018, p. 70) and Dany Prince's analysis of Maika's demonic possession in *Monstress* (2021, p. 79). This chapter contributes to this discourse by exploring patterns in the representation of young, female, and feminine characters throughout Marvel Comics' publication history.

Barbara Creed's The Monstrous-Feminine

In *The Monstrous-Feminine*, Barbara Creed (2015) argues that the female monster is not simply an inversion of the male monster, but rather is horrifying precisely because of its femininity (p. 25). Her work draws on Julia Kristeva's *Powers of Horror: An Essay on Abjection* (1982), which articulates the concept of abjection and its relation to sex and gender. Kristeva describes the abject as "what disturbs identity, system, order. What does not respect borders, positions, rules. The in-between, the ambiguous, the composite" (p. 4). This concept of the border is key to Creed's analysis of monstrosity, as she argues that "the function of the monstrous ... [is] to bring about an encounter between the symbolic order and that which threatens stability" (p. 45).

While Creed addresses several "faces" of the monstrous-feminine, this chapter addresses two in particular: woman as witch and woman as possessed monster. The figure of the witch, often depicted as female, challenges boundaries and realities with her magic, unsettling the symbolic order (Creed, 2015, p. 213). Women portrayed as possessed—by power, external forces, or demonic influence—attack the symbolic order and expose its vulnerabilities (p. 119). The vulnerability and liminal state of adolescence make young female characters particularly susceptible to being portrayed as monstrous (Smith & Moruzi, 2018, p. 15). Each character discussed in this chapter is portrayed as having developed or discovered magical abilities during their adolescence or teenage years, a time when they are particularly vulnerable to outside influence.

Illyana Rasputin/Magik

Illyana Rasputin first appeared in *Giant-Sized X-Men* #1 as the 6-year-old sister of the X-Man Colossus (Wein et al., 1975). She underwent a dramatic transformation in 1983's *Uncanny X-Men* #160, when she was lured through a portal to Limbo, a hell dimension outside of time and space, by the demon lord Belasco (Claremont et al., 1982, p. 3). When she is pulled back through the portal to Earth, she emerges as a 13-year-old girl—although she was separated from the X-Men for just a moment, she spent seven years growing up in Limbo (Claremont et al., 1982, pp. 21–22).

A miniseries titled *Magik* addressed Illyana's lost childhood in Limbo via flashbacks. The exposition labels Illyana as "the in-between, the ambiguous, the composite"—traits Kristeva ascribes to abjection (Kristeva, 1982, p. 4). From the start, her split identity primes Illyana to follow one of two diametrically opposed paths: good or evil; light or darkness.

Illyana's magic power was activated by the creation of "bloodstones," artifacts that contain portions of her soul extracted by Belasco. The corruption of an innocent soul is a great source of power in Limbo. Belasco abducted Illyana precisely because she was "delightfully pure and unspoiled"—a pure, innocent soul vulnerable for corruption (Claremont et al., 1983, p. 5). The creation of bloodstones can be read as symbolic of the onset of menstruation: Illyana must give her blood and become a woman to access her true power. As is often the case in horror, the narrative constructs menstruation and women's blood as a source of abjection for their transformative powers (Creed, 2015, p. 223). As Illyana matures, she also grows darker, becoming more corrupted by Belasco's demonic influence.

Illyana's thoughts of Belasco become perversely erotic and sexual as the miniseries progresses. In *Magik* #3 she narrates: "I thrill to Belasco's voice, his touch, his very presence. He is my lord and master—" (Claremont et al., 1984c, p. 2). Here, Illyana constructs abjection through her lustful, carnal response to

Belasco's extraction of her soul and his plans to use her as a "gate" for demonic gods to pass through. This recalls Kristeva's description of abjection as "a terror that dissembles, a hatred that smiles, a passion that uses the body for barter" (p. 4). Illyana's corruption is described in particularly sexual terms in *New Mutants* #72, where she is described as a "pretty pastel present" to be opened, revealing a grotesque inside (Simonson et al., 1989a, pp. 2–3). This implied sexual corruption at the hands of Limbo demons echoes Creed's (2015) definition of stereotypical feminine evil—"beautiful on the outside/corrupt within" (p. 122). This description also aligns with her description of the monstrous-feminine as highly sexual, with its thinly veiled euphemisms for the loss of virginity and aggressive sex (Chare et al., 2019, p. 102). To escape Limbo, Illyana uses her magic to create a "soulsword," a physical manifestation of her life force energy, with which to battle Belasco (Claremont et al., 1984b, p. 18). Wielding a phallic sword of her own creation, Illyana threatens established rules of sexual difference, presenting as both generative and destructive (Kristeva, 1982, p. 71).

After escaping Limbo, the now-13-year-old Illyana takes on the moniker Magik and joins the New Mutants, a team of heroes in training. Even when she demonstrates her heroism and commitment to her teammates, Illyana's peers regard her as *other* because they do not understand the true nature of her powers. After a misunderstanding in the heat of battle, Cannonball lashes out, saying: "Rahne had you pegged from the start, witch—Lord forgive me for not list'nin' to her! The evil side o' you take over, girl?! You figure this was the time t' show your true colors—t' join up with your own kind?!!" (Claremont et al., 1984a, p. 13). Despite their shared mutant identity, she is not of *"their kind"*— she is viewed first and foremost as a *witch*.

In the "Inferno" storyline, a demon called N'astirh manipulates Magik into opening a portal between Limbo and Earth that she is afterwards unable to close, resulting in a wave of demons invading New York City (Simonson et al., 1989b, p. 17, 21). The narrative once again constructs her as abject, because her actions allowed comingling between the normal and the supernatural, between good and evil, threatening the stability of the symbolic order (Creed, 2020, p. 216). After Magik closes the portal to Limbo with her soulsword, she seemingly dies, although her "innocent" child-self is later found within her crumpled armor (Simonson et al., 1989c, p. 40). When Magik flings her soulsword into Limbo, she effectively purges herself of all magic and, in doing so, becomes a child again. By "dying," Illyana serves as a self-sacrificing child, destroying a version of herself for the good of the world (Brooks de Vita, 2014, p. 390). These events draw a clear line between magic and burgeoning female sexuality. Without the corrupting force of magic—and without her phallic soulsword—Illyana reverts to the pure, innocent state of a six-year-old child.

Illyana featured prominently in Josh Boone's 2020 film *The New Mutants*. As with her comic origin, film Illyana's magical abilities develop in response to a loss of innocence. The film adaptation recalibrates Illyana's traumatic backstory, infusing it with unambiguous real-world abuse by gangsters. This modified origin story accentuates her emotional detachment, thereby sowing seeds of apprehension within her team. She is referred to as "the crazy one" and assumed to be the source of an attack on the facility where the New Mutants live (Boone, 2020). Film co-writers Boone and Lee's interpretation is perhaps more insidious, since it shifts her teammates' fear from the destructive potential of Illyana's demonic power to a fear of Illyana herself, a survivor of assault who has become emotionally distant in response to her trauma.

Megan Gwynn/Pixie

Pixie first appears as a member of the Paragons training squad, one of several teams of trainee X-Men. Her mutation is a pair of insect-like wings that allow her to fly, as well as the ability to emit a hallucinogenic "pixie dust" (DeFilippis et al., 2004). While she initially served as a supporting character and occasional comic relief, Pixie eventually becomes one of the most prominent New X-Men and earns a place on the primary X-Men roster. This is, in part, due to her acquisition of magical teleporting abilities and a souldagger after she is kidnapped to Limbo by an alternate Magik, who performs a blood ritual to extract a portion of her soul. Magik tells Pixie: ". . . of all the children I felt come into Limbo, your soul was most pure. In this place, you have the most power, more than any other X-Man" (Yost et al., 2007, p. 16). Magik makes a direct connection between innocence and power—the more innocence one has, the more power they can access by sacrificing it, corrupting their soul in the process. Marvel Comics' presentation of innocence is both gendered and sexualized, focusing on the spiritual and sexual purity of the heroes, with puberty and sexuality framed as corrupting forces that draw them closer to the supposed evils of dark magic.

Like Magik's soulsword, the souldagger is a physical embodiment of Pixie's magical power, the hole in her soul externalized as a weapon. As she comes to rely on this phallic externalized weapon, Pixie becomes more aggressive and violent, which are stereotypically masculine-coded traits (Fraction et al., 2008, p. 19). Like Magik, she is at times ostracized due to her magical nature and incomplete soul. While her newfound abilities make her an indispensable asset to the senior

X-Men team and her peers, they often comment on her "darker" attitude, especially when wielding her souldagger, and how her incomplete soul might make her a liability—or enemy—even though she has proven herself a dedicated X-Man time and time again (Cebulski et al., 2009, p. 11; Immonen & Pichelli 2010b, p. 16). By overstepping the "natural" boundaries of gender roles and violently wielding a phallic dagger, Pixie is constructed as monstrous (Cohen, 1996, p. 9).

Author Kathryn Immonen explains Pixie's affinity for magic by revealing that her mother is an actual fairy and her true father is the villain Mastermind, who Pixie describes as "a schemer and a murderer" (Immonen & Pichelli 2010a; Immonen & Pichelli 2010c, p. 23). Pixie's hybrid nature can be viewed as a rejection of the borders between human and supernatural beings, resulting in a monstrous birth (Weinstock, 2020, p. 8). Her magical parentage, paired with her blood-magic-based abilities, positions Pixie as "magic just as much as mutant"—a being at the border (Immonen & Pichelli 2010b, p. 7). Interestingly, although Pixie's father was a villain who has used his power to manipulate and prey on women[4], it is the magic inherited from her mother that causes her teammates to question her stability and self-control, illustrating a double-standard that privileges patrilineal inheritance.

Nico Minoru

Nico Minoru is introduced in *Runaways* #1 as the daughter of powerful, evil witches (Vaughan et al., 2003a). Like Illyana and Pixie, Nico's magic is embodied in a phallic weapon (a staff) that is generated by her body. Nico first discovers her power when her mother attempts to stab her with The Staff of One. Rather than suffering a killing blow, Nico's body absorbs the staff, effectively taking ownership of it from her mother (Vaughan et al., 2005b, p. 17). From then on, to summon the magical Staff of One, Nico must bleed—exchanging blood for magic power (Vaughan et al., 2003b, p. 17). Nico's self-inflicted cuts and subsequent emission of blood mark her as impure, as they violate the skin border between internal and external (Creed, 2015, p. 223). She later learns that menstruation allows for immediate access to her magic without the need to cut herself (Vaughan et al., 2005a, p. 10). A key source of abjection in horror, and indeed superhero comics, is blood—specifically menstrual blood. Creed (2015) writes of menstrual blood as a source of abjection, saying: "its powers are so great it can transform woman into any one of a number of fearful creatures: possessed child, killer and vengeful witch" (p. 223). According to Kristeva (1982), it "stands for the danger issuing from within the identity (social or sexual)" (p. 71).

Interestingly, Nico's means of casting spells also threatens the inside/outside boundary. She must speak the name of her spells out loud ("Freeze," "Heal," "Float"), although the Staff of One cannot cast the same spell twice. This forces Nico to rely on synonyms and creative workarounds when in need of a spell similar to one that she has already cast. Kristeva suggests that "sin" comes from within and is spoken by the subject (Kristeva, 1982, p. 114). This might suggest that, with each new utterance and spell, Nico is releasing additional sin into the world.

Nico is initially unsure of where the Staff goes when she falls asleep, as it was always gone when she wakes up. Her teammate Alex Wilder suggests that she "reabsorbs it" in her sleep (Vaughan et al., 2003c, p. 12). The Staff of One, emerging and reentering Nico's body, takes on a decidedly sexual nature. The feeling she gets when the Staff "sinks back inside her" is later described as ". . . like a snake slithering into her chest. Like someone else's soul coming home to roost in her body" (Rowell & Anka 2018a, p. 3). This idea is further developed in the fifth volume of *Runaways*, when the Staff of One is revealed to be an ancient, evil, *male* magician called The One (Rowell & Anka 2019). Nico makes a deal with the magician, renegotiating their relationship's terms so that, rather than shedding blood to summon the Staff, The One will bleed a portion of himself *into her* (Rowell & Anka 2018b, p. 20). Whereas Nico previously spoke her magic into the world, she now allows a little bit of evil to enter her with each spell. Nico is thus marked as impure, as the phallic source of her power is established as a penetrating, corrupting force that resists the boundary between self and other.

Of the four heroes discussed, Nico is perhaps the least feared by her teammates and the superhero community. While her magic is initially mysterious and the full extent of her power is seemingly limitless, her teammates are more often concerned with the emotional toll that Nico's magic—and requisite bloodletting—takes on her. Still, the immense power of the Staff of One is deemed beyond Nico's control by adults including her mother and a male magic-user who describes the Staff as "far too powerful for a child" (Moore & Miyazawa 2009, p. 20). More notably, after Nico renegotiates her pact with The One, she begins to fear *her own* magic use, afraid that too much of him will enter her. She planned to use the Staff's magic less frequently but ends up repeatedly using magic to save herself and her friends from danger. Afraid that her frequent magic use could eventually allow The One to take over, she entrusts her girlfriend to hide the Staff in distant space (Rowell et al., 2021, p. 30). Here, Nico seems to view *herself* as abject, as she comes to question the stability of the boundary between herself and The One (Creed, 2015, p. 96).

Nico also appears in the Hulu television series *Marvel's Runaways,* which ran for three seasons from 2017 to 2019. As in the comics, her magic powers derive from the Staff of One, which she obtained from her mother. While her magic's unpredictable—and potentially dangerous—nature is apparent from the start, it isn't until late in the series that Nico and her teammates develop serious concerns about the Staff of One. While becoming intimate with her girlfriend Karolina, Nico's eyes become blackened with dark magic and the Staff of One begins to shake violently, causing Nico to panic (Moore & Liddi-Brown, 2019). This scene draws an explicit connection between the Staff of One's influence over Nico and her same-sex desire for Karolina. Creed argues that "Possession becomes the excuse for legitimizing a display of aberrant feminine behaviour which is depicted as depraved, monstrous, abject—and perversely appealing" (Creed, 2015, p. 94). By giving in to her sexual impulses and unwittingly using her dark magic, Nico embodies Creed's "woman as possessed monster."

Billy Kaplan/Wiccan

Billy Kaplan, also known as Wiccan, was introduced as a member of the Young Avengers (Heinberg et al., 2005). I include Wiccan with this cohort of heroes because he is a gay male who is consistently feminized by the narrative of *Young Avengers.* As a gay man, Billy's "deviant" sexual identity makes him especially vulnerable to alignment with the monstrous (Cohen, 1996, p. 9). However, it is his connection to his mother and his reality warping powers that makes him monstrous-*feminine.* De Dauw's (2018) skillful analysis of the character points out that Wiccan's origin as the "spiritual" son of the Avenger the Scarlet Witch, magically created without fatherly input, "plays into stereotypical views of homosexuality caused by the domineering mother, who overtly feminises her son and does not allow for any stabilising, masculine influence" (p. 70). He is further presented as the feminized counterpart to his masculine boyfriend Hulkling (p. 62). Billy's very existence presents a challenge to patriarchal culture, as his fatherless birth demonstrates the generative power of woman without man (Weinstock, 2020, p. 11).

Wiccan's magical, familial connection to the Scarlet Witch not only frames him as abject and monstrous, but positions him as a threat, doomed to repeat her actions. Although she is typically cast as a hero, the Scarlet Witch has inadvertently used her reality-warping powers, in a moment of mental crisis, to cause mass destruction in the Marvel Universe, including the decimation of the mutant race in 2005's *House of M* miniseries. Because his magical reality-warping powers closely mirror his mother's, the superhero community fears that Wiccan has the potential to cause similar levels of destruction. As a reality warper, he "polices the border of the possible," bending the world to his whim, and so must be destroyed (Cohen, 1996, p. 16).

The scope of Billy's magical reality-warping powers is examined when Loki suggests that Wiccan used his powers to literally create the perfect boyfriend—Hulkling, a shapeshifting alien—and make him fall in love via magic. He points out the seemingly impossible odds that Wiccan and Hulkling would even meet, implying that Wiccan's magic has the potential to alter reality even into the far reaches of space (Gillen et al., 2013, p. 14). What's more, Loki implies that, if Wiccan created Hulking, he may not have done so intentionally: "Whims and daydreams are all that it takes," he offers (Gillen et al., 2013, p. 15). Billy is further constructed as monstrous because his nearly limitless powers are implied to be activated by his sexual desires.

Marvel's Magical Youth

This chapter has illustrated how, like horror films, superhero comics can be interpreted as "a project designed to perpetuate the belief that woman's monstrous nature is inextricably bound up with her difference as man's sexual other" (p. 225). This analysis of Illyana Rasputin/Magik, Megan Gwynn/Pixie, Nico Minoru, and Billy Kaplan/Wiccan highlights the complex interplay between magic, gender, and monstrosity within Marvel Comics. By wielding magical powers that operate outside the established rules of their reality—a reality that ironically includes countless super-beings of non-magical origin—these young heroes disrupt the symbolic, masculine, scientific order of the Marvel Universe. Notably, Pixie, Nico, and Wiccan each embody the threat of matrilineal inheritance. Their magic, or at least their potential for magic, is passed down from their mothers and their mothers before them. Pixie is half-fairy; the women of Nico's family have been witches at least as far back as her great-grandmother; and Wiccan is the spiritual child of the Scarlet Witch, one of Earth's most powerful magic-users.

The development or use of their magical powers also evokes feminine blood, which Barbara Creed identifies as an "abject substance" that aids in the construction of their monstrosity (Creed, 2015, p. 198). Magik and Pixie are empowered by blood magic performed in the hell-dimension Limbo, and Nico Minoru must shed blood to summon the magical Staff of One that grants her power. Each wields a phallic weapon—the soulsword, souldagger, and Staff of One—which blurs the line between masculine and feminine power.

They represent the intersection of various threats—magic, femininity, hybridity, and alternative possibilities—that provoke discomfort within their fictive universe. As their power grows, so too does their ability to rewrite the narrative. No longer a supplemental element of the team, they become a powerhouse capable of determining the outcome of battle. This power cannot go unchecked, so the narrative presents these heroes as monstrous. Each character discussed in this chapter emerged as a threat—a source of fear and apprehension for their communities, their teams, and even themselves. The masculine leadership of the superhero community has cast them out, targeted them for destruction, and otherwise suppressed them. Still, they emerge as fan-favorite characters, maintaining a transmedia presence within the Marvel Comics universe that extends beyond their books of origin (Buxton, 2017; Diaz, 2020; Schlesinger, 2022; Wyatt, 2019). In a genre often focused on masculine power and scientific explanations, these characters introduce a new dimension by embracing the mystical, the feminine, and the uncertain. They prompt readers to reconsider the boundaries of what is possible, question the established norms, and challenge the deep-rooted fears that underlie the rejection of the abject. In doing so, they offer a unique perspective on the potential of *embracing* the abject, inviting readers to explore the complexities of power, identity, and transformation in ways that transcend the traditional superhero narrative. The juxtaposition of power and vulnerability, purity and corruption, innocence and monstrosity, offers a multifaceted exploration of the monstrous-feminine in the context of superhero comics.

While superhero comics have traditionally marginalized and suppressed characters that embody abjection, these heroes challenge that narrative. They demonstrate resilience, determination, and an unyielding commitment to heroism. Their stories are engaging because they *celebrate* abjection, showing that empowerment and strength can emerge from the very qualities that are feared and rejected. Barbara Creed (2015) explains this duality of abjection, stating, ". . . abjection by its very nature is ambiguous; it both repels and attracts" (p. 55), echoing Kristeva's description of abjection as ". . . a composite of judgment and affect, of condemnation and yearning, of signs and drives" (1982, p. 9). This ambiguity enriches the complexity of these characters and their narratives. While their monstrous-femininity might lead to isolation within the superhero community, it simultaneously distinguishes them as unique, compelling individuals amidst the expanding roster of superheroes in comics and film.

Notes

1 See, for example, the X-Men's Jean Grey/Phoenix, Storm, and Rogue, or The Avengers' Black Widow, Ms./Captain Marvel, and She-Hulk.
2 See *Strange Academy* (2020) by Skottie Young (w) and Humberto Ramos (a), which follows the exploits of magical youths training in the mystic arts under Doctor Strange, Doctor Voodoo, The Scarlet Witch, and other adult mages (Young & Ramos 2020).
3 Marvel often claims to represent "the world outside your window" (Lee et al., 2019), accounting for real-world events and reflecting real-world values.
4 Most notably Jean Grey, serving as the catalyst for her transformation into Dark Phoenix beginning in *Uncanny X-Men* vol. 1 #122 (Claremont et al., 1979).

References

Boone, J. (Director). (2020, August 28). *The new mutants*. 20th Century Studios.
Brooks de Vita, A. (2014). Descent into the pit of the redeemer: The sacrificial child in international film and literature. *Extrapolation, 55*(3), 369–392. https://doi.org/10.3828/extr.2014.20
Buxton, M. (2017, February 3). 40 X-Men characters who haven't appeared in the movies but should. *Den of Geek*. https://www.denofgeek.com/movies/40-x-men-characters-who-havent-appeared-in-the-movies-but-should/
Cebulski, C. B. (w), Camuncolli, G. (p), & J. Delperdang (i). (2009). Soul Survivors. *X-Infernus* vol. 1 #1. Marvel Comics.
Chare, N., Hoorn, J., & Yue, A. (Eds.). (2019). *Re-reading the monstrous-feminine: Art, film, feminism and psychoanalysis* (1st ed.). Routledge. https://doi.org/10.4324/9780429469367
Claremont, C. (w), & Sienkiewicz, B. (a). (1984a). Badlands. *New Mutants* vol. 1 #20, Marvel Comics.
Claremont, C. (w), Anderson, B. (p), & Wiacek, B. (i). (1982). Chutes and ladders. *Uncanny X-Men* vol. 1 #160, Marvel Comics.
Claremont, C. (w), Buscema, J. (p), & Palmer (i). (1983). Little girl lost. *Magik (Illyana and Storm Limited Series)* vol. 1 #1, Marvel Comics.
Claremont, C. (w), Buscema, J. (p), & Palmer (i). (1984b). Darkchild. *Magik (Illyana and Storm Limited Series)* vol. 1 #4, Marvel Comics.
Claremont, C., Byrne, J. (w), Byrne, J. (p), & Austin, T. (i). (1979). Cry for the Children! *Uncanny X-Men* vol. 1 #122, Marvel Comics.
Claremont, C. (w), Frenz, R. (p), & Palmer (i). (1984c). Soulquest. *Magik (Illyana and Storm Limited Series)* vol. 1 #3, Marvel Comics.
Clover, C. J. (2015). *Men, women, and chain saws: Gender in the modern horror film* (First Princeton classics edition). Princeton University Press.
Cocca, C. (2016). *Superwomen: Gender, power, and representation*. Bloomsbury Academic, an imprint of Bloomsbury Publishing Inc.

Cohen, J. J. (Ed.). (1996). *Monster theory: Reading culture*. University of Minnesota Press. https://doi.org/10.5749/j.ctttsq4d.

Creed, B. (2015). *The monstrous-feminine: Film, feminism, psychoanalysis*. https://www.taylorfrancis.com/books/9780429236143

Creed, B. (2020). Horror and the monstrous-feminine: An imaginary abjection. In J. A. Weinstock (Ed.), *The monster theory reader* (pp. 211–225). University of Minnesota Press.

De Dauw, E. (2018). Homonormativity in Marvel's young avengers: Wiccan and Hulkling's gender performance. *Journal of Graphic Novels and Comics*, 9(1), 61–74. https://doi.org/10.1080/21504857.2017.1288641

DeFilippis, N., Weir, C. (w), Ryan, M. (p), & Avalon Studios (i). (2004). Choosing sides 5 of 6: Above the law. *New X-Men* vol. 2 #5, Marvel Comics.

Diaz. (2020, August 5). *Avengers' LGBTQ power couple to marry in new Marvel comic*. Nerdist. https://nerdist.com/article/marvel-lgbtq-couple-marrying-empyre/

Donohoo, Ti. (2023, October 3). *10 Pieces of miles Morales lore every new reader needs to know*. Comic Book Resources. https://www.cbr.com/miles-morales-spiderman-important-history-lore/

Fraction, M., Brubaker, E. (w), Land, G. (p), & Leisten, J. (i). (2008). Beginning to see the light. *Uncanny X-Men* vol. 1 #503, Marvel Comics.

Giancola, G., & Coleman, J. (2018). The Gwenaissance: Gwen Stacy and the progression of women in comics. In M. D. Goodrum, T. Prescott, & P. Smith (Eds.), *Gender and the superhero narrative* (pp. 251–84). Jackson: University Press of Mississippi.

Gibson, M. (2018). "Yeah, I Think There Is Still Hope": Youth, ethnicity, faith, feminism, and fandom in Ms. Marvel. In M. D. Goodrum, T. Prescott, & P. Smith (Eds.), *Gender and the superhero narrative* (pp. 23–44). University Press of Mississippi.

Gillen, K. (w), McKelvie, J., Norton, M. (p), & McKelvie, J. (i). (2013). Deus ex machine gunner. *Young Avengers* vol. 2 #4. Marvel Comics.

Goodrum, M. D., Prescott, T., & Smith, P. (Eds.). (2018). *Gender and the superhero narrative*. University Press of Mississippi.

Gramuglia, A. (2019, March 2). *10 LGBTQA Characters who should be introduced to the MCU*. Screen Rant. https://screenrant.com/lgbtqa-characters-marvel-cinematic-universe-diversity/

Hallum, D. (w), & Walker, K. (a). (2012). Worse things. *Avengers Arena* vol. 1 #1, Marvel Comics.

Heinberg, A. (w), Cheung, J. (a). (2005). Sidekicks. *Young Avengers* vol. 1 #1, Marvel Comics.

Immonen, K. (w), & Pichelli, S. (a). (2010a). Pixie: Strikes back! Part two. *Pixie Strikes Back* vol. 1 #2, Marvel Comics.

Immonen, K. (w), & Pichelli, S. (a). (2010b). Pixie: Strikes back! Part three. *Pixie Strikes Back* vol. 1 #3, Marvel Comics.

Immonen, K. (w), & Pichelli, S. (a). (2010c). Pixie: Strikes back! Part four. *Pixie Strikes Back* vol. 1 #4, Marvel Comics.

Kristeva, J. (1982). *Powers of horror: An essay on abjection*. Columbia University Press.

Kvaran, Kara M. (2017, April). Super daddy issues: Parental figures, masculinity, and superhero films. *The Journal of Popular Culture*, 50(2), 218–38. https://doi.org/10.1111/jpcu.12531.

Lee, S., Gerber, S., Michelinie, D., Claremont, C., & Lobdell, S. (2019). *Marvel comics: The world outside your window*. Marvel Worldwide, Inc.

Moore, K. A. (Writer), & Liddi-Brown, A. (Director). (2019, December 13). Lord of Lies (No. 3.3) [Broadcast]. In *Marvel's Runaways*. Hulu.

Moore, T. (w) & Miyazawa, T. (a). (2009). Rock zombies (Conclusion). *Runaways* vol. 3 #9, Marvel Comics.

Prince, D. (2021, February). 'No One Made Me; I Was Always Like This': The *Monstress* in Us. *The Journal of Popular Culture*, *54*(1), 67–87. https://doi.org/10.1111/jpcu.12995.

Robinson, J., Gonzales, D., & Edwards, G. (2023). *MCU: The Reign of Marvel Studios* (First edition). Liveright Publishing Corporation, a division of W.W. Norton & Company.

Rowell, R. (w), Genolet, A., Anka, K., Alphona, A., (p), Genolet, A., Anka, K., & Alphona, A. (i). (2021). Come away with me (Part 7). *Runaways*, vol. 5 #38 Marvel Comics.

Rowell, R. (w), & Anka, K. (a). (2018a). Best friends forever pt I. *Runaways* vol. 5 #7, Marvel Comics.

Rowell, R. (w), & Anka, K. (a). (2018b). Find your way home pt III. *Runaways* vol. 5 #3, Marvel Comics.

Rowell, R. (w), & Anka, K. (a). (2019). That was yesterday pt III. *Runaways* vol. 5 #15, Marvel Comics.

Schlesinger, A. (2022, September 3). X-Men's Magik has marvel's best character arc. *Screen Rant*. https://screenrant.com/xmen-magik-illyana-rasputin-new-mutants-character-arc/

Shendruk, A. (2017). *Analyzing the gender representation of 34,476*. Comic Book Characters. The Pudding. https://pudding.cool/2017/07/comics/.

Simonson, L. (w), Blevins, B. (p), & Williamson, A. (i). (1989a). Demon reign. *New Mutants* vol. 1 #72, Marvel Comics.

Simonson, L. (w), Blevins, B. (p), & Williamson, A. (i). (1989b). Limbo. *New Mutants*, vol. 1 #71 Marvel Comics.

Simonson, L. (w), Blevins, B. (p), & Manley, M., & Williamson, A. (i). (1989c). The gift. *New Mutants* vol. 1 #73, Marvel Comics.

Smith, M. J., & Moruzi, K. (2018). Vampires and witches go to school: Contemporary young adult fiction, gender, and the gothic. *Children's Literature in Education*, *49*(1), 6–18. https://doi.org/10.1007/s10583-018-9343-0.

Standlee, K. (2015, August 23). 2015 Hugo award winners announced. *The Hugo Awards*. https://www.thehugoawards.org/2015/08/2014-hugo-award-winners-announced/

Vaughan, B. K. (w), Alphona, A. (p), & Newbold, D. (i). (2003a). Pride and joy, chapter one. *Runaways* vol. 1 #1, Marvel Comics.

Vaughan, B. K. (w), Alphona, A. (p), & Newbold, D. (i). (2003b). Pride and joy, chapter five. *Runaways* vol. 1 #5, Marvel Comics.

Vaughan, B. K. (w), Alphona, A. (p), & Yeung, C. (i). (2003c). Teenage wasteland, chapter one. *Runaways* vol. 1 #7, Marvel Comics.

Vaughan, B. K. (w), Alphona, A. (p), & Yeung, C. (i). (2005a). True believers, chapter one. *Runaways* vol. 2 #1, Marvel Comics.

Vaughan, B. K. (w), Alphona, A. (p), & Yeung, C. (i). (2005b). True believers, chapter four. *Runaways* vol. 2 #4, Marvel Comics.

Wein, L. (w), Cockrum, D. (p), Cockrum, D., & Iro, P. (i). (1975). Deadly genesis! *Giant-Sized X-Men* vol. 1 #1, Marvel Comics.

Weinstock, J. A. (Ed.). (2020). *The monster theory reader.* University of Minnesota Press.

Wyatt, L. (2019, October 28). Runaways: 10 reasons why Nico Minoru might be Marvel's most powerful character. *CBR.* https://www.cbr.com/runaways-nico-minoru-true-powers/

Yost, C., Kyle, C. (w), & Young, S. (a). (2007). The quest for Magik: Conclusion. *New X-Men* vol. 2 #41, Marvel Comics.

Young, S. (w), & Ramos, H. (a). (2020). 1st story. *Strange Academy* vol. 1 #1, Marvel Comics.

8

Saving Herself and Turning Rhetorical Tropes in Disney Films: Subverting the Monstrous-Feminine in Supernatural Genre Conventions

ERIKA M. THOMAS

In the Disney+ web series, "Bridging the Gap," two episodes focus on Disney's animated films, *Encanto* (Bush & Howard, 2021) and *Turning Red* (Shi, 2022), addressing the importance of their "type" of story or, as Director Domee Shi explains it, "redefining what the universal story is" ("Coming of Age with Pixar"). The episodes unintentionally reveal similarities in themes, such as "coming of age," diverse representations, and personal vulnerabilities and trauma ("Multigenerational Storyytelling" and "Coming of Age"). For me, a white, cis-gendered, hetero, middle-class viewer, the films did not just subvert one storyline. In fact, both films' themes, as told through supernatural framings, showcase another identifiable subtext: the notion of the monstrous feminine and its reversal. Though not explicitly mentioned by any of the creators, this sub-plot exists and directs the affective reactions toward the films' protagonists. Thus, in this chapter, I am interested in exploring that very trend: how contemporary animated Disney films are referencing and creatively addressing "women-as-monster" (Creed, 1993; Kelly, 2016). In doing so, these texts are relevant to a new category of films coined "New Wave Feminism" by Creed (2022). Films that meet the definition may be created by women, inter-generic, and are directly contrary to or protesting sexist messages. Creed generally recognizes the films based on their tackling of subjects like misogyny, racism, violence, and sexual assault against women but also acknowledges films' explicit reference to the monstrous feminine and the ability to undermine the myth. The supernatural in Disney's films not only draws upon a recognizable trope in the films, but it shows that progressive "New Wave Feminist" storytelling approaches can extend to children's films and deconstruct some overused tropes.

This chapter examines the ideological messages in *Encanto* and *Turning Red* to illustrate how they cite a "traditional" characteristic of the monstrous feminine (Creed, 1993) and reclaim it. I use ideological, feminist, and psychoanalytic reading lenses to identify abject qualities that define monstrous feminine depictions in horror and supernatural films and to trace how Disney's films reference the familiar body horror (Rapoport, 2020) but also alter the trope.

I begin by exploring Disney's changing reputation regarding representation and, next, describe how Disney's twenty-first century supernatural stories are unique from previous feature length films, but also consistent with the company's responsiveness to critics and their significance in children's entertainment. I then explore monstrous feminine qualities and, finally, analyze the two Disney films, showing how supernatural characters ultimately deconstruct the harmful imagery of adolescent girls with mysterious and threatening bodily "powers." I conclude with discussion on the significance of subverting the monstrous feminine/body horror conventions and its contribution to New Wave Feminist media.

Disney's Historical and Changing Representations

As a prominent contributor to family entertainment, the Walt Disney Company remains a powerful, global influencer in relaying stories and teaching "the ways in which these presentations change over time" (Davis, 2007, p. 13). It is important to examine popular and far-reaching animated films by Disney since storytelling operates pedagogically and leads to social learning for audience members (Giroux & Pollock, 2010; Cuenca-Orellana & López-Heredia, 2020). Today, with access to the large archive of both old and new films on the streaming application, Disney+, critical examinations of texts help young audiences navigate portrayals of lived experience.

Despite the label, "family-friendly," Disney texts are also egregiously known for contributing to Hollywood's history of problematic and offensive representations. Scholars have fixated critiques on Disney's representations of social roles, including stereotypical, racist, and sexist imagery (Bell et al., 1995; Davis, 2007; Giroux & Pollock, 2010; Forman-Brunell & Hains, 2015). Racist portrayals were highly common in the early twentieth century, but also continued throughout the 1990s as films were criticized for their approach to multiculturalism, including the studios' animated features *Aladdin* (1992), *The Lion King* (1994), *Pocahontas* (1995), and *Mulan* (1998) (Chatters & Roberts, 2020; Ghisyawan, 2020; Lee-Oliver, 2020). Also, despite attempts to address sexism and patriarchy, Disney films still contained representations centered on traditional views of romance and femininity and limited social advancement (Hains, 2014; Higgs, 2016).

Today, scholars acknowledge that Disney executives have listened to academic and cultural discourse and present more progressive messages to revise the problematic past of Disney's early mediated images (Hains, 2014). For example, films encapsulate a range of human experiences, characters of various cultures, and contain "inclusive stories with protagonists that challenge gender stereotypes (e.g., *Frozen*) and/or feature people of color (e.g., *Coco* or *Moana*)" (Holcomb & Latham-Mintus, 2022, para. 1). Such trends are also found in recent live-action remakes of earlier animated films that address the critiques of original films (Banh, 2020; Ghisyawan, 2020; Weidman-Winter, 2020) and in Pixar known for generally progressive messaging (Giroux & Pollock, 2010; Cuenca-Orellana & López-Heredia, 2020; Schiele et al., 2020; Holcomb & Latham-Mintus, 2022). Most recently, Pixar's *Lightyear* (2022) and *Strange World* (2022) made strides in representations of gay/lesbian identities.

Thus, Disney films have stayed relevant and notable because their cultural artifacts reflect political changes, and their producers are open to reflexivity. "Disney works to avoid appearing out of touch ... constantly adjusting its position as a cultural force; one that mirrors the current times, providing entertainment and memories that feel authentic to the costumers it wishes to serve for decades to come" (Roberts, 2020, p. 14). In addition to their socially relevant content and responses to criticism, their recent approaches to constructing supernatural youth are particularly relevant since it incorporates original storytelling with a direct reversal of overused tropes less common in children's films.

The Supernatural Genre and Disney

In relation to the book's theme on supernatural youth, this chapter specifically examines these two films because of their apparent qualities. Disney is an obvious hegemon in texts with fairy tale or fantasy plots, but the supernatural genre contains more limited characteristics, and, thus, for Disney, are a recent trend. *Encanto* and *Turning Red* are contemporary, unique examples of Disney's engagement with this genre. First, they heavily contain horror-like/gothic qualities, such as those tales featuring suspenseful mysteries, witchcraft, and other types of "monstrous" creatures with superpowers. A significant quality of supernatural stories includes the "wrongness" or a threat which derives from a creature or supernatural encounter in the *real world* instead of another, fictional land (Clute & Grant, 1997). Thus, this quality distinguishes previous "fantasy" tales with focus on fairies, villainous witches, and faraway lands. While some Disney films have always incited fear in audiences with characters, like the Evil Queen in *Snow White* (1937), Maleficent in *Sleeping Beauty* (1959), and Ursula in *The Little Mermaid* (1989), the sense of mystery and fearful scenarios in these recent films are persistent throughout the narrative, rousing suspense, or fear throughout the storyline, over the excitement of action or adventure.

Disney's recent "supernatural" storylines are likely deliberate. Since the late twentieth century, supernatural and horror genres have grown in popularity as evidenced by stories frequently consumed among all types of audiences, like witches in teen literature, television, and films in the 1990's (Nash, 2015). Additionally, the supernatural is frequently an allegory for identity, quality, or an insecurity, which results in an audience's response to understanding themselves or others through magical creatures/people (Nash, 2015). Supernatural fiction also includes physical or bodily elements to stand in for marginalized sexualities, racial and ethnic differences, or bodily changes, like puberty or pregnancy. *The Encyclopedia of Fantasy* adds that such supernatural fictional literature focuses on "the body, with violations of the body, with conversions and immurements and seductions of the body" and explains that "the relationship between the supernatural and the mundane may best be understood in terms of the minglings of flesh" (Clute & Grant, 1997).

Strategic, rhetorical elements of supernatural fictions provide Disney with a means to share messages about accepting Otherness and promoting inclusivity. Such efforts help to address Disney's long history of stereotyping, Othering non-white races, and providing fewer diverse representations. Furthermore, supernatural texts help individuals find meaning in our material world and develop corporeal relationships with oneself and one another. Due to the supernatural's rich subtext, audiences consume diversity and experience(s), making it a useful genre for contemporary storytelling. Just as Disney likely chose supernatural qualities to represent diverse protagonists, Disney's ability to "play" upon common tropes, overturn them, and "correct" them indicates that Disney and Pixar story teams were likely attuned to the filmic tropes in the horror genre.

The Horror of Feminine Bodies: Women as Monster and Abject

Tracing the extensive history of monstrous imagery throughout primarily Western cultures, Creed (1993) asserts that "all human societies have a conception of the monstrous-feminine, of what it is about women that is shocking, terrifying, horrific, abject" (p. 1). Society projects the feelings of lust but also terror and repulsion onto women's bodies where it "has found a home for decades in film and literature" (Rapoport, 2020, p. 619) and has been studied as a trope in media, film, and rhetorical scholarship. (Clover, 1992; Creed, 1993; Wee, 2011). Wee (2011) argues that "Western culture has a more deliberate tradition of aligning femininity/the female with motherhood, monstrosity and/or death" (p. 159). In a comparison of the Japanese film *Ringu* (1998) to the American version, *The Ring* (2002), Japanese folklore subtexts are exposed to reveal women as monsters because of men's betrayals, whereas Western cultures see the association of femininity to evil as innate. These supposed inherent "conditions" are replicated and commonly found in cultural texts and artifacts.

Additionally, as noted about supernatural genres, the monster has identity-based associations, so "to search for the promises attendant to monsters is to search for the ways exclusionary cultural norms of gender, race, sexuality, class, and ability may be contested and unsettled" (Langsdale, 2020, p. 395). Our affective responses, anxieties or desires, and experiences of repression, difference, acceptance, and personal or sexual empowerment are then transcribed onto the monsters, broadening our understanding of culture, social interaction, and the self.

Creed (1993) approached the cinematic trend psychoanalytically to reveal hidden and repressed fears, building upon Kristeva's work, which developed the association between gender qualities, like femininity, motherhood, and horror. She determined "the monstrous-feminine horrifies her audience" in ways "different from why the male monster horrifies his audience" (p. 3). It is the fear, disgust, and loathing surrounding characteristics like gender difference, sexuality, and maternal elements that is signified in plots and images of the horror genre. Creed also differentiates her theory from Freud's, arguing that women terrify, not simply due to the Freudian state of "castration," but because they are viewed unconsciously as an active monster which incites fears on the part of men, and "dread . . . from her eviscerating power" (Creed, 1993; Clover, 1992; Kelly, 2016, p. 86).

The theories of repression which play out in the fictional texts represent patriarchal norms and the dominance that subverts feminist ideals and emphasizes bodily political correctness. For example, the reactions to abjection (blood, urine, vomit, etc.) coincide with sphincteral training and paternal laws, mandating a "clean and proper body" (Creed, 1993, p. 13). Imagery of blood and gore illustrate how the culturally constructed notions of horrific reactions develop from detachment from childhood. As such, psychoanalytic criticism remains a productive tool when investigating origins and patterns of tropes.

Studying monstrosity and body horror, then, explains our assumptions toward women and marginalized others and the source of treatment that results in everyday, material experiences. The cultural predisposition to portray the feminine, menstruation, and coming-of-age discourse in horror films and raunchy comedies makes women's bodies horrific. It sensationalizes womanly qualities and bodily responses, like menstruation, through film imagery portrayed as repulsive, evil, embarrassing, or dangerous. It creates "aspects of the taboo" and reaffirms "cultural myths" that have negative impacts on adolescent women (Thomas, 2017, p. 23).

When comparing this genre against the innocence, purity, and, "family-friendly" label typically affiliated with Disney programming, the monstrous feminine seems far-fetched from the content directed toward Disney's intergenerational audiences. However, Davis (2007) reminds us that many attributes in horror genres also appear in Disney's animated films, such as the plot device of "good versus evil" as well as "the heroine/victim, the monstrous Other, the victorious hero who defeats the monster and re-establishes order" (p. 22). Characters like Maleficent, a vengeful evil fairy first introduced in *Sleeping Beauty* (1959), and Ursula, a sea witch in *The Little Mermaid* (1989, 2023), are both sinister monsters, capable of wicked curses that need to be overpowered by a hero or protagonist so that romance and disciplined femininity can be rewarded in the plot. As Davis observes, "Disney films and horror films tend to deal [...] with such themes as what is proper/improper behavior for women, what is/is not the 'natural order,' issues of coming of age and sexuality, and other gender-based concepts" (p. 23).

Given this history, inter-generic quality of horror continues in the storylines of *Encanto* and *Turning Red*, but it is now even more relevant, given the films and their themes to tackle more sophisticated coming-of-age content. "Stories surrounding women and their bodies often tend to include elements of the supernatural as an excuse to write about the otherwise natural functions of the body such as desire, sex, menstruation, etc." (Rapoport, p. 621). However, as my psychoanalytic and feminist examinations in the next sections will show, these supernatural and monstrous feminine narratives curtail horrific endings and, instead, portray a reconciliation of the feminine with bodies, self-esteem, identities, and others. While many contemporary scholars in such disciplinary areas as the humanities, film studies, and rhetorical criticism are tracing and analyzing progressive representations in Disney films and texts, none have explicitly examined such depictions through the lens of the supernatural nor have they extended or compared their examination of children's' films to trends in other films targeted toward older audiences. Building upon Creed's categorization of films that qualify as "New Wave Feminist," this analysis extends the label to the selected Disney films. Such subtexts positively alter women's understandings of changing bodies/sexuality and affective qualities. Ultimately, I argue that these family films revolt against patriarchal assumptions in this Western contemporary moment (Creed, 2022).

Feminist/Psychoanalytic Film Analyses

Encanto: Mirabel as Witch

Encanto, a fictional tale, follows a Colombian family, the Madrigals, with magical powers. The matriarch and grandmother, Abuela Alma, once received a mysterious miracle that is passed down as supernatural "gifts" to each generation ("Disney's 'Encanto,'" 2022). Even the house, which the family calls "Casita," is a product of the miracle and unexplainably holds magical, ever-growing, interactive powers. However, Mirabel, the grandchild and protagonist, does not receive a power, inciting feelings of inferiority. She overcompensates for her insecurity by assisting her family. When the Madrigals' powers unexpectedly dissipate, Mirabel grows determined to find the cause, which leads to more internal conflicts. *Encanto*'s themes of supernatural monstrosity construct Mirabel as a witch. I argue that although Mirabel can be understood as the trope initially, by the end, the film overturns the fears associated to this monstrous feminine state.

Based on the Madrigals' backstory, Disney's *Encanto* follows a similar trend in other popular culture texts, such as *Practical Magic* (1998) and *Charmed* (1998–2006), which feature supernatural qualities and magical protagonists as "morally good" (Nash, 2015, p. 21). The Madrigals' gifts—which include reading the future, conjuring plants, controlling the weather, and more—are embraced by the community and are a source of pride, despite their mysterious origin. Like trends in films and series about teenage witches, *Encanto* establishes an inverted construction of what and who should be feared in this plot. Though I contend Mirabel represents woman-as-monster in the form of a "witch," it is Mirabel's inexplicable *lack of a gift* that leads to others' fearing her. Since "normalcy" is the source of her difference, the community casts doubt around Mirabel and her intentions. Mirabel is further assumed to be a witch and treated like one because she seems connected to a power that can take away the family's supernatural abilities.

Despite the lack 'of labels or dialogue explicitly using the word, "witch," in the film, Mirabel's initial "witch" status is supported by the film's context involving horror qualities. Although endearing characters and cheerful songs are sprinkled throughout the story, there are also many dark, gothic characteristics and scenes, a plot mystery, suspenseful music/sound effects, and frightening imagery. The signs and symbols include lightning and thunderstorms, rats, shadowy figures, and creepy, entrapping spaces, which contribute to a horror genre and the familiar characterization of Mirabel as monstrous feminine.

Second, it is important to note that Creed (1993) also traces the witch's supernatural power to "the female reproductive system—particularly menstruation" since the trope is commonly associated with young girls in puberty (p. 77). While there are no explicit connections to Mirabel's menarche, and it is not referenced in any way, Mirabel is at a critical coming-of-age moment when her emotions seem inexplicably linked to strange and destructive happenings occurring around the Casita. According to the Disney fan site and wiki, Mirabel is fifteen years old ("Mirabel Madrigal," 2021), which clarifies her mark as an adolescent.

Given the history of the trope of adolescence and the media's persistent reading of it as horrific or monstrous, Mirabel can be read through this view. Causations or correlation between the two are implied, as in the scene after Antonio receives his gift. Mirabel croons that she is waiting for her own "miracle," and, after, a tile from their magical Casita falls and cracks. When she investigates it, Mirabel cuts her hand, a symbol of the abject (00:22:29-00:24:48). Creed (1993) notes that open wounds represent "reproductive functions" and the "alliance with the world of nature" (p. 83). As Casita begins crumbling and cracking, Mirabel notifies everyone, but upon investigation, everything has returned to its original state. It is unclear if Mirabel witnessed actual destruction, imagined it, or had a premonition. Regardless, she is treated with skepticism or fear. Creed notes that in the history and social reactions to the witch, "a young girl who had prophetic dreams at the time of her menarche was frequently singled out as a future shaman or witch" (p. 74).

In these subtle ways, the film affirms the monstrous feminine trope and its connection to Mirabel in a state of adolescence. Although it is unclear if Mirabel is intentionally hurting the Madrigals' magic, her strong emotions seem unexplainably tied to the destruction of their home, powers, and Abuela's fear that something is, indeed, hurting the magic.

According to Creed (1993), the witch is a figure who, throughout history, has been met with both "awe and dread" (p. 74), as mystical abilities come from evil origins. Creed explains that the representations in popular culture, specifically horror films, derive from an ideological function to portray "women's monstrous nature" as connected "with her difference as man's sexual other" (p. 83). In short, it is Mirabel's feminine qualities, her inexplicably mysterious differences, and her rejection of Abuela's "ordering" that make her a witch. Thus, Mirabel is made into "an abject figure" not only for her lack of gift but due to her determination to operate "within patriarchal discourses as an implacable enemy of the symbolic order" (76). With each attempt to help her family, Mirabel is blamed, scapegoated, and otherized. The construction of Mirabel as someone to fear begins at the start of Antonio's gifting ceremony. Some members of the family are noticeably nervous about her presence given her own failed ceremony. As inexplicable supernatural conditions develop and the loss of magic continues, family members direct suspicion and doubt towards Mirabel. Her cousin Dolores asserts that Mirabel is "gonna destroy the magic" and exclaims that they are "all doomed!" (00:52:39-00:52:43) At the story's climax, when Mirabel confronts Abuela and insists that she can help "fix" the family, Abuela dismisses her offer and blames her: "I don't know why you weren't given a gift, but it is not an excuse for you to hurt this family!" (01:12:20-01:12:27) In these instances, Mirabel is marked as monstrous, a witch or the source of fear, as power struggles develop between her and Abuela.

Even Mirabel begins to blame herself. In Bruno's vault, Mirabel searches for his *terrible* vision [emphasis added] and discovers she is at the center of it (00:38:09-00:38:10). During her epiphany of her monstrous state, Bruno's room is destroyed. Mirabel later hypothesizes the association to her father: "I ... broke into Bruno's tower, I found his last vision, the family's in trouble, the magic is dying, the house is breaking, Luisa's gift is fading, and I think it's all because of ... me?" (00:49:46-00:49:55). Creed (1993) explains that the witch "is thought to be dangerous and wily, capable of drawing on her evil powers to wreak destruction on the community" (p. 76). Though evidence points to her as responsible for ending the family's powers, Mirabel seeks more answers and eventually disproves the theory.

Mirabel (and Bruno): The "Good" Witch

Encanto eventually reverses the trope of the monstrous feminine in two notable ways. First, the monstrous, outcast characters, specifically Mirabel, are determined not responsible for the Madrigals' loss of supernatural power. In the case of Mirabel, she is the source of healing the magic and the family. This theme begins subtly but is revealed by the end of the film. A direct example of subversion of Mirabel's monstrosity develops when Mirabel meets Bruno and asks him directly whether she is the source hurting her family. Since this vision was different than his previous ones, the outcome is not foretold and it changes, making her fate unknown to Bruno. After listening to Mirabel and making another vision at her request, Bruno convinces Mirabel that she can save the magic. "You're exactly what this family needs. You just have to see it" (01:05:47-01:05:54).

Another apparent sign that Mirabel is a savior and not a monster occurs when Mirabel helps her sister, Isabela, recognize that she is not yet ready for marriage and, if true to herself, is capable of her own unique beauty. When Isabela and Mirabel hug, the candle glows brighter and the cracks in the house begin to disappear. Finally, Mirabel reveals that Abuela is responsible for the family's vulnerabilities and is the real source of danger for the Madrigals, who are repressed by her standards. Despite an angry confrontation between Mirabel and Abuela, Mirabel's encouragement, her willingness to listen, understand, and forgive Abuela brings the family and their community together to rebuild and find strength in each other. Once Casita's structure is complete and the front door has been added, the family presents Mirabel with her own doorknob, acknowledging her brightness and bravery and asking her to view herself in this same way, as "the real gift" (01:28:57-01:28:58). When she turns the knob, Mirabel restores the magic in Casita and the candle. Like her Abuela, Mirabel's power is a source of her family's magic, and each family member regains their original gift. However, given this second chance, they now use their magic in a way that is honest and genuine, rather than for the expectations of others.

Second, *Encanto* alters the traditionally *feminine* trope of the witch by constructing Bruno as similarly witch-like. Bruno, a man, is also scapegoated, feared, and shunned, equally as much as any (female) witch. He becomes a fearful figure through tales and rumors, like his alleged "seven-foot frame" (00:47:19-00:47:21) but also through his association with rats and decrepit surroundings. Creed (1992) notes that the witch is often connected to "abject things" like cobwebs, decay, and rats (p. 76). By introducing Bruno and his role as a source of fear for the family, *Encanto* deconstructs the trope's monstrous *feminine* as one that inextricably upholds the patriarchal order.

However, the film also does more than simply projecting fear onto another; it eliminates the fear altogether. Mirabel helps Bruno recognize that he has merely become a scapegoat and is not a source that is evil or to be feared. She assures him that if his new vision is bad, she will not blame him. She tells him he doesn't "make bad things happen" and that "sometimes family weirdos just get a bad rap" (01:02:23-01:02:35). Mirabel restores Bruno's reputation by bringing him back to the family and helping him and others recognize their value. The message stands that qualities which make individuals non-normative are not reason to ostracize or fear them. The supernatural plot successfully uses its expected affect to reverse the plot and challenge traditional horror representations. Overall, Mirabel (and Bruno's reemergence) reverses the damage to the magic. It reveals *Encanto* as subverting a supernatural trope to positively alter the critique of otherness it initially represented.

Turning Red: Mei as Monstrous Womb and Possessed Monster

Turning Red tells the story of a 13-year-old, Chinese Canadian girl, Meilin Lee, growing up in Toronto in 2002. Life is good for the high-achieving, academically successful, loyal daughter, and friend, but Mei is also changing. She encounters her budding sexuality, a growing interest in boys, and ongoing tension with her mom. After an embarrassing encounter, a horrified Mei awakens to discover that she has turned into a giant red panda overnight. Mei learns that the transformation is inherited, a "gift" bestowed by ancestor, Sun Yee. Mei also learns that a ritual on an evening with a red moon can ward off the powers indefinitely. Until then, Mei learns to control her powers with the help of her friends, while also using her transformative powers to secure tickets to see their favorite boy band, 4-Town. Everything goes according to plan until the concert conflicts with the red moon ritual. After a confrontation with Mei's mother and a falling out with her friends, Mei seems resolved to complete the ritual while her girlfriends attend the concert. However, Mei changes her mind, chooses to keep the red panda, and joins her friends at the concert, which results in Ming releasing her rage and red panda. The concert is disrupted and focus turns to containing Ming's red panda. The film has coming-of-age themes, and the red panda serves as an obvious analogy for the experience of puberty, especially when a teenage girl "is torn between family loyalty and the chaos of puberty and the growing pains of middle school" (Lattanzio, 2022).

The film's blatant connection to puberty themes explicitly connects it to the monstrous feminine. Mei's story and transformation relates to many monstrous characteristics, but it best qualifies as two types of tropes; first, the monstrous womb, and, second, the woman as possessed monster. In the first instance, Mei is a child monster in the form of a red panda, the monstrosity is produced and read as a physical manifestation of women's "enraged psyche" (p. 45). Creed (1992) explains that women's biological, reproductive functions "links her directly to the animal world," or a bestial, human/animal figure (p. 47), like how Mei's pubescent alter ego becomes expressed through a red panda. Though the monstrous womb can be understood as an evil child in utero, it can also be understood as women's "desire ... represented as a form of internal rage—a rage against the mother, which is shown to stretch back in time, passing from one generation to the next" (p. 46). The conflicts that instigate the red panda derive from Mei's own tension between her child-like, repressed persona, controlled and directed by her mother, and her independent and adolescent identity that is emerging.

Consistent with the trope, Mei's powers are also presented at the "threshold of puberty" (Creed, 1992, p. 77) and constructed as "monstrous" (p. 81). Briefel (2005) explains "female monsters menstruate. Violence in the horror film is often initiated by the female monster getting her period, an event that is either suggested or overtly displayed" (p. 21). When Mei first transforms into a red panda and hides in the bathroom from her unknowing mother, Ming asks, "Did the red peony bloom?" referencing a period euphemism. Mei, unsure how to respond, says "maybe," inciting a horrific reaction. Mei's dad, Jin, is shown freezing in the hallway with a look of horror on his face, slowly backing up and running off while Ming screams, "it's happening!" (00:17:10-00:17:26). Mei's parents react with fear and horror in response to Mei's expected bodily and reproductive changes, while, unbeknownst to them, their daughter is a literal monster. While read humorously, it is also a problematic representation, replicating mainstream films' tendency "to illustrate the conditions and contexts responsible for illuminating the modern beliefs and logic of the American menstruation taboo" (Thomas, 2017, p. 2). In turn, this affirms reproductive changes as something to be feared.

Second, Mei's uncontrollable possession which forces her body to transition into a red panda is another illustration of how a "good girl" can also hold "evil" within. Mei is pure, innocent, and obedient on the outside, but also portrayed as dangerous and troublesome internally. Creed explains the construction of woman "as possessed when she attacks the symbolic order, highlights in its weaknesses and plays on its vulnerabilities; specifically, she demonstrates that the symbolic order is a sham built on sexual repression and the sacrifice of the mother" (p. 41). Not surprisingly, the symbolic order as understood through Mei's cultural and protective parents is targeted when Mei seeks to escape repressive boundaries and navigate the world and identity outside of those limits. Mei is a red panda instead of an abject figure, but the representation replicates horror film characters who enact possession as they struggle with coming-of-age and "mommy issues" (Bayar, 2022, p. 4).

Mei's sexual awakening is explicitly linked to her monstrous transition. The night prior to Mei's first conversion, Mei starts fantasizing about Devon, her crush. As Mei sketches him, she is comically and dramatically animated as sweating, slobbering, and unable to focus on anything else. She continues to draw him under her bed, implying the action was shameful and inappropriate. Later, after her mom goes to the Daisy Mart to confront Devon, Mei also acts horrified by her own actions. She asks herself, "What were you thinking?" She references her thoughts and drawings as "horrible, awful, sexy things" and tells herself it "will never happen again" (00:14:24-00:14:54). mimicking her mom and repressing herself. Throughout, Mei's budding sexual desire for boys is portrayed as similarly uncontrollable and as animalistic as the red panda itself. While attempting to remain calm at school, Mei notices one of her classmates. The animation moves in slow motion, and romantic music plays while her heartbeat pounds rapidly and her eyes glisten in a "Kawaii"/anime aesthetic. Even when she turns into the red panda at school and flees to get home as quickly as she can, she seems unable to stop herself from stomping her foot and screaming "Awooga!" when she sees Devon (00:24:45-00:24:49).

Just as sexual awakening represents her possession, Mei's independence, emotions, especially her temper, also sprout when her red panda emerges. She shows explosive but also repressed reactions toward her mother throughout the film. For example, in reaction to her mother barging into the bathroom and assuring her all will be okay, Mei shouts back: "No it's not, will you just get out!!" Mei, shocked by her own impulsive response, covers her mouth and yells at herself, "stop it, stop talking" before slapping herself in the face (00:17:35-00:17:48). Incited by her mother embarrassing Mei at school, Mei "explodes" in a cloud of pink smoke, roaring and becoming the panda when she cannot control her emotions any longer. In another scene, Mei reveals to her friends her fiery anger after Ming tells Mei she is not permitted to go to the 4-Town concert. Her friends validate her by shouting "Fight the power!" (00:41:20-00:41:21). Even after learning to "control" her panda, the film treats Mei's ongoing strong emotional reactions as horrifying and requiring repression. Her "disobedience" slips out as she struggles regulating her thoughts.

Mei also has shocking, severe, and impulsive outbursts toward others. Angered, Mei grows enraged, turning on her classmate, Tyler, slamming him to the ground and screaming, "I hate you!" (00:59:31-00:59:38). On the night of the ritual, when she flashes back to that moment, she shudders at the memory of her "bestial" actions. Mei is overcome by rage in the temple when she learns about Sun Yee and asks: "Are you serious? You cursed us?" And accusatorily screams at her ancestor's picture, "it's all your fault!" (00:28:18-00:28:25). Mei's eyes glow red, she bares her teeth and is overcome with fury. That night, Mei overhears her parents describing her rage as horrific. As she grieves uncontrollably on her mattress, she triggers transformation into the red panda.

To further mark Mei's changes, including her emotional and sexual awakenings, the film's color and shading frequently change to red to represent anger or desires. Red represents Mei's "monster" and menarche. Foreshadowing begins with images of red lanterns in Mei's neighborhood and red doors on the temple. Shades of red appear on or around Mei throughout the story, representing her physical and emotional changes. After the eve of her initial transformation, Mei's eyes and hair change indefinitely to the color, red-orange, and shades of red dominate the dreams she has that night.

In addition to turning Mei into a literal monster, Mei and other characters explicitly label monstrosity and associate it with requiring repression. In various scenes, Mei internalizes her status and identity as "monster." She describes herself as "sloppy" and "smelly" and concludes "I'm a freak" (00:32:56-00:33:21). She tells her parents that she's "a gross red monster!" (00:17:43-00:17:46) and warns them to not look at her. Ming compares the panda to "darkness" and worries she will "get whipped up into a frenzy and panda all over the place" (00:38:09-00:38:12) Grandma Wu acknowledges the challenge of keeping the "unruly beast at bay" while Mei's aunts express surprise that a child can "control such a beast" (00:49:58-00:50:49) After her outburst at Tyler's party, Mei is called an "animal" and, when she runs from the school, someone shouts: "It's a monster!" (00:24:30-00:24:32). These examples and her own reactions convince Mei that she is a problem just as society's tropes create similar problematic constructions for women. Mei internalizes the fear dismissing those who try to persuade her to see the panda as good, arguing she is "dangerous" and "outta control." Eventually, the end of the film operates to work against the assumption that a woman's emotions and her reproductive functions are something to fear, control, or repress.

Mei's Positive Panda Power

Turning Red, like *Encanto*, initially perpetuates problematic tropes of the monstrous womb/possessed woman but ultimately subverts the narrative/trope that frames women's bodies as monstrous wombs or in states of possession. In numerous scenes, the connotation of the panda begins to shift. Audiences learn that Sun Yee used her gift for good, during wartime, protecting family, the village, and herself, which helped Mei's ancestors thrive and survive. Though Mei originally adopts Ming's belief that the panda is a modern "inconvenience" and "curse," eventually, friends and family change Mei's opinion of her power.

Mei's friends suggest she consider not completing the ritual and keeping the panda, claiming, "You're not the same feather-dustin' straight-A, goody goody, who we never saw, like, ever, you're such a rebel now ... you've really changed, and I'm proud of you. Just don't get rid of all of it, you know?" (00:57:27-00:00:57:53). Likewise, her friend, Miriam also encourages Mei to see herself as confident and in control. When Mei calls herself "a furry ticking time bomb," Miriam cuts her off and responds, "Of awesomeness. And now you can control it" (00:35:37-00:35:43) The storyline reveals the panda as empowering. It rejects suppression, because it denies a side of Mei that is an essential part of her identity. By accepting her friends' and family's love, and most importantly, trusting herself, Mei not only learns to manage emotions, but she also gains a better understanding and acceptance of herself.

Mei's father, Jin, sums it up when he tells Mei that people have many sides and that some "are messy." He states: "The point isn't to push the bad stuff away, it's to make room for it, live with it." He tells her that she can "erase it," but also shares that recordings of the panda made him laugh (00:01:05:15-00:01:05:45). As Jin characterizes both Mei's panda and her mother's panda in a positive light, it leads Mei to reflect more carefully on what she is giving up. This conversation ultimately helps Mei recognize that what society normalizes us into seeing as "bad" is not necessarily behaviors or parts of our identity that should be eliminated.

This culminates during the red moon ritual, when Mei is spiritually sent to the astral plane to walk through a circle to sever her panda. The circle displays her reflection like a mirror. Like Lacan's mirror stage, Mei sees her ideal ego, pre-panda. The mirror acts as the gap between Mei's authentic psychological identity and the symbolic mask she wears. As she attempts to separate herself from the panda, she screams and strains representing her symbolic castration. As Mei pulls, the panda resists, expressing agony, pain, and the sorrow Mei will experience if she loses a part of herself. In a montage of brief flashbacks, Mei remembers all the positive and genuinely good times she had as the panda, reminding her of what she is giving up. She shouts "No" as she reunites with it and crashes down from the plane in a cloud of smoke. Mei announces she intends to keep the panda before running to the concert. Mei tells her friends: "I couldn't do it. The panda is a part of me, and you guys are too" (01:11:52-1:11:58).

Despite this resolution, Mei's decision to keep the panda sets off a chain of events, provoking Ming's fury and unleashing her red panda. Despite Mei's initial fear, she continues to stand up for herself to her mother. She taunts: "I'm not your little Mei-Mei anymore." She admits to lying, to "hustling" the panda, choosing to go to Tyler's party and admitting to liking "boys," "loud music," and "gyrating." (01:16:10-01:16:30). The message, though hostile, is authentic and used to distract her mother so Mei can save her. The pubescent Mei/red panda is not evil; she is compassionate, loving, still a "good" daughter, and now honest. Once they return to the astral plane, Mei leads her mother back to her family and the circle. Grandma Wu blesses Mei and Mei's aunts accept her decision, acknowledging "It's her life" (01:24:25-01:24:23). Likewise, even though Ming confessed her fear of losing her daughter, she accepts and respects Mei's choice.

In the film's epilogue, Mei is empowered by her panda. Mei defends her choice to wear her red panda ears and tail to karaoke, and reminds her, "My panda, my choice, mom"—the phrase becoming Mei's own feminist mantra (01:28:10-01:28:12). The final lines of the film further subdue the pressure to repress or assign horror to what we become. Mei concludes: "We've all got an inner beast . . . a messy, loud, weird part of ourselves hidden away." She admits we tend to not let it out, that she did, and poses the question back to the audience: "How about you?" (01:28:42-01:28:56). By the end of the film, the narrative to fear or repress the "beast" is reversed by the realization that Mei's strong emotions are natural and common. Likewise, the color, red, reemerges as a dominant color in the same scenes where Mei accepts her panda and values her identity and newfound independence. In *Turning Red*, we have an example of a "new female/feminist imaginary" as Mei's voice, her journey in a state of abjection comes through in a coming-of-age film, a filmic "feminine space" for others to reside (Creed, 2022, p. 16). In this subtle way, the film's visual qualities reverse the color red's meaning, just as it alters the messages about monstrosity.

Conclusion

As globally recognized staples in cultural imaginations with impressive and lasting social/cultural impact, Disney films and their messages require evaluation of their influential, intersectional, and trans-mediated discourses. In this chapter, I textually analyzed *Encanto* and *Turning Red* to examine the portrayals of supernatural youth. More than just coming-of-age stories and tales of difference and marginality, each film sets up a monstrous feminine trope that portrays woman as abject, exposing the oppressive ways society tends to project monstrous qualities and discourse onto women. Previous and contemporary portrayals, especially in horror films, fueled repressive messages, resulting in feelings of shame and insecurities associated with women's physical and emotional changes. Initially, Disney's utilizes the references to the well-known, monstrous feminine archetypes and appear to reify them as threats to women in the context of puberty and adolescence.

However, despite the initial constructions, the supernatural characters in these Disney films are empowered in the stories, which can extend feelings of positivity toward the bodies and identities of adolescent girls. They overcome the tensions within their psyches and their families by staying true to their identity and resisting fear, insecurities, and power imbalances. The films reverse the genre of body horror by allowing a witch and a possessed womb/monster to save their families, ultimately de-monstering the women and altering traditional, normative imagery of adolescent girls. Furthermore, the film's inclusivity of diverse, non-Anglo qualities fuels minimization of otherness and endorses messages of acceptance. Although more future examinations of the films are justified to interrogate the neoliberal implications behind these films' messages, I counted the alternative representations of feminine qualities are refreshing. The subversion of the monster/body horror conventions, especially in diverse characters, operate to help adolescents accept themselves, view their changing bodies as nothing to fear, and adopt personal and cultural inclusivity.

Additionally, this study could expand to analyze additional representative patterns and explore use of additional tired tropes, such as those focused on maternal qualities. The films reveal and engage in reclamation of the trope of the "Archaic/Castrating Mother" by centering of maternal relationships and the generational trauma impacting the protagonists. Though both deserve additional analysis, they are beyond the scope of this chapter. Nonetheless, it points to the progressive, feminist messaging subtly operating in the film and questioning traditional tropes.

Returning to Creed's latest project on the identification of "New Wave Feminism" discourse in film, this analysis can serve as further evidence that such messages are extending to and present in family/children's films. The films examined in this essay upend or reverse the harmful assumptions tied to women and their bodies. Consistent with New Wave Feminist films, these films all focus on the protagonist's identification and her journey. The character is threatened but emerges transformed but only after engaging in revolts that are "political, personal, and intimate" (Creed, 2022, p. 15). By confronting and reverting the monstrous, girls and women socially learn to resist oppressive structures, directed toward them, or brewing in their own psyche. The audience's appreciation of such portrayals of women signals an embrace of future identities and forwards liberating resistant through individualism and the act of reinventing views of oneself.

References

Banh, J. (2020). #MakeMulanRight: Retracing the genealogy of Mulan from ancient Chinese tale to Disney classic. In S. Roberts (Ed.), *Recasting the Disney princess in an era of new media and social movements* (pp. 129–146). Lexington. https://doi.org/10.1080/14680777.2022.2104905

Bayar, H. (2022). Turning red: Tradition, repression, mommy issues, and a millennial way of growing up. *Markets, Globalization & Development Review, 7*(1), 1–8. https://doi.org/10.23860/MGDR-2022-07-01-02

Bell, E., Haas, L., & Sells, L. (1995). *From mouse to mermaid: The politics of film, gender, and culture.* Indiana University Press.

Briefel, A. (2005). Monster pains: Masochism, menstruation, and identification in the horror film. *Film Quarterly, 58*(3), 16–27. https://doi.org/10.1525/fq.2005.58.3.16

Bush, J., & Howard, B. (Directors). (2021). *Encanto* [Film]. Walt Disney Pictures.

Chatters, A., & Roberts, S. (2020). Explaining #BlackLivesMatter through *Zooptopia*. In S. Roberts (Ed.), *Recasting the Disney princess in an era of new media and social movements* (pp. 263–279). Lexington. https://doi.org/10.1080/14680777.2022.2104905

Clover, C. J. (1992). *Men, women, and chainsaws: Gender in the modern horror film.* Princeton University Press.

Clute, J., & Grant, J. (1997). Supernatural Fiction. *The Encyclopedia of Fantasy.* https://sf-encyclopedia.com/fe/supernatural_fiction

Coming of Age with Pixar. (2022, May 17). *Bridging the Gap [Video] Disney+ YouTube.* https://www.youtube.com/watch?v=Fqp7NzOOEyw

Creed, B. (1993). *The monstrous-feminine: Film, feminism, pyschoanalysis.* Routledge.

Creed, B. (2022). *Return of the monstrous-feminine: Feminist new wave cinema.* Routledge. https://doi.org/10.4324/9781003036654

Cuenca-Orellana, N., & López-Heredia, P. (2020). Male and female workers. Gender treatment through Pixar's films. *index.comunicación, 10*(1), 97–123.

Davis, A. M. (2007). *Good girls and wicked witches: Women in Disney's feature animation.* John Libbey.

Disney's "Encanto": Neither fairytale nor fantasy. (2022, February 02). https://www.proquest.com/wire-feeds/disneys-encanto-neither-fairytale-nor-fantasy/docview/2624767753/se-2

Forman-Brunell, M., & Hains, R. C. (2015). *Princess cultures: Mediating girls' imaginations and identities*. Peter Lang. https://doi.org/10.3726/978-1-4539-1322-2

Ghisyawan, K. (2020). A Whole new worldview: Gender norms, Islamophobia, and orientalism. In S. Roberts (Ed.), *Recasting the Disney princess in an era of new media and social movements* (pp. 181–196). Lexington. https://doi.org/10.1080/14680777.2022.2104905

Giroux, H. A., & Pollock, G. (2010). *The mouse that roared: Disney and the end of innocence*. Rowman and Littlefield.

Hains, R. C. (2014). *The princess problem: Guiding our girls through the princess-obsessed years*. Sourcebooks.

Higgs, S. (2016). Damsels in development: Representation, transition, and the Disney princess. *Screen Education, 83*, 62–69.

Holcomb, J., & Latham-Mintus, K. (2022). Disney and disability: Media representations of disability in Disney and Pixar animated films. *Disability Studies Quarterly, 42*(1), n.p. https://doi.org/10.18061/dsq.v42i1.7054

Kelly, C. R. (2016). Camp horror and the gendered politics of screen violence: Subverting the monstrous-feminine in *Teeth* (2007). *Women's Studies in Communication, 39*(1), 86–106. http://dx.doi.org/10.1080/07491409.2015.1126776

Langsdale, S. (2020). Moon girls and mythical beasts: Analyzing race, gender, and monstrosity. *Signs: Journal of Women in Culture and Society, 45*(2), 395–420. https://doi.org/10.1086/705281

Lattanzio, R. (2022, March 9). 'Turning Red' cast speaks out after controversial review drew outrage, was pulled by outlet. *Indie Wire*. https://www.indiewire.com/features/general/turning-red-cast-speaks-out-cinemablend-review-1234706371/

Lee-Oliver, L. (2020). Pocahontas: Digital coloniality, coercive fiction, and "renewing" western hegemonic power. In S. Roberts (Ed.), *Recasting the Disney princess in an era of new media and social movements* (pp. 163–180). Lexington. https://doi.org/10.1080/14680777.2022.2104905

Maribel Madrigal. (2021, July 8). In *The Disney Wiki*. https://disney.fandom.com/wiki/Mirabel_Madrigal

Multigenerational Storytelling. (2022, September 14). *Bridging the Gap [Video] Disney+ YouTube*. https://www.youtube.com/watch?v=izrmagr0iEI

Nash, I. (2015). The princess and the teen witch: Fantasies of the essential self. In M. Forman-Brunell & R. C. Hains (Eds.), *Princess cultures: Mediating girls' imaginations and identities* (pp. 3–23). Peter Lang. https://doi.org/10.3726/978-1-4539-1322-2

Rapoport, M. (2020). Frankenstein's daughters: On the rising trend of women's body horror in contemporary fiction. *Publishing Research Quarterly, 36*, 619–633. https://doi.org/10.1007/s12109 020-09761-x

Roberts, S. (2020). Recasting the Disney princess in an era of new media and social movements. In S. Roberts (Ed.), *Recasting the Disney princess in an era of new media and social movements* (pp. 199–210). Lexington. https://doi.org/10.1080/14680777.2022.2104905

Schiele, K., Louie, L., & Chen, S. (2020). Marketing feminism in youth media: A study of Disney and Pixar animation. *Business Horizons, 63*, 659–669. https://doi.org/10.1016/j.bushor.2020.05.001

Shi, D. (Director). (2022). *Turning Red* [Film]. Walt Disney Pictures.

Thomas, E. M. (2017). Crimson horror: The discourse and visibility of menstruation in mainstream horror films and its influence on cultural myths and taboos. *Relevant Rhetoric: A New Journal of Rhetorical Studies, 8*, 1–27. http://www.relevantrhetoric.com/

Wee, V. (2011). Patriarchy and the horror of the monstrous feminine: A comparative study of *Ringu* and *The Ring*. *Feminist Media Studies, 11*(2), 151–165. https://doi.org/10.1080/14680777.2010.521624

Weidman-Winter, R. (2020). Belle: Beyond the classic story for the modern audience. In S. Roberts (Ed.), *Recasting the Disney princess in an era of new media and social movements* (pp. 199–210). Lexington. https://doi.org/10.1080/14680777.2022.2104905

9

A Zambian Fairytale: Shula and The Magic of Rungano Nyoni's *I Am Not a Witch*

HOPE L. RUSSELL

Rungano Nyoni's award-winning film *I Am Not a Witch* (2017) is a stunning critique of misogyny, forced labor camps, witch-hunting, and neocolonial tourism. At its center is a nine-year-old African girl named Shula who is accused of witchcraft and enslaved in a "witch camp." Although the film's plot is fictional, writer-director Nyoni was inspired by modern-day witch hunting and real-life witch camps in African countries like Zambia and Ghana. Nyoni was born in Lusaka, Zambia and, from a young age, raised in Wales, United Kingdom. While researching the film, she learned that most of the women incarcerated in witch-camps had "become a burden to their families, or were cast off by their spouses, deemed eccentric or outspoken" (Page, 2017). Nyoni's bicultural background, combined with the film's setting and dramatization of contemporary conflicts in Africa, establish *I Am Not a Witch* as one of many postcolonial and diasporic texts in African cinema, a field that has flourished in recent decades due to the rise of streaming services like Netflix and the subsequent shift away from national cinemas to global ones (Harrow, 2024, pp. 1–3). Nyoni's film is further situated within African cinema through her portrayal of Shula who, unlike many characters in Western supernatural media, is not a white protagonist who knowingly deploys flashy supernatural powers to save others or the world. Dark-skinned Shula is instead positioned as a supernatural youth who seems not to deliberately, or even consciously, wield her magical powers. Far from the celebrated "girl power" ethos in Western supernatural media, Shula's subtle magic is steeped in African folk-logic, which differentiates between supernaturalism and witchcraft, and the natural and supernatural worlds. Nyoni's use of African traditions, her genre mixing, and her characterization of Shula as an innocent child who is morally superior to the adults who oppress her, combine to make a powerful statement about youth and magic alongside the film's wider critique of oppressive social practices. One of the few academic analyses of this film appears in Kenneth Harrow's *African Cinema in a Global Age* (2024). In addition to discounting the possibility of real magic, as presented in the film, Harrow's interpretation depends on viewing Shula in the dual role of a child-adult. In contrast, I argue that Shula's status as a child is vital to the film's meanings. While the adult characters believe in and fear the dark magic of witchcraft, *I Am Not a Witch* suggests that real magic is gifted only to the young and innocent by unknown supernatural forces, and for the benign purpose of surviving a patriarchal, misogynistic society. To support my analysis, I draw upon film reviews from both critics and audiences, published interviews with the film's writer-director, Zambian folktales which may have been used as source material for the film, and scholarship on African folktales, literature, and film.

Throughout this chapter, I analyze Nyoni's use of African belief systems and African conventions of storytelling in her portrayal of Shula as a supernatural youth. In so doing, I expose two distinct sets of challenges that emerge from the opposing forces of witchcraft and supernaturalism as they unfold onscreen: challenges inside the film related to its story and challenges outside the film related to its genre and reception. First, I explore the film's juxtaposition of witchcraft and supernaturalism to highlight the stark differences between the adults' perception of Shula as a malevolent witch and Nyoni's portrayal of her as a benevolent supernatural youth. Second, I investigate what it means for Shula to embody the supernatural and how that embodiment is specifically connected to her youth, her innocence and benevolence, and to African lore regarding the natural and supernatural worlds. The related challenges inside the film regarding its story are laid out in these two sections.

Third, I examine how Nyoni's use of African conventions of storytelling, specifically magical realism and supernaturalism, makes it difficult for reviewers to classify the film's genre.

Additionally, Nyoni's subtle positioning of Shula as a supernatural youth is further hinted at through these storytelling conventions and the various plot and character ambiguities they produce in that Shula is the only girl in the witch camp and the only accused witch who is linked to scenes involving magical realism and supernaturalism. In this section, I also explore Nyoni's subtle use of recognizable, Western fairytale tropes and unrecognizable (to Western viewers) Zambian fairytale tropes in the making of her film. This mixing of genres, as Nyoni attests, is another African convention of storytelling that she employs to prefigure Shula as a supernatural youth (Kasman, 2017). For these reasons, I posit that *I Am Not a Witch* can be best understood as a Zambian fairytale, one that mixes fairytale tropes from two different cultural traditions. The fairytale tropes, conventions, and ambiguities combine to represent challenges outside the film related to genre and reception.

Lastly, I analyze the phenomenon of Western viewers' inability to understand Nyoni's film as the Zambian fairytale she intended since Shula embodies magic in subtle, unexpected ways, more in keeping with an African aesthetic than a European-American one. To these ends, I discuss how deeply entrenched, Western worldviews constrain some viewers' imaginations and responses to the film, thus creating another set of challenges related to genre and reception.

Witchcraft Vs. Supernaturalism[1]

The plot of the film establishes a conflict between true supernatural magic derived from a mystical source and human-made beliefs in witchcraft. *I Am Not a Witch* begins with a young girl suddenly appearing in a field in a remote African village, startling a woman who spills her bucket of water and then accuses a woman of witchcraft. The girl is brought to the local police station where the villagers, a witch doctor, and a corrupt government official named Mr. Banda denounce her as a witch on spurious evidence. Found guilty, she is sentenced to live in a state-run labor camp alongside other accused witches who name the preternaturally silent girl Shula. When Shula and the women labor in the fields, they are prevented from escaping by long white ribbons clipped to their backs. At the end of the film, Shula performs a rain dance to end the drought in the village. She dies that night under mysterious circumstances. As the women mourn Shula's death, thunder rumbles overhead and heavy rain pours from the sky. In the final scene, the ribbons that bound the women are flying free in the wind—and the women have vanished from sight.

The villagers and some of the power-hungry men that Shula encounters believe that she is a witch because her sudden, unexplained appearance coincides with other strange occurrences in the village. Their attendant beliefs in witch doctors as arbiters who can detect witches, and in labor camps as places in which to enslave accused witches, seal Shula's fate. However, Shula's experiences beyond the camp and her likely involvement in freeing the women from their bondage suggests that she has true supernatural magic. As it plays out in the film, the conflict between Shula's authentic magic and the adults' artificial beliefs in witchcraft originates from her youth and innocence: she is the only child in the camp and the only accused witch who is linked to real supernatural magic.

Throughout *I Am Not a Witch*, there is no evidence that Shula and the older women are actual "witches" in the way their culture defines the term. Even though Shula never proclaims the bold words in the film's title, it speaks for Shula when she cannot speak for herself. The title also establishes an important distinction between witchcraft and supernaturalism. Shula is "not a witch," but she is connected to the supernatural. In the eyes of the villagers, the men who run the labor camp, the witch doctor, Mr. Banda, and the tribal queen, Shula is a witch. They conspire to convict her of witchcraft and enslave her in the camp based solely on hearsay. Shula is accused of using witchcraft to teleport, taint the well water, and physically harm a man in his dream. Tellingly, none of the other "strange things" the villagers blame Shula for are ever explained (Nyoni, 2017, 5:42).

In these cases, Shula incites fear in the villagers who believe that she has used witchcraft for malevolent purposes. However, Shula is nothing but benevolent throughout the film, thus suggesting that she is morally superior to the patriarchal adults who persecute her. This is evident in the scenes where Shula thoughtfully refills the water bucket of the woman whom she had startled, and when she does not respond to the villagers with the same anger and hatred that they repeatedly cast upon her.

Petrus and Bogopa's (2007) research on African lore is useful in understanding the relationship between Shula's benevolence and the supernatural. The authors state that witchcraft is considered a reality in "most, if not all" African communities, whether rural or urban, and these communities view witchcraft as "a viable cause of misfortune, illness or death" (Petrus & Bogopa, 2007, p. 2). Differentiating between witchcraft and divining or traditional healing, they explain that witchcraft deploys the supernatural for evil or harmful purposes whereas the latter practices engage the supernatural for benevolent reasons (p. 3).

Contrary to what the villagers believe, Shula uses her supernatural powers for benevolent as opposed to malevolent purposes. Shula approaches her mission in Mr. Banda's sham of a kangaroo court with the utmost sincerity. When Mr. Banda brings her before suspected petty thieves and asks her to identify the guilty party, she accurately divines the thieves on several occasions. In these scenes, the conflict between real supernatural magic and human-made witchcraft further establishes Shula as morally superior to adults like Mr. Banda who clearly manipulates her for his own gain. Although some viewers, such as my own students, have argued that Shula was coached or made a lucky guess, the ambiguous nature of these scenes suggests that Shula has access to mysterious powers.

In a film review published in *African Studies Review*, Katherine Luongo (2020) explains how the adults in the film perceive Shula and the other accused witches. Not only do they condemn the accused witches to perform forced labor in the fields, but they also restrict their freedom of movement to prevent them from flying and killing people. As such, viewers learn that witches "are dangerously powerful and deeply vulnerable, [they are] women who have no friends, no relations, no one, and thus no social standing or protection. They are at once malevolent actors who inspire fear and hapless victims who invite incarceration" (Luongo, 2020, p. E39). More to the point, Shula is not a woman but a girl who is perceived as a malevolent witch.

Similarly, in *African Cinema in a Global Age*, Harrow downplays Shula's youth when he argues that "Shula is a child, but in the persona of an old woman" (Harrow, 2024, p. 220). He also claims that she represents "both witch-as-old-woman and witch-as-little-girl" and points to the "disjuncture between her appearance as helpless little girl and her function as old woman" (Harrow, 2024, p. 222). The assertion that Shula embodies both a child and an old woman is problematic in many respects. First, there is no suggestion in the diegesis of the film, or in Shula's portrayal, that she is meant to approximate the figure of an old woman. Second, Harrow's argument minimizes the violent realities of Shula's lived experience as a vulnerable child; he claims that the witchcraft accusations levied against Shula bring viewers "into the world of old women who are the real targets of the accusations" (Harrow, 2024, p. 218). Throughout the film, however, it is painfully obvious that Shula is also a "real" target of her accusers' misogyny, exploitation, and violence. By placing Shula in the same age category as the other accused witches, Harrow implies that her experience of enslavement is on par with that of the much older women. As a girl, however, she is even more vulnerable and victimized on account of her age; she also has even less social standing and no friends or family members to protect her from violence and exploitation. Harrow's argument ultimately robs Shula of her youth and innocence, effectively denying her the racial innocence so often afforded to white children yet denied to Black children in the real world (Epstein et al., 2017, pp. 6–8). In so doing, he also forecloses the possibility that Shula, unlike all the older "witches" around her, has truly supernatural powers; instead, he suggests that she is simply a falsely accused witch like the other women in the labor camp. Harrow's reading ignores the film's repeated hints that Shula, as the camp's only child, has access to mystical abilities not given to adults. In Nyoni's film, it is the misogynistic, patriarchal culture of adult society that delimits and denigrates accused witches. It is only through Shula's magic, which results in her mysterious death and the older women's liberation, that she and the women can escape their oppression. The film subtly suggests that mysterious, mystical forces have gifted Shula with magic for this very purpose.

Overall, Shula is framed as a witch by the adults in the film who uphold traditional African beliefs in witchcraft; however, that same tradition also positions her as a supernatural youth who uses her "powers for benevolent purposes" (Petrus & Bogopa, 2007, p. 3). Shula possesses true supernatural magic, not by choice or "craft," but as a gift from an unknown mystical source or divine being. She is gifted these powers because she is the youngest and most innocent person in the camp. It is perhaps a reward for her benevolence and the very thing she and the women need to escape the horrors they endure. The film ultimately suggests that the magic of a blameless young girl is the kind of magic that cannot be named, detected, or contained. The adults' view of magic, what they call witchcraft, is portrayed as morally and ideologically inferior in comparison. Although Shula dies at the end of the film, she remains uncorrupted by those in power.

Understanding Shula's physical embodiment and the natural and supernatural worlds that she inhabits is also critical to understanding her positioning as a supernatural youth. In *The Body and Embodiment: A Philosophical Guide*, Frank Chouraqui (2021) states that embodiment is not only "the experience of having a body" (p. 52) but also "a structure of being: it separates the world into the realm of the actual and the realm of the possible" (p. 54). Applied to Shula, her world and her experience of her body split in two at some point: the realm of the actual/natural and the realm of the (im)possible/supernatural. What is possible for Shula—the acquisition of supernatural powers—is impossible for the other characters in the film; the women in the camp lack youthful innocence as do the power-hungry men and tribal queen. For Shula, embodying the supernatural means that she is connected to larger, unknown and unknowable powers that imbue her with magic. Shula, like the film itself, cannot be easily classified. She is not a witch, nor is she a vampire, zombie, or other named and therefore known fantastical being.

In "Nature and the Supernatural in African Literature," Amy Riddle's (2020) explanation of the supernatural world provides a useful context for further understanding Shula's embodiment of, and connection to, the supernatural. Riddle writes, "The supernatural genre, a common avenue of representation in African cultural production, combines fantasy and horror as it deals with the social and psychological anxieties surrounding the unknowns of its time" (p. 80). In contrast to the known and somewhat knowable natural world, the supernatural world is unknown, largely unknowable, and inapprehensible (Adejunmobi, 2017, as cited in Riddle, 2020, p. 80). First, Shula "cannot be apprehended" as a supernatural youth precisely because she embodies the unknown (Adejunmobi, 2017, as cited in Riddle, 2020, p. 80). The word apprehension invokes "the feeling of dread, anxiety or fear, together with the anticipation of future events. As it stems from the Latin term prehension (meaning 'to seize or grasp'), apprehension can also be attached to mental processes of anticipation, comprehension and understanding" (Walton, 2018, p. 251). Apprehension "can also involve legal action such as the seizing or arrest of a suspect" (Walton, 2018, p. 261). Ironically, Shula *is* apprehended when she is brought to the police station and accused of witchcraft in what amounts to a bogus witch trial. Shula's trial occurs before a de facto judge (Officer Josephine), two "witnesses" who accuse her of witchcraft, and an angry "jury" gathered outside. In this same scene, however, Officer Josephine cannot apprehend Shula; that is, she cannot understand or fully grasp the silent girl sitting before her. The villagers also cannot apprehend Shula—who she is and where she has come from. As a result, they blame her for their misfortunes, accusing her of witchcraft and making her the scapegoat for their own "social and psychological anxieties" (Riddle, 2020, p. 80). Shula's mysterious arrival and elusive presence, combined with strange happenings, produces heightened anxiety, fear, and dread amongst the villagers. In other words, she who cannot be apprehended causes apprehension.

Second, Shula is part of "the unknown and potentially unknowable" supernatural world in that she seems to have appeared out of nowhere in the village (Adejunmobi, 2017, as cited in Riddle, 2020, p. 80). She has no one who can claim her or protect her from the abuse she endures in the village and beyond. Shula remains an elusive and mysterious figure throughout the entire film. Her backstory and the origins of her supernatural powers are aptly ambiguous and must remain unknown and ultimately unknowable for that is precisely how the supernatural world functions. Shula's name, which means "uprooted," is a fitting appellation for a girl who has been uprooted from the unknown and thrust into the natural, known world of the village and the supernatural, unknown world of the beyond (Nyoni, 2017, 27:24).

Throughout the film, Shula is repeatedly exposed to violence and dehumanization in ways that seem to heighten her embodiment of, and connection to, the supernatural. Even though the adults accuse her of causing harm, they are the ones who repeatedly inflict harm on her. For instance, one man threatens to stone her and bury her alive. Another claims that she ate his relatives and tries to physically attack her. On a talk show, Mr. Banda boasts about Shula's alleged powers while she sits in silence and painfully cries. She also witnesses an angry mob of townspeople physically and verbally accost Mr. Banda's wife, an accused witch named Charity. After a failed rain dance, Mr. Banda verbally abuses Charity and then punishes Shula by making her spend the night inside a grotesque, plastic clown's head; the next day, heartless tourists gawk and take photos of the crying girl sitting alone inside. Shula's youth, and her lack of social standing, leave her vulnerable and victimized in these moments. At the same time, her use of supernatural magic seems to grow after each of these experiences.

In the end, Shula harnesses the full extent of her magic to perform the rain dance and free the women. In yet another nod to her benevolence, she dances to help not only the kind women but also the cruel villagers. As Shula dances, she looks up into the blinding light of the sun as it shines across a perfectly blue, cloudless sky. This moment can be interpreted as Shula calling upon supernatural powers to darken the sky and make it rain. Significantly, the villagers think that Shula has malevolently used witchcraft to cause the drought, but this scene suggests that she uses her magic to end it.

The events surrounding the rain dance and Shula's death are the strongest indications of her supernatural powers. Back at camp, she tells the women that she wishes she had chosen to be a goat instead of a witch. This relates to an earlier scene when Mr. Banda forced the child to make a choice between being a goat or a witch, to make a choice, as it were, between freedom and servitude. That night, Shula slowly gathers her white ribbon to its end, which can be interpreted as her freeing herself and choosing to "become" a goat. As the women mourn Shula's death the next day, torrents of rain begin to fall from the sky. In the final scene, the women—magically freed from their own ribbons—have vanished from sight. Goats are heard bleating in the background. Here, the girl who was the unwilling scapegoat for the villagers' misfortune presumably becomes the willing sacrificial goat who gives her own life so the women could live theirs freely.

Shula's death can be attributed to her magic and her connection to the supernatural world. It is possible that she died because she overexerted her powers during the rain dance. More compellingly, Shula sacrificed her life for the women because it was the only way to free them. Either way, Shula had to die to make it rain and to liberate the women. The ambiguity surrounding her death suggests that she is a vessel for true magic which emanates from her but without her conscious control. In death, she remains morally superior to those who persecuted her. Ironically, her oppressors created their own worst nightmare by harming Shula to the point where she freed the women using not the witchcraft of their own making but true supernatural magic.

Nyoni's Zambian Fairytale

Interestingly, professional film critics and audiences alike have variously referred to the film as a satire, tragicomedy, fantasy, or fairytale (Obenson, 2018; Carrier, 2017; Hall, 2018; Simpson, 2019). As such, the film elides easy classification into one specific genre primarily due to Nyoni's use of three conventions of African storytelling: magical realism, supernaturalism, and genre mixing. In this section, I posit that Nyoni's film can be best understood as a Zambian fairytale based on the incorporation of these African traditions. While many Western fairytales are, by definition, about magical beings, this African film presents magic not in the form of, say, a fairy godmother but in the very real figure of a girl. Unlike Western fairytales, Shula's powers are not made obvious through the flick of a magic wand or the invocation of a powerful spell; instead, magic seems to unconsciously work through her in mysterious and unexplainable ways.

Magical realism, a subgenre of film that incorporates magic and fantasy within real-world settings, is incorporated into two of the film's major symbols: an enchanted funnel and the white ribbons. Shula's magical interactions with these objects suggest that she has supernatural powers. Additionally, she is the only accused witch in the film who is linked to its magical realism. In one scene, Shula holds a makeshift blue funnel close to her ear and smiles sweetly as she hears the perfectly audible sounds of a nearby schoolhouse. The students' voices seem to be magically carried on the wind much to Shula's delight. The magical realism in this scene suggests that Shula has used magic to enchant the funnel. Contrary to the adults' belief that witches practice dark magic, Shula uses magic for the benign purpose of education and connection with other children, for happiness as opposed to harm. While some viewers, including my students, have suggested that Shula is simply imagining the sounds of the classroom, this does not seem likely since she earlier admits that she has never been to school. The ambiguous nature of this scene can only be explained by Shula's connection to, and embodiment of, the supernatural.

In several other scenes, the white ribbons represent Nyoni's use of magical realism as a means in which to subtly suggest that Shula has supernatural powers. Magical realism occurs through the film's juxtaposition of enchanted white ribbons within the realistic settings of an African village and witch camp. Nyoni's use of magical realism is intensified through her clever camerawork and juxtaposition of the rain dance scene and the film's final scene. Before the camera pans out to reveal that the women have vanished from sight, a close-up reveals several white ribbons rippling in the wind and reaching upward into a perfectly blue, cloudless sky. Shula had looked toward a similar sky while performing the rain dance. Contrary to the laws of physics, the ribbons seem like they are being magically pulled upward into the sky. These factors, combined with the women's disappearance and the quiet, symbolic bleating of goats, suggest that Shula used her supernatural powers to free the women. Since the circumstances surrounding their disappearance are unexplained, the ambiguity of the final scene firmly positions Shula as a supernatural youth.

Furthermore, a film critic for *The Guardian* suggests that "the motif of women restrained from flight by vast lengths of white ribbon has a touch of Charles Perrault or the [B]rothers Grimm—a magical-realist conceit that brilliantly dramatises the down-to-earth reality of the ties that bind" (Kermode, 2017). Shula's magical transformation of the ribbons from tools of oppression to symbols of freedom is yet another factor that distinguishes her as a supernatural youth.

In addition to magical realism, Nyoni's use of supernaturalism also makes it difficult for reviewers to place this film into one specific genre. In keeping with Norbeck's earlier definition of supernaturalism, Shula's supernatural powers are subtly suggested through her characterization. A mysterious character with unknown origins, Shula's very presence on screen is haunting and ethereal. She rarely speaks and her facial expressions provide little insight into what she is thinking. Since her magic arises from an unknown supernatural source, it is no match for the cruel adults and their human-made beliefs in witchcraft. The supernatural world is on Shula's side; it imbues her with magic so she can free the women. Shula's youth and innocence are precisely what allow her to remain uncorrupted by the power-hungry adults and their patriarchal, misogynistic culture.

Overall, Nyoni's use of magical realism and supernaturalism further complicates genric classification and produces much plot and character ambiguity. These ambiguities heighten not only the potentiality but also the probability of Shula's connection to the supernatural. Nyoni's use of these African traditions also encourages viewers to engage in a willing suspension of disbelief—to believe, as it were, in the impossible. But as the title of the film suggests, Nyoni does not want viewers to believe that Shula is a witch. Rather, she wants them to believe in the possibility of a supernatural youth whose magic works in mysterious and unexplainable ways.

When film critics variously describe *I Am Not a Witch* as a satire, tragicomedy, fantasy, or fairytale, they often add modifiers like feminist, surrealist, absurdist, or cautionary ("I Am Not a Witch," n.d.; Greenwood, 2017; Dalton, 2017; Simpson, 2019). In several interviews, Nyoni acknowledges that she conceived of the film as a fairytale (Kasman, 2017; Lazic, 2018) and, more specifically, a "Zambian fairytale" (Wise, 2018). She also explains that she closely collaborated with cinematographer David Gallego to explicitly make the film "look like a fairytale" (Barber-Plentie, 2017, p. 8). Nyoni's use of recognizable (or known) fairytale tropes familiar to Western viewers and unrecognizable (unknown) fairytale tropes of Zambian fairytales subtly combine to create a powerful film about an African girl who is gifted magical powers to help herself and the other accused witches survive a patriarchal, misogynistic society.

In brief, the recognizable fairytale tropes include the orphaned child, the malevolent witch, the utmost importance of female docility and marriage (which Shula learns from Charity), and the power of magical transformation (e.g., the enchanted ribbons, the symbolism of the goat). Other recognizable fairytale tropes are more subtly represented through the film's evil villains and angry mobs. But Shula does not encounter villains in the familiar form of a cunning wolf or old witch; instead, she confronts villains in human form. The suggestion is that real evil exists not in witches and witchcraft but in humans and their misogyny. As a supernatural youth, Shula uses magic to combat these evil forces.

In addition to recognizable fairytale tropes, Nyoni also employs unrecognizable—to Western viewers, that is—Zambian fairytale tropes in her film. Two such tropes include the mixing of genres and the character of the witch doctor. In an interview with Daniel Kasman (2017) of *Notebook*, Nyoni explains why she depicted her story like a fairytale instead of a realistic account of modern-day witch camps. She observes that she "found a really good Zambian way of saying the story, without making it about Zambia" and that she was trying to get away from the beleaguered "arc" of filmic storytelling (Kasman, 2017). In essence, Nyoni wanted her film to resemble the fairytales that she grew up with; in the Zambian tradition, these unique stories mixed genres and were infused with magical realism.

Like many of her viewers, Nyoni grew up with fairytales and used the specific fairytale tropes of her childhood in her film. Especially interesting is Nyoni's statement that Zambian fairytales mix genres because, again, film critics lack consensus regarding the film's genre. The supposition that this film is not solely a fairytale, but a Zambian fairytale, also speaks to this mixing of genres. Furthermore, in the African worldview, the natural and supernatural are not two separate worlds; instead, like Nyoni's mixing of genres, they "blend and merge together" to form "part of the same world" (White et al., 2021, 52:37; Deme, 2010, pp. 27–8). Perhaps Shula's magical abilities "blend and merge together" in unseen ways in the natural world, so much so that they are undetected by other people in the film (White et al., 2021, 52:37).

Nyoni succeeds in her attempt to defy the typical filmic arc because her fairytale does not conclude with a happy-ever-after. Instead, Shula dies mysteriously, the villains do not get their comeuppance, and the conflicts that the protagonist faced throughout the film are not satisfyingly resolved. This is Nyoni's "Zambian way of saying the story, without making it about Zambia" (Kasman, 2017). Additionally, some viewers are left questioning whether Shula truly has supernatural powers given Nyoni's use of subtlety and ambiguity right up until the very end of the film. None of this is what Western viewers, raised on the Brothers Grimm and Disney, expect from their fairytales.

In the same interview, Nyoni adds that the witch doctor is a popular character in Zambian fairytales (Kasman, 2017). For example, in Parvathi Raman's (1979) *Kalulu the Hare and Other Zambian Folk-Tales*, the witch doctor, Kalulu, figures prominently. In one illustration, Kalulu is clothed in ritual attire; he dances above a near-dead animal and waves a giant feather in the air. The caption reads: "Kalulu made a great show of dancing rhythmically" (Raman, 1979, p. 13). This is similar to the scene where the witch doctor beheads a chicken and performs a ritual dance. He too puts on "a great show" (Raman, 1979, p. 13) not only while he dances, but also when he removes his clothing and repeatedly assures his audience that he is "a real witch doctor" (Nyoni, 2017, 12:47). Furthermore, his ritual attire is nearly identical to Kalulu's clothing. Both witch doctors wave a giant feather in the air and wear a feathered headdress, grass skirt, cowrie necklace, and bangles.

Somewhat relatedly, Nyoni has stated that the white ribbons were her own fairytale invention (Rife, 2018; Bucey, n.d.) inspired by real-life witch camps (Lazic, 2018). A reporter for *Film Journal International* explains that Nyoni's use of this "brilliant magic-realist touch" was inspired by Alphonse Daudet's book *Monsieur Seguin's Goat*—a French fairytale about a farmer and his beloved goat (Garcia, 2018). To protect the goat from a prowling wolf, the farmer ties her to a tree. In her desire for freedom, however, the goat would rather cut the rope that binds her to the farm and run away to live in the mountains where, as the farmer has warned, she will surely be eaten by a wolf. Although the goat puts up a mighty fight against the wolf, she inevitably meets this fate (Sfetcu, 2017). Like the goat, the price for Shula's freedom is her life.

Despite the plethora of fairytale tropes in *I Am Not a Witch*, Western viewers have often failed to see it as a fairytale—let alone a Zambian fairytale. To be sure, the sample size for this claim is relatively small because Nyoni's film is an independent, foreign language film that has had limited distribution and viewership in the United States and other Western countries. Nonetheless, a thorough investigation of the comments sections on Internet Movie Database (IMDb), Rotten Tomatoes, Amazon Prime, and other websites featuring the film reveals three primary, interconnected responses from Western viewers. They contend that the film is confusing, potentially alienating, and decidedly not a fairytale.

On Amazon Prime, a reviewer named Elijah ended his five-star review by stating: "Side Note: I didn't see this as a 'satiric feminist fairy-tale'" ("Do Not Allow Yourself," 2019). Here Elijah is disagreeing with the specific film description provided by Film Movement (the film's North American distributor) and often repeated in the press. On IMDb, David speaks to white, Western viewers' expectations of the film and their potential confusion and alienation from it. He writes that its "long, lingering shots [are] asking us—especially the white, Western observer, just what it is we are waiting or expecting to see" (Meldrum, 2019). He then suggests that Nyoni "runs the risk [of] alienating the more casual Western viewer" with some of her directorial choices (Meldrum, 2019). An unnamed Metacritic reviewer echoes these claims when they write that viewers will be confused by the film's end and that "it is not something that would be easily understood or easily appreciated for its vagueness" ("Beautiful," 2018). Overall, Western viewers seem unable to understand the film as the Zambian fairytale that Nyoni intended since it does not traffic solely or plainly in Western fairytale tropes.

Other Western viewers have also struggled to see the film as a fairytale because fairytales, whether the traditional Brothers Grimm tales or the Disney films, are depicted quite differently in Western countries. For three semesters, I have taught Nyoni's film in my Fairytale and Fantasy course at Niagara University, a small, private, liberal arts college near Niagara Falls, New York. Despite being immersed in traditional and contemporary fairytales for almost an entire semester, my undergraduate students often find it difficult to identify the fairytale tropes in the film. Aside from the familiar figure of the witch, they are nonplussed by Nyoni's assertion that her film is a fairytale because it does not resemble any of the fairytales they grew up with and still enjoy watching. This can be attributed to two factors. First, *I Am Not a Witch* is a foreign language film set in a non-Western country. It features a mostly African and Black cast and was written and directed by an African and Black woman. Second, the majority of my students are white and, growing up, they were exposed to media that largely prioritized the stories of white women and girls. The same is true for my students of color. As a result, my students, and many online reviewers, reject the notion that this film is a fairytale.

Lastly, it is quite possible that Western viewers would initially fail to recognize Shula as a supernatural youth because they are unaccustomed to the reality of a young, Black heroine with supernatural powers. (See also Chapter 10 by Winfield et al. in this volume.) They are unprepared for the supernatural heroism of a young, Black girl who sacrifices her life—not for the white protagonist, but for other Black women. Far too often, Black girls like Rue in *The Hunger Games* film (2012) and Bonnie the witch on *The Vampire Diaries* (2009–17) are represented as "sacrificial victims" who die while trying to help their white friends (Thomas, 2019, p. 47).

In *The Dark Fantastic: Race and the Imagination from Harry Potter to the Hunger Games*, Ebony Elizabeth Thomas (2019) argues that the West is suffering from a widespread "diversity crisis in children's and young adult media" which she refers to as an "imagination gap" (p. 5). In Western literature, television, and film, young Black girls are often positioned as Dark Others in the fantasy genre due to the imagination gaps of their white creators and largely white audiences (pp. 4–7). In such roles, Black girls are often the only characters of color on the page or screen, and they are the antagonists or supporting characters in stories that center young white girls. Hence Thomas contends that white people especially have unconsciously and uncritically developed Eurocentric and Western worldviews that define and thereby limit their understandings of the role that race plays in the fantasy genre.

Thomas' theories can be applied to Western viewers whose geographic and cultural locations prevent them from seeing Nyoni's film as the fairytale she intended, in addition to those viewers who may not recognize Shula as a supernatural heroine. Nyoni's film is incredibly significant, therefore, because it tells relatively new stories about Black girls and the supernatural. Significantly, *I Am Not a Witch* was written and directed by a Zambian-Welsh woman; the film is set in a remote African village; the protagonist is a Black, African girl; and the supporting characters are mostly Black, African women.

Through its writing, directing, and casting, Nyoni's film can be understood as engaging in the complex project of "emancipating the imagination"

(Thomas, 2019, p. 29). The imagination in question is multiple and can include Western and African viewers alike such as: the imaginations of those who view Nyoni's film, especially young people who, as Thomas argues, need to see more racial diversity in literature and popular culture; the imaginations of those who view Nyoni's film and then proceed to emancipate their own and others' imaginations through their own creative works; and perhaps Nyoni's own imagination since she was born in Zambia, raised in Wales, and attended college in England. Recall that Nyoni was trying to move away from the traditional arc of filmmaking with her debut film. Her film demonstrates not only a movement away from the arc of Western films, but also the arc of Western fairytales. As argued throughout this chapter, Nyoni has created her own arc, and her own distinctly African fairytale, through her inconspicuous use of Western and Zambian fairytale tropes, in addition to her subtle characterization of Shula as a supernatural youth who, in her innocence and benevolence, is gifted magic to survive and liberate others. In these ways, she has also created her own supernatural heroine.

In this chapter, I have examined the ways in which Shula is prefigured as a supernatural youth through Nyoni's use of African belief systems and African conventions of storytelling. These African traditions rely on subtlety and produce various ambiguities related to the plot and its protagonist—all of which reinforce Shula's positioning as a supernatural youth. Moreover, these traditions create distinct challenges inside and outside of the film related to its story, genre, and reception. The storytelling conventions create a cultural divide wherein European-Americans are unable to understand Nyoni's film as the fairytale she intended. Firmly placed within recent trends in African cinema, I have argued that Nyoni relies on these traditions to subtly position Shula as a supernatural youth whose benevolence and innocence make her morally superior to those who oppress her. The film suggests that youth-magic is real magic and that it defies adult understanding. It is mysterious, unknowable, and seems to be gifted only to the young and innocent for the benign purpose of surviving a patriarchal, misogynistic society. Shula's magic is presented as a corrective to the real-world corruption and cruelty of adults, and it thus serves as a feminist indictment of witch camps and oppressive social practices. With its Black and African writer-director and cast, and its African setting, traditions, and storyline, *I Am Not a Witch* is a necessary intervention into a Western media landscape that largely fails to represent the full humanity of Black women and girls and to show Black girls as heroines.

Note

1 For the purposes of this chapter, the supernatural is defined as "all that is not natural, that which is regarded as extraordinary, not of the ordinary world, mysterious or unexplainable in ordinary terms" (Norbeck, 1961, as cited in Petrus & Bogopa, 2007, p. 2). In contrast, witchcraft, particularly in African communities, is generally understood as the use of psychic or other powers for evil or harmful intent (Petrus & Bogopa, 2007, pp. 2–3). Therefore, the terms witchcraft and supernatural are not used synonymously, or viewed as mutually constitutive, in this chapter. They are considered distinct entities in the context of this particular film and film analysis.

References

Adejunmobi, M. (2017). Mediating religion: Daniel Fagunwa, Mike Bamiloye, and JK Rowling. *Celebrating DO Fagunwa*. Bookcraft.

Barber-Plentie, G. (2017, November). I put a spell on you. *Sight and Sound, 27*(11), 8–9. https://www.proquest.com/magazines/i-put-spell-on-you/docview/1961360496/se-2

Beautiful, but uncomfortably confusing. (2018, November 25). Review by smijatov89 of I am not a witch, directed by R. Nyoni. *Metacritic*. https://www.metacritic.com/user/smijatov

Bucey, M. (n.d.). I am not a witch. *Spirituality and Practice*. https://www.spiritualityandpractice.com/films/reviews/view/28625/i-am-not-a-witch

Carrier, D. (2017). Zambian-set tragicomedy of superstition and exploitation. *Camden New Journal*. https://www.camdennewjournal.co.uk/article/zambian-set-tragicomedy-of-superstition-and-exploitation

Chouraqui, F. (2021). *The body and embodiment: A philosophical guide*. Rowman & Littlefield.

Dalton, S. (2017, October 18). I am not a witch: We're in a time when it's fashionable to get Black female directors. *British Film Institute*. https//www.bfi.org.uk/interviews/i-am-not-witch-interview-rungano-nyoni

Deme, M. K. (2010, April 1). The supernatural in African epic traditions as a reflection of the religious beliefs of African societies. *Studies in World Christianity*. https://doi.org/10.3366/E1354990110000730

"Do not allow yourself to become allergic to comfort." (2019, April 7). Review by Elijah of I am not a witch, directed by R. Nyoni, *Amazon Prime*. https://www.amazon.com/gp/customer-reviews/r1gf0jrxq2ewg1/ref=cm_cr_getr_d_rvw_ttl?-ie=utf8&asin=b07klg6jpr

Epstein, R., Blake, J., & González, T. (2017, June 27). *Girlhood interrupted: The erasure of black girls' childhood*. Center on Poverty and Inequality, Georgetown University. https://doi.org/10.2139/ssrn.3000695

Garcia, M. (2018, September 6). Film review: I am not a witch. *Film Journal International*. https://www.fj.webedia.us/reviews/film-review-i-am-not-witch

Greenwood, D. (2017, June 2). The film about feminism and witchcraft that you need to see. *Another Magazine*. https://www.anothermag.com/design-living/9888/the-film-about-feminism-and-witchcraft-that-you-need-to-see

Hall, S. (2018, April 18). I am not a witch review: Grotesque fantasy is sadly plausible. *Sydney Morning Herald*. https://www.smh.com.au/entertainment/movies/i-am-not-a-witch-review-grotesque-fantasy-is-sadly-plausible-20180418-h0ywzc.html

Harrow, K. W. (2024). *African cinema in a global age*. Routledge.

I Am Not A Witch. (n.d.). *Film movement*. https://www.filmmovement.com/product/i-am-not-a-witch

Kasman, D. (2017, May 31). A Zambian fairy tale: Rungano Nyoni discusses her debut I am not a witch. *Notebook*. https://www.mubi.com/notebook/posts/a-zambian-fairy-tale-rungano-nyoni-discusses-her-debut-i-am-not-a-witch

Kermode, M. (2017, October 22). I am not a witch review—Magical realism. *The Guardian*. https://www.theguardian.com/film/2017/oct/22/i-am-not-a-witch-review-magical-surrealism-margaret-mulubwa-rungano-nyoni

Lazic, E. (2018, March 2). Director Rungano Nyoni on her Zambia-set debut I am not a witch. *Seventh Row*. https://www.seventh-row.com/2018/03/02/rungano-nyoni-talks-i-am-not-a-witch/

Luongo, K. (2020). Film review: I am not a witch. *African Studies Review*, *63*(1), E38–9. https://doi.org/10.1017/asr.2019.64

Meldrum, D. (2019, January 13). Artful, funny and gently powerful—promising debut. Review of I am not a witch, directed by R. Nyoni. *Internet Movie Database [I.M.D.B.]*. https://www.imdb.com/title/tt6213284/reviews

Norbeck, E. (1961). *Religion in primitive society*. Harper & Brothers.

Nyoni, R. (Director). (2017). *I am not a witch* [Film]. Curzon Artificial Eye.

Obenson, T. (2018, September 17). I am not a witch: How a satire about misogyny is transforming Zambia's film industry. *Indiewire*. https://www.indiewire.com/2018/09/i-am-not-a-witch-rungano-nyoni-interview-zambia-1201999906/

Page, T. (2017, May 29). I am not a witch: Film explores plight of Zambians accused of witchcraft. *CNN*. https://www.cnn.com/2017/05/29/africa/cannes-i-am-not-a-witch-rungano-nyoni/index.html

Petrus, T. S., & Bogopa, D. L. (2007). Natural and supernatural: Intersections between the spiritual and natural worlds in African witchcraft and healing with reference to Southern Africa. *Indo-Pacific Journal of Phenomenology*, *7*(1), 1–10. https://doi.org/10.1080/20797222.2007.11433943

Raman, P. (1979). *Kalulu the hare and other Zambian folk-tales*, retold and illustrated by Parvathi Raman, A.H. Stockwell.

Riddle, A. (2020). Nature and the supernatural in African literature. *African Identities*, *18*(1–2), pp. 80–94. https://doi.org/10.1080/14725843.2020.1773238

Rife, K. (2018, September 7). Tradition and technology collide in the spellbinding, bone-dry satire of I am not a witch. *AV Club*. https://www.avclub.com/tradition-and-technology-collide-in-the-spellbinding-b-1828889737

Sfetcu, N. (2017, February 7). The goat of Mr. Seguin, by Alphonse Daudet. *MultiMedia*. https://www.telework.ro/en/goat-mr-seguin-alphonse-daudet/

Simpson, N. (2019, May 23). Revisiting surreal absurdist fairytale "I am not a witch" two years on. *Headstuff*. https://www.headstuff.org/entertainment/film/i-am-not-a-witch-review/

Thomas, E. E. (2019). *The dark fantastic: Race and the imagination from Harry Potter to the Hunger Games*. New York UP.

Walton, S. (2018). Cruising the unknown: Film as rhythm and embodied apprehension in L'inconnu du lac/Stranger by the lake (2013). *New Review of Film and Television Studies*, *16*(3), 238–263. https://doi.org/10.1080/17400309.2018.1479183

White, M. (Host), Deighan, S., & Seams, S (Guest co-hosts). (2021, August 25). I am not a witch (No. 535) [Audio podcast episode]. In *Projection Booth*. Weirding Way Media. https://www.projectionboothpodcast.com/2021/08/episode-535-i-am-not-witch-2017.html

Wise, D. (2018, February 16). I am not a witch director Rungano Nyoni worked with non-professionals overseas on super-ambitious Zambian fairy tale. *Deadline*. https://www.deadline.com/2018/02/i-am-not-a-witch-rungano-nyoni-baftas-interview-news-1202291631/

Part III

Confronting Exclusions in Supernatural Identities

10

Where Are All of the Black Kids?: A Contemporary Search for Black Youth in the Fantastic World

ASHA WINFIELD, MEGHAN SANDERS, ROCKIA HARRIS, HOPE HICKERSON, AND TIFFANY R. SMITH

With so many fantasy worlds and alternate realities in our current media landscape, one must wonder where the Black children are. In this chapter, we ask: *Where are the supernatural, superpowerful, magical, and brilliant Black children and youth[1] in contemporary fantasy media?* In our systematic and introspective review, we located two major types of fantasy worlds where Black children and youth thrive: supernatural (magical) and superpowered (imbued with powers from scientific means or STEM brilliance rather than mysticism). We differentiate between superpowered and supernatural youth, leaning on the conceptualization that anything framed as scientific, by definition, cannot be "supernatural," which is mystical. Ultimately, this text explores historical and contemporary, satisfactory and limited examples of Black youth in fantasy worlds while also interrogating how the presence of Black youth has come with conditions and consequences—genetically modified (*Raising Dion, Naomi, Black Lightning*); supernatural (*Wednesday, Chilling Adventures of Sabrina*); STEM-based (*See You Yesterday, Jingle Jangle*); while also addressing the material and historical consequences of race relations in their real and imagined worlds. For superpowered and supernatural Black youth, not saving the world or someone in it could lead to hyperinvisibility or erasure of their issues, particularly if their issues intersect race, age, and gender on the margins.

For this project, we utilized Ebony E. Thomas' (2019) "dark fantastic" theory to consider the presence, absence, and characterization of Black youth in fantastic worlds, including contemporary television, streaming series, and films. We noted Black youths' patterns of representation, and we critically interrogated their significant underrepresentation. In our introspective analysis of each genre, we found that Black children are present in media about the superpowered, often deriving superpowers from a physical object or a genetic modification—but noted they are more absent—less centered—in narratives specifically focused on the magical and supernatural, in which powers are an inexplicable gift without roots in scientific or sci-fi sources. But both sci-fi and fantasy yield an inadequate number of narratives focused on Black youth.

As context for these findings, we begin this chapter by examining the literature on stereotypes and the psychological effects of seeing Black bodies and specifically, Black youth in futuristic, imaginative, sci-fi, and fantasy roles. We then turn to an in-depth explanation of our introspective analysis of contemporary Black youth characters, in which we detail our findings that these works are characterized by the presence of (1) Black joy, (2) Black brilliance, (3) genetic mutations, and (4) Black tributes and sacrifices. In addition to those major recurring themes, we discuss additional findings: (a) the decentering of magical Black girls in fantasy worlds; (b) the significance of portraying Black youth as having gained superpowers via genetic and familial mutations; and (c) these texts' depictions of Black brilliance as both a natural occurrence and a superpower used for saving the world.

As we undertook this project, we were informed by a shared concern that Black children are not allowed in the imaginative, speculative, mainstream spaces of media where freedom and creativity thrive. We asked ourselves: What are the implications of this omission? This crucial question led to our critical interrogation as reported in this chapter, as well as our search for Black children in media spaces as sources of new representations and portrayals transcending stereotypes that have persisted for more than a century. We differentiate our findings into two groups: satisfactory and limited presentations. For us, a satisfactory presentation of Black youth in fantastic worlds allows the children to explore their supernatural or superpowered experience in its fullness (full of joy, limitlessness, and freedom of youth expressions) without the adultification presented in many limited examples that force Black youth to solve society's identity issues (e.g., race, sex, gender, sexuality, religion, class). We specifically seek representations that avoid problematic stereotypes, for research has shown that Black children's self-concept can be significantly affected by the representations they see of their own identities on screen.

Our work is a departure from previous studies, as it adds to the conversation of fantastic worlds with Black youth, and more specifically looks at their characterizations in contemporary media and popular culture. While many of the media texts we examine have ended their seasons, have been canceled, or were singular films that are not part of a larger series, we make space for those stories as valuable media texts.

Stereotypes, Counter-Storytelling, and Psychological Impacts

Many psychological theories and models explain the effects of stereotypes, and also how, when and why we may use them (Sanders & Whitenack, 2019). For example, cultivation theory proposes that time spent consuming media content is associated with how similarly we perceive the real world to be with the mediated one (Busselle & Van den Bulck, 2019). Extant research has found that in the context of news consumption, this often translates into audience beliefs that Black individuals are threatening, violent, perpetrators of crime, are less educated, and have lower income levels (Dixon & Linz, 2000). Historically, in terms of fantasy and science fiction literature, this may translate into audience beliefs that Black individuals are either marginal to the story, are the key antagonists, or are the text's "personified, embodies, and most assuredly racialized" darkness, ultimately serving as metaphors for the value (or devaluation) of Black individuals in society (Thomas, 2019, p. 20).

Theories such as social identity and self-categorization argue that social categories such as racial and ethnic identity are important aspects to a person's self-concept. In an effort to establish self and collective worth, individuals compare favorable characteristics of the group to unfavorable characteristics of a similar and proximate outgroup (Fiske & Taylor, 1991). To take this a step further, social categorization theory argues that media can trigger emotionally relevant and accessible categories for an individual, drawing closer connections to not just group identity, but personal identity as well. Media representations can encourage and nurture the need for positive social and personal identities (Trepte & Loy, 2017). In this case, positive representations hold the ability to bolster psychological well-being, individual and collective esteem. Black audiences may turn to fantastical worlds to see Black heroism, strength, positive political messaging and the range of possibilities that exist for themselves to become more than what may be possible in the real world, depending on their own lived experiences.

Traditional narratives may marginalize characters of color or otherwise present allegories, metaphors, and entities (e.g. dark forces, werewolves, witches, etc.) that allude to people of color in negative ways, but audience members may even reclaim these with additional perspective. Thomas (2019) identifies this as the *dark fantastic*, referring to racial difference's importance in the consumption and interpretation of written and mediated fantasy fiction in the genres of fairy tales, superhero comics, science fiction and other imagined worlds. *The Dark Fantastic* presents a critical race counter-storytelling in which racialized, sometimes embodied characters become the focal point from which the story is told. In such counter-storytellings, racialized characters cease to be the danger, the violence, the challenge, the thing to be feared and thus violently destroyed, and the object that must be overcome in order to protect the natural order of things and the light (e.g. whiteness). Instead, racialized characters become fully realized characters, through which cultures are represented and new stories are told—through which readers of color can find themselves whole and centralized to the story. They are not incidental to the story; rather, the story cannot exist without them.

The most recent wave of fantasy narratives features an array of counter-stereotypes, representations that challenge widely held beliefs about a given group. From a psychological perspective, they are impactful because they move marginalized groups to the center of narratives, and they allow audiences to see heterogeneity of experiences and individuals that exist within various social groups (Ramasubramanian et al., 2020). These presentations thus serve as counterpoints to stereotyped beliefs (see Tan et al., 2000). Often, scholars cite Marvel's *Black Panther* and related films as offering critical and important counter-stereotypical representations of Black people within superhero narratives (El-Nasir et al, 2021). In *Black Panther*, audiences saw images of a prosperous, technologically advanced African nation with critical value to an entire narrative universe. Sanders and Banjo (2022) found that for white and non-Black adult audiences, the impact of the film's counter-stereotypes were associated with perceptions about power and status of Black Americans. Likewise, González-Velázquez et al. (2020) found some connection between viewing the film and feelings of empowerment and self-esteem among youth of color.

Though the primary audiences for content featuring fantastic children may not indeed be children, the effects of limited, lacking, and/or absent representation have substantial effects on child audiences. Media scholars have found that underrepresentation is associated with lower self-esteem, internalization of negative perceptions, or even lack of power and ability to influence the world around them (Sanders & Banjo, 2013). As Xie (1999) argued, if one considers racial/ethnic "Otherness" in the context of postcolonialism, children are the most impacted and negatively impacted by colonialist ideas because they are in their formative years. This places even more importance on characters like the titular *Naomi* (2021), a teenage girl who finds out she is from another Earth, with different parents and superpowers; and Dion (*Raising Dion*, 2019–2022) whose genetics were altered forever after this late father was in a scientific accident that gave him super-powers. For child audiences, stories featuring dynamic, non-stereotypical, non-fetishized Black characters and cultures can improve their self-esteem and their belief in their own abilities (Bandura, 1982; Stroman, 1986). Black children have historically used comics' narratives in particular as a source for observing Black heroism and strength, as well as a vehicle through which to see the potential to become something bigger than themselves (Howard & Jackson, 2014). With this in mind, our research team sought to find, list, and describe the satisfactory and limited presentations of Black youth in the fantastic worlds in contemporary media.

An Introspective Analysis of Black Youth in Fantasy Worlds

For this chapter, the research team used an introspective analysis after an extensive online search yielded limited results for Black youth in contemporary media (television series and film) on cable, networks, premium, and streaming services. Our inclusion criteria helped us to answer the guiding research question: how is contemporary media portraying supernatural and superpowered Black children over the last two decades? First, we searched on Internet Movie Database (IMDb) for Black American children, youth, in the last 23 years (2000–2023) in "Feature films," "TV specials," "TV series," and "TV episodes" with genres "action," "family," "comedy," "horror," "mystery," "sci-fi," "adventure," "fantasy," "animation," and "thriller" in the United States in the English language for a more systematic review of titles. Those results yielded only one title and without Black children. We altered the search to remove "horror" and yielded 139 titles including only 3 series. After adjusting the search measures again for only "fantasy" titles between 2000–2023, we yielded 4,798 titles, with no way to decipher if those titles featured and centered Black children within the advanced search. However, the search yielded recent and popular titles like *The Little Mermaid* (2023) remake starring Halle Bailey and *Spider-Man: Across the Spider-Verse* (2023). At first scan, it appears that scientifically [em]powered Black youth are seen in science fiction programs like *Black Panther*, *Black Lightning*, and *Raising Dion*.

After reviewing the titles, we categorized the titles into the most recurring themes (Black joy, Black STEM brilliance, genetic mutations, Black tribute/sacrifices) where Black children are centered in fantasy worlds. Each author chose a media text and genre on which to perform an introspective analysis (Stamps, 2021). According to previous studies, an "introspective analysis allows researchers to examine specific issues to gain a greater understanding of their application in society, highlighting marginalized experiences" (Stamps, 2021; p. 106; Elo & Kyngas, 2008). Our findings are separated by genres and themes where Black youth are presented even if in limited ways.

Decentered Magical Girls: Prudence and Bianca

A recent example of the dark fantastic is the character of Bianca on the Netflix streaming series, *Wednesday*. Initially presented as a foil or antagonist to the main character, Bianca is everything Wednesday is not. Even their physical appearances present a strong juxtaposition: Wednesday is white with very pale skin and very dark, long hair that emphasizes her whiteness while Bianca has a very dark complexion and wears her natural hair cut close to the scalp (a fade). She is a siren with stunning good looks and the power to entrance others to do her bidding. Bianca (whose name means "white" and "pure" in Italian) is very popular and as one of the strongest Nevermore Academy students, she is almost fearfully respected. She is even referred to as a queen whose crown is slipping, presumably into Wednesday's reluctantly waiting hands. The two young women regularly compete against one another in and outside of the classroom, each experiencing wins and losses. While the series writers do not tell the narrative from her perspective, they allow viewers to see more of the narrative world from her vantage point as the series progresses. Bianca confides to Wednesday her worries of never trusting anyone's true nature because she is a siren. Viewers learn that Bianca is hiding from her mother, who previously coerced her into using their joined siren songs to swindle others. She later advises the mayor's son, a character who regularly antagonized and played cruel jokes on Nevermore students, to avoid a mobile app designed by her mother to target victims more easily. Even though in an early episode Wednesday explicitly tells Bianca that she isn't better than everyone, just Bianca, by the end of the series it is abundantly clear that

Wednesday could not have succeeded in saving the Nevermore students from a deadly threat without having Bianca as an ally. So, whether an application of the dark fantastic or simply good character development, Bianca ceases to become the danger or threat to the protagonist, the obstacle that Wednesday must outwit. Bianca is a well-rounded, complex character that viewers are allowed to connect with and develop empathy for.

In another recent example, Netflix's *The Chilling Adventures of Sabrina* (2018–2020), Prudence Blackwood, a teen witch presents another limited presentation. Prudence, played by Tati Gabrielle, is a biracial teenage girl, and leader of a trio of mean girls called the weird sisters. Her father, Father Blackwood, is the leader of the Church of the Night and together they are antagonists to the series lead, Sabrina. In the first season, Prudence is set against Sabrina and often causes Sabrina great pain in her maturation into a young witch (particularly when Sabrina transfers to another academy). However, even in their complex relationship, writers create a nuance in Prudence's character where she fights for other young women when she is not their nemesis.

In fact, when Sabrina wants to enact revenge on a group of teen boys whose bigotry and sexism lead to violence against one of the high school girls, she asks Prudence and the weird sisters for their help. Prudence and the other girls lure the teenage boys into a cave and use their sexuality to trick the boys into a serious make-out session with each other. Before they realize they have been duped, Sabrina takes a picture and Prudence removes some of their physical abilities leaving them impotent.

Prudence is characterized as oversexual, a bully, evil, and cruel—all of which play on many of the historical stereotypes for Black women. Prudence believes that she and other girls must give up their freedom in order to have power and to her, power is the most important. Most interesting in Part One of the series is the insistence of Prudence calling Sabrina a "half-breed" because of her witch and mortal ancestry and for this she hates Sabrina and offers her nothing beyond jealousy, violence, torture, and torment. Prudence may offer us a contemporary feminist media reading of today's magical media landscape, but falls short in Black youth presentations making her a limited presentation. This does not mean that we believe she has to be a good character in order to be a satisfactory presentation but her secondary roles as antagonist, with historical stereotypes does not present her as free and full. In contrast, Sabrina's best friend, Roz is another Black teenage girl with connections to the Christian church. Roz's characterization is not that of a witch in the first season but later Roz is revealed as a Sentinel or Seer, another type of witch. Roz is another secondary character but the depth of her characterization and stereotypical casting is much more satisfactory, though still limited.

From Familial Genetic Mutations to Unexplainable Accidents: Black Superpowers

Within the last five years, mass audiences have seen a number of Black youth whose creative imaginations can only be matched by their youthful, sometimes uncontrollable, recently discovered superpowers. In this section, we briefly discuss mainstream media's Black youth whose powers were gained through gene-altering accidents occurring in their parents. CW's *Black Lightning* and *Naomi*, and Netflix's *Raising Dion* are three examples of young Black superheroes whose quest to learn more about their powers is also a discovery into their young, growing selves.

Raising Dion (2019–2022) features a young Black child, Dion, who realizes he has superpowers. His mother, Nicole, a widow and now single parent, fights to keep her joyful and excited young son safe from the harms of the world while also allowing him to enjoy the youthful adventures of his imaginative superhero life with his band of friends. Unfortunately, his father's untimely death is what endows Dion with power and places him in the line of fire from governmental forces and The Crooked Man, who want to capture, study, and destroy the young boy. While Dion enjoys traveling through the city with teleportation, making fish fly with his thoughts alone, and freezing objects in motion, his existence as a super-powered young Black boy makes him a double target in the fictional, fantasy world where he exists.

In another example, *Naomi* features a young Black teenager's discovery of her own superhero abilities as she and her friends search for answers about a battle between Superman and an unknown foe that occurs in the center of her hometown. Further, her previously unknown powers, which include super-hearing, x-ray vision, clairvoyance, and invulnerability, are activated by this event. Her abilities are considered magically supernatural by those on Earth, but we later learn that Naomi is an alien from an alternative Earth. The audience sees other aliens, living in plain sight, attempting to help her discover and strengthen her powers, while her human friends help solve mysterious happenings in town. Like other superhero aliens (e.g. Superman, Supergirl, etc.), Naomi seeks to learn about her past and heritage, driving her to search for a true sense of home. However, her road to the truth is full of deception and betrayals by those she most trusts and considers family. Naomi is not able to enjoy her youth or her powers because she is constantly burdened with the well-being of others. These truths, in a sense, leave her orphaned again which is an outcome not often experienced by other youths in the DC Universe. Naomi's characterization is satisfactory as she is removed from earthly stereotypes and her fight is for her own truth versus society's evil; she is the main character and her deep characterization allows her freedom on her journey.

In the final example, we highlight the daughters of *Black Lightning* and their hybrid presentation of satisfactory and limited presentation of Black youth in fantastic worlds. Inside of this family of superheroes (or masked vigilantes, depending on your perspective) is Black Lightning/Jefferson Pierce and his daughters, Anissa/Thunder and Jennifer/Lightning—who recently discovered their abilities to produce light, power, and super strength, as well. They seek to right racist, systemic, and institutional oppressions in their fictional town of Freeland, Georgia. The Pierce sisters are empowered by genetic mutations from their father, who was a part of a city-wide spread of power-inducing drugs from his youth. With the help of the scientific genius of their mother, Lynn, Thunder (Anissa) and Lightning (Jennifer) are charged with powers and support from within, and without. The sisters are also assisted by Uncle Gambi who has a secret lair of technological advancements and security. Between fighting the organized crime of Tobias Whale, The 100, the A.S.A, and the local government, the sisters find joy in the regenerative power of the atmosphere. Much like their names, Thunder and Lightning are too powerful to be ignored but fight to remain invisible to society to keep their families and friends safe from the harms of their visibility.

So far, we have explored the Black youth characters who are present in the fantasy world and yet lacking the joy of youthfulness and their magic and power. This is not to say that the Black teens in *Black Lightning* don't find a smile in the sky where their thunder is recharged, or that Dion doesn't laugh at his teleportation powers but those same powers he enjoys also removed his father from this world. The Black youth feel the weight of the power their superidentities bring.

Black STEM Brilliance as a "Superpower"

In other examples of fantasy media, Black youth are depicted as possessing special "powers," but without the presence of magic added to their genius: a brilliant intelligence with science, technology, engineering, or math. Recent examples include the young women of the fictional Wakanda: Shuri in *Black Panther* (2018) and Riri Williams from *Black Panther: Wakanda Forever* (2022), as well as the characters of CJ from Netflix's *See You Yesterday* and Journey from the Netflix family film *Jingle Jangle: A Christmas Journey*. In each case, the heroines demonstrate exceptional scientific knowledge, but with mixed results of being satisfactory or limited. In the *Black Panther* movies, the scientifically gifted Shuri and Riri are older teenagers, closer to adulthood than the other characters discussed in this chapter so far—illustrating the necessary space for younger Black youth representation to fill. One reviewer described Shuri as having "a Nobel Prize mind for devising medical treatments, weapons and gadgets galore" (Breznican, 2018, p. 28). To witness Shuri and Riri in their elements is almost like a "magic" or colloquially referred to as "Black girl magic." For some Black youth audiences, to simply see Black young women successfully wielding scientific, intellectual power was "magical" and inspiring for those in similar fields. It contrasts with typical non-fiction narratives in which high-achieving Black women's intellectual aptitude is unacknowledged, instead presented within the context of grim realities and oppressive social structures (Bucciferro, 2021). Shuri's intellectual aptitude is loud, bold, and unapologetic, creating a sense of "superheroism" through her confidence and agency (Reed, 2018). For our team, we find STEM-related superpowered youth present a more complex, nuanced, well-rounded and joyous presentation of Black youth. We also recognize that not all STEM-related superpowered youth are satisfactory; some brilliant Black youth are still required to right the wrongs of society and save loved ones from ultimate defeat.

In another example, Netflix's *See You Yesterday* shows high school students Claudette "CJ" Walker and her best friend, Sebastian, use scientific abilities to time-travel to an incident that took the lives of her brother and her best friend. With CJ's youthful spirit, brilliant mind, and loyal character, audiences see her capable of taking on society's problems, mirroring the superwoman or strong Black woman stereotype (Donovan & West, 2014). However, a deeper look at CJ's characterization reveals both her joys inside the inner city and her intentional use of intelligence as a weapon of freedom and resistance (Winfield, 2020). Ultimately, these Black teenage girls became the communities' saviors, providing representation for Black girls and engaging their stories; but at the same time, it perpetuates the strong Black women trope, placing it on Black girls who are mourning and seeking survival in a sci-fi land ravaged by colonialism, violence, death, and racist ideologies.

But we do see a Black girl portrayed with childlike innocence, *and* exceptional STEM intelligence, in *Jingle Jangle: A Christmas Journey*. The protagonist, Journey, is a young girl filled with confidence, intelligence, persistence, and swag. Her story offers a joyful counterpoint to those found in mainstream news media, where reports abound of both police brutality against Black bodies and political warfare against teaching critical race theory to youth, causing emotional stress, psychological triggers, fatigue, and other negative emotional responses (Hawkins, 2021; Hickerson & Stamps, 2023). Counteracting the trauma of real-world on-screen news, *Jingle Jangle: A Christmas Journey* offers a story of joy, triumph, and peaceful existence in this world, with a Black a child at the center.

Set in a town heavily inspired by steampunk, *Jingle Jangle* is the tale of Journey inspiring her toymaker/inventor grandfather and bringing an entire town back to life after both lost their hope and "spark." As an inventor herself, Journey both taps into magic and unapologetically leans into her intelligence, confidence and creativity, finding joy in math and science—a compelling portrayal, as young girls tend to lose confidence in math abilities by third grade, despite initially having greater STEM career aspirations than peer boys ("The STEM gap," 2022). As a result, Journey's portrayal as proficient at math/science is powerful. The Christmas magic she returns to her grandfather's inventions is both literal and metaphorical. Journey knows how smart she is and isn't afraid to show it. She expresses her desires and dreams and actively goes after them, and as her story lacks the adultification common in stories about Black girls ("Research Confirms that Black Girls," 2019), child-like wonder permeates her on-screen world. Finding it a soothing balm against the painful realities that some must endure, we argue that the media landscape needs more stories with characters like Journey, to show that trauma is not inevitable for Black people.

Given the real paucity of Black youth with magical or superpowers, we also examined sci-fi and fantasy media with young Black characters who do not embody special powers. In some cases, Black youth in such roles exist to be sacrificed; their deaths make them special. This is the case with the character of Rue, close friend of the heroine Katniss in the novel and film series *The Hunger Games* (2012–2015), a science-fiction adventure that shows a dystopian future where citizens compete in fatal games for survival (Calta, 2014; Washington & Washington, 2015). When Rue is killed in the games, her death has narrative importance, and her innocence and humanity are signaled by Katniss' honor of her death by placing flowers around Rue's body (Collins, 2024). This serves as a more positive counternarrative of the established stereotypes and norms of how Black death and murder, especially of little Black girls, are mourned. Scholars assert that Black girls are stereotyped as being more independent, wiser about adult topics like sex, and less in need of protection, support, and comfort than white girls (Epstein et al., 2017). Such stereotypes rob Black girls of the opportunity to be seen as innocent children (Morris, 2016; Muhammad & Haddix,

2016; Sealey-Ruiz, 2016), so *The Hunger Games* gives a mixture of satisfying and limited messages about Black youth.

Disney + Pixar's Black Princesses

Disney is a top animation studio, known for crafting fantasies where children and adults gain life lessons through distinctive obstacles. Despite their positive reputations, in our analysis, we quickly noticed the lack of Black youth in the Disney/Pixar worlds, locating them only in princess roles: Tiana in *The Princess and the Frog* (2009), which presented the first Black Disney princess and was the first animated film with a Black lead; and the live-action version of *The Little Mermaid* (2023), which reimagined Ariel as a Black mermaid.

In *The Princess and the Frog*, a majority Black cast shares New Orleans' culture and a tale of magical kisses. Unfortunately, one such kiss turns lead character Tiana into a frog early in the film, and she spends the vast majority of it in this alternative form. Tiana's screen time in frog form reflects an ongoing problem at Disney, and its subsidiary Pixar, too. In their feature films, Black leads are too often portrayed as animals, lessening these characters' physical value and agency. This trope is seen in productions including *Brother Bear, The Emperor's New Groove, Soul,* and *Spies in Disguise* (2019). Like these films' Black adult characters, once Tiana is transformed into a frog, she is no longer subjected to the societal issues she faces while living in her physical Black body. So, while in some ways one could argue that Black youth representation occurs in *The Princess and the Frog*, invisibility and erasure also occur. We are left to conclude that movies, even feature films and animated entertainments, do a mediocre job at portraying Black characters as they often replace them with animals or limit their roles.

When Tiana returns to her human form, it is due to her compelled dependence on her non-black co-lead—a problem across several of these films, in which the co-leads are essentially white saviors, heroes who save Black characters from tragedy (Murphy & Harris, 2018). Given this pervasive problem, Tiana's case in context makes clear that we need more Black animations that allow Black youth (and adults) to exist in their Black bodies and identities. In contrast to the problems of *The Princess and the Frog*, *The Little Mermaid* (2023) spotlights a young heroine whose racial identity is neither erased nor the center of the narrative. In the live-action remake, we see Halle Bailey portray an Ariel who experiences joy, new adventures, and love both in mermaid form and after turning into a human being.

While Bailey's depiction of a Black mermaid sparked triumph and jubilation for many viewers, it also drew controversy similar to that which surrounded Rue in *The Hunger Games:* Some audience members could not fathom the idea of the 1989 animated Ariel, who was pale white with bright red hair, being recast as a Black woman with locs. Racist backlash led to many individuals "review bombing" the film on IMDb, or flooding the site with negative reviews about the film to negatively impact its rating (Murphy, 2023). Audience members have done the same for other films that have been rebooted with Black characters in roles previously played by white actors, such as *Ghostbusters* (2016). The reactions to Bailey as Ariel, taken in this broader context, reiterates the existence of a societal fragility among some mass audiences who expect fictional, majestic characters to still reproduce Eurocentric standards of beauty on land and sea. While *The Little Mermaid* did not address racial realities or inequities, her presences meant something to Black youth viewers searching for themselves in fantasy worlds without identity trials and tribulations.

Discussion

Superpowered, Supernatural, and "Super" Black Kids

In examining patterns of representation for this chapter, we found that Black youth with superpowers are presented as either hero, savior, or vigilante. Their existence in the role of savior or hero has often been linked to self-sacrificial services, despite their young ages. For example, the teenage witch Bonnie Bennett in the popular CW series *The Vampire Diaries* regularly sacrificed her body, well-being, happiness, and at times even her own powers to protect the show's white human and supernatural characters (Thomas, 2019). When put into the context of the Black American experience, media featuring superpowered Black youth there often presents a need to save their families and friends from systemic and institutional oppressions. White children with superpowers tasked with such life-threatening responsibilities (e.g. Buffy, Sabrina, etc.) do not also have racial systemic structures overtly or implicitly conveyed by the narrative as barriers to their success but do often face barriers related to sexism and sexuality. Even though Bonnie's character was limited and not satisfactory, she gave stellar performances when she did appear in the series.

In many instances, Black youth are presented as mythical heroes. While the same may be said of white youth, many Black youth heroes serve in the capacity of hero for their community and savior for the broader world placing an added layer on the importance of their heroic abilities and success. In fact, since 2000, mass audiences have seen many examples of Black children with superhero capabilities, such as CW's *Black Lightning* (2018–2021) and *Naomi* (2021–2022), as well as Netflix's *Raising Dion* (2019, 2022) and *See You Yesterday* (2019); and the films *Fast Color* (2018) and *The Darkest Minds* (2018). Across genres and decades, the media have depicted Black children with abilities that derive from their parents or some mutation, including the previously mentioned *Fast Color, Black Lightning,* and *Raising Dion*, as well as *Spiderman: Into the Spider-verse* (2018), and *Cloak and Dagger* (2018–2019). And within their various superhero roles, is often added responsibility for family, and respect for culture and community.

There are more Black youth in speculative media now than before, but there is still room for improvement. The first Black Disney heroine, Tiana, is the subject of enchantment but has no powers of her own: her world is filled with magic, but she is not. Even when youths do have superhero or mystical powers, they often suffer burdens and griefs that go with it. Of course, the supernatural genre makes its white protagonists unhappy and burdened, too. But it's more problematic in the case of Black children, because of history and the reality of real-world racism that seeps into the fantastic. It is thus especially concerning that high-profile, famous characters like Prudence from *The Chilling Adventures of Sabrina* and Dion from *Raising Dion* are depicted with an excess of grief and anxiety, and a scarcity of safety and joy.

Across many media texts, Black children are depicted as tasked with saving the world, rather than enjoying the imaginative truths and freedoms found in Afrofuturism. Afrofuturism was coined in Mark Dery (1994) to describe how African American speculative fiction addresses the concerns of Black Americans. Ytasha Womack later defined the term as a "way of looking at the future and alternate realities through a Black cultural lens ... it intersects the imagination, technology, Black culture, liberation and mysticism ... bridging literature, music, visual arts, film and dance" (Pratt Institute, 2021). So, while media about Black youth *could* depict them enjoying lives full of excitement, joy, creative freedom, and unbound imagination (often seen in the Afrofuturism and speculative fiction spaces), they are instead relegated time and again to reluctant heroes, full of society's responsibilities without society's love.

In this critical introspective analysis of Black youth in fantasy worlds, we extensively explore Black youths' portrayals in contemporary media fantasy worlds. Multiple genres, from comics to science fiction, showcase Black youth in ways that interrogate historical tropes and reconstruct how magical youth can be viewed. We contend that audiences turn to these types of media for a fulfillment that may be inaccessible in other fantasy worlds without Black bodies. Additionally, seeing Black youth on screen in supernatural worlds may encourage a generation who wish to see their identities valued in entertainment media.

We describe multiple media texts like *Hunger Games, Jingle Jangle, Raising Dion, Naomi,* and *Black Lightning,* and how fantasy worlds can be corrupted and complicated by continuous racial and social injustices. Simultaneously, these texts' main characters utilize their powers and abilities for good, combating racist challenges. Some characters' inherited traits and genetic modifications are part of their uniqueness of being magical Black youth. Some Black youth characters are also depicted as being empowered by a distinct brilliance that sets them apart, similar to films where Black youth and STEM influence are interconnected. Through this centralized notion of magical Black youth utilizing their knowledge and skills for solutions and ease, it is evident that their superpower is their brilliance in science, technology, engineering, arts, and mathematics. Shuri from *Black Panther* and Riri from *Black Panther: Wakanda Forever* show unapologetic and bold brilliance that is not criticized, and their value is seen through other characters.

Though some Black youth characters, from Anissa Pierce/Thunder of *Black Lightning* to Princess Tiana, were impacted by genetic mutations, magical worlds, and fantasy worlds differently, media with these depictions have still inspired Black youth to believe they deserve happy endings, love, justice, and equity in the real and imagined worlds. Black magical youth have moved beyond historical tropes and can exist outside of the societal challenges: Joy exists on screen for some Black youth.

Ultimately, while Black youth are not leading the fantasy or science fiction genres, they are visible in multiple fantasy-world genres. In texts such as *Black Panther,* and *Naomi,* Black youth can captivate the screen with their cultural richness, intelligence, and deep commitments to saving their communities from the woes of society despite the personal cost to themselves. Their self-discovery through their powers remains an identity-making process for all who engage. Satisfactory and limited presentations of Black youth in fantastic worlds exist in contemporary media and continue to grow. We look forward to the thoughtful creation and deep characterization of supernatural and superpowered Black youth across multiple genres and forms as the diversification of creators and producers change the stories and outcomes for our young Black heroes and leads.

Note

1 For this chapter, we define Black youth and children as those under the age of adulthood (typically 18 years in American contexts) and whose racial and ethnic identity are linked to Black/African American ancestry.

References

Bandura, A. (1982). Self-efficacy mechanism in human agency. *American Psychologist*, 37(2), 122. https://doi.org/10.1037/0003-066X.37.2.122

Breznican, A. (2018, February 9). The women of Wakanda roar: A Q&A with the female warriors of "black panther." *EW.com*. https://ew.com/movies/2018/02/09/black-panther-women-of-wakanda-interview/

Bucciferro, C. (2021). Representations of gender and race in Ryan Coogler's film Black Panther: Disrupting Hollywood tropes. *Critical Studies in Media Communication*, 38(2), 169–182. https://doi.org/10.1080/15295036.2021.1889012

Busselle, R., & Van den Bulck, J. (2019). Cultivation theory, media, stories, processes, and reality. In M. B. Oliver, A. Raney, & J. Bryant (Eds.), *Media effects: Advances in theory and research* (4th ed. pp. 69–81). Routledge.

Calta, A. (2014, August 26). *The hunger games: Class, politics, and marketing.* American University. https://www.american.edu/cas/news/hunger-games-class-politics-marketing.cfm

Collins, S. (2023). *The Hunger Games*. Scholastic Australia.

Dixon, T. L., & Linz, D. (2000). Overrepresentation and underrepresentation of African Americans and Latinos as lawbreakers on television news. *Journal of communication*, 50(2), 131–154.

Donovan, R. A., & West, L. M. (2014). Stress and mental health: Stress and mental health: Moderating role of the strong Black woman stereotype. *Journal of Black Psychology*, 41(4), 384–396. https://doi.org/10.1177/0095798414543014

Dery, M. (1994). *Flame wars: The discourse by Cyberculture*. Duke University Press.

El-Nasir, M. (2021). The fusion of activism and imagination in Ryan Coogler's *Black Panther*. *African Scholar Journal of Humanities and Social Sciences*, 21(6), 83–92.

Elo, S., & Kyngäs, H. (2008). The qualitative content analysis process. *Journal of Advanced Nursing*, 62(1), 107–115. https://doi.org/10.1111/j.1365-2648.2007.04569.x

Epstein, R., Blake, J., & Gonzales, T. (2017). *Girlhoood interrupted: The erasure of Black Girls' childhood.* https://www.law.georgetown.edu/poverty-inequality-center/wp-content/uploads/sites/14/2017/08/girlhood-interrupted.pdf

Fiske, S. T., & Taylor, S. E. (1991). *Social cognition* (2nd ed.). Mcgraw-Hill Book Company.

González-Velázquez, C. A., Shackleford, K. E., Keller, L. N., Vinney, C., & Drake, L. M. (2020). Watching Black Panther with racially diverse youth: relationships between film viewing, ethnicity, ethnic identity, empowerment, and wellbeing. *Review of Communication*, 20(3), 250–259. DOI: 10.1080/15358593.2020.1778067

Hawkins, D. S. (2021). "After Philando, I had to take a sick day to recover": Psychological distress, trauma and police brutality in the Black Community. *Health Communication, 37*(9), 1113–1122. https://doi.org/10.1080/10410236.2021.1913838

Hickerson, H., & Stamps, D. (2023). COVID-19, digital media, and health| health messaging and social media: An examination of message fatigue, race, and emotional outcomes among Black audiences. *International Journal of Communication, 17*(20).

Howard, S. C., & Jackson, R. L. (2014). *Black Comics: Politics of race and representation.* Bloomsbury.

McGee, E. O., & Bentley, L. (2017). The troubled success of black women in Stem. *Cognition and Instruction, 35*(4), 265–289. https://doi.org/10.1080/07370008.2017.1355211

Morris, M. W. (2016). *Pushout: The criminalization of black girls in schools.* The New Press.

Muhammad, G., & Haddix, M. (2016). Centering Black girls' literacies: A review of literature on the multiple ways of knowing of Black girls. *English Education, 48*(4), 299–336.

Murphy, J. K. (2023, June 1). "The little mermaid" user rating weighted by IMDB after "unusual" influx of negative scores. *Variety.* https://variety.com/2023/digital/news/little-mermaid-review-bombing-imdb-ratings-change-1235630089/

Murphy, M. K., & Harris, T. M. (2018). White innocence and black subservience: The rhetoric of white heroism in "The Help." *Howard Journal of Communication, 29*(1), 49–62. https://doi.org/10.1080/10646175.2017.1327378

NCES. (2022, September 30). Number of STEM degrees and certificates awarded in the United States from 2008–09 to 2020–21, by race/ethnicity [Graph]. *Statista.* https://www-statista-com.libezp.lib.lsu.edu/statistics/828874/number-of-stem-degrees-awarded-in-the-us-by-race/

Pratt Institute Libraries. (Ed.). (2021). *Afrofuturism: Home.* LibGuides – Afrofuturism. https://libguides.pratt.edu/afrofuturism

Ramasubramanian, S., Winfield, A. S., & Riewestahl, E. (2020). Positive stereotypes and counterstereotypes: Examining their effects on prejudice reduction and favorable Intergroup relations. In A. Billings & S. Parrot (Eds.), *Media stereotypes: From ageism to Xenophobia* (pp. 257–276). essay, Peter Lang Publishing, Inc.

Reed, A. (2018, February 16). 5 Ways that 'Black Panther' celebrates and elevates Black women. *USA Today.* https://www.usatoday.com/story/life/2018/02/16/5-ways-black-panther-celebrates-and-elevates-black-women/338779002/

Research confirms that Black girls feel the sting of adultification bias identified in earlier Georgetown Law Study. (2019). https://www.usatoday.com/story/life/2018/02/16/5-ways-black-panther-celebrates-and-elevates-black-women/338779002/

Sanders, M. S., & Banjo, O. (2022). The power of Black Panther to affect group perceptions: Examining the relationships between narrative engagement, narrative influence, and perceived vitality of African Americans. *Imagination, Cognition and Personality, 41*(4), 439–459. https://doi.org/10.1177/027623662110638

Sanders, M. S., & Banjo, O. (2013). Mass media and African American identities: Examining Black self-concept and intersectionality. In D. L. Lasorsa & A. Rodriguez (Eds.), *Identity and Communication: New agendas in communication* (pp. 126–148). Routledge.

Sanders, M., & Whitenack, S. (2019). The role of media in perpetuating stereotypes. In E. P. Downs (Ed.), *The dark side of media & technology: A 21st century guide to media and technological literacy* (pp. 73–84). Peter Lang.

Sealey-Ruiz, Y. (2016). Why Black girls' literacies matter: New literacies for a new era. *English Journal, 48*(4), 290–298. http://www.jstor.org/stable/26492571

Stamps, D. L. (2021). B(l)ack by popular demand: An analysis of positive black male characters in television and audiences' community cultural wealth. *Journal of Communication Inquiry, 45*(2), 97–118.

Stroman, C. (1986). Television viewing and self-concept among Black children. *Journal of Broadcasting & Electronic Media, 30*(1), 87–93. https://doi.org/10.1080/08838158609386610

Tan, A., Fujioka, Y., & Tan, G. (2000). Television use, stereotypes of African Americans and opinions on affirmative action: An affective model of policy reasoning. *Communication Monographs, 67*(4), 362–371. https://doi.org/10.1080/03637750009376517

The STEM Gap: Women and girls in science, technology, engineering and mathematics. AAUW. (2023, August 29). https://www.aauw.org/resources/research/the-stem-gap/

Thomas, E. E. (2019). *The dark fantastic: Race and the imagination from Harry Potter to the Hunger Games*. New York University Press.

Trepte, S., & Loy, L. S. (2017). Social identity theory and self-categorization theory. *The International Encyclopedia of Media Effects*, 1–13. 10.1002/9781118783764.wbieme0088

Washington, P., & Washington, D. (2015). *The Hunger Games*: Confronting innocence and deconstructing Black prejudice through Rue. *Humanity & Society* (pp. 1–3).

Winfield, A. S. (2020, February 4). A new blerd?: Recognizing and reimagining the brilliant Black Girl image through spike Lee's "See You Yesterday." *Media Res*. http://mediacommons.org/imr/content/new-blerd-recognizing-and-reimagining-brilliant-black-girl-image-through-spike-lee%E2%80%99s-%E2%80%9Csee

Xie, S. (1999). Rethinking the identity of cultural otherness: The discourse of difference as unfinished product. In R. McGillis (Ed.), *Voices of the other: Children's literature in the postcolonial context* (pp. 1–16). Routledge.

11

Queering Teen Supernatural TV Dramas: Fandom's Impact on LGBTQ Youth

VICTOR EVANS

Since the early 1900s, the supernatural other has had an impervious link to homosexuality. Vampires, werewolves, fairies, goblins, and witches all resonate with the LGBTQ community because they are "othered" as outliers in society. In *Monsters in the Closet*, Benshoff (1997) wrote: "monster is to 'normality' as homosexual is to heterosexual" (p. 2). Benshoff theorized that just as society has viewed monstrous characters as unnatural, it has often applied the same label to the LGBTQ community—which is why supernatural and horror genres draw queer audiences (Benshoff, 1997). Historically these depictions have demonized, victimized, or otherwise ostracized queer people, through repeated tropes like the transgender killer (*Murder!* [1930]), the lesbian vampire (*Dracula's Daughter* [1936]) or the sad, gay werewolf (*Werewolf of London* [1935]). Despite such heinous depictions of the monstrous queer, monsters became a focus of identification for queer audiences.

When the film industry imposed the Hays Production Code on Hollywood films during the 1930s and 1940s, prohibiting filmmakers from depicting anything considered obscene, including homosexuality, directors used subtext to code characters as queer. Queer director James Whale's 1931 film *Frankenstein*, based on Mary Shelly's novel, exemplifies this. Victor Frankenstein's relationship with the monster implies an underlying queer context, and the monster's unnatural appearance startles the "normal" townsfolk who immediately ostracize and shun the creature for his abnormality, which parallels how queer individuals have faced isolation and condemnation for centuries (Rigby, 2017).

Today, queer monsters of all kinds appear in fiction. Since the early 2000s, they have become longstanding staples in online fandom spaces. Many fans, mostly LGBTQ youth, create queer content that aligns with their experience of the world as they explore their sexual orientations. Much of this fandom content is inspired by popular supernatural television shows targeting teens. Given the connection between monstrosity and queerness, it is understandable that many supernatural television series include LGBTQ characters in their diverse casts, particularly when targeting younger adolescents. Adolescents are arguably more open to such inclusion: Because of improvements in the acceptance of homosexuality in the U.S., more Gen Z young adults identify as LGBTQ than in any previous generation (G.L.A.A.D., 2022). I argue that LGBTQ youth see these shows as conceits full of creative and even radical potential for queer readings.

Several factors influence fantasy fandoms' discourses, particularly those surrounding the supernatural and horror genres. For example, as Halberstam (1995) notes, postmodern Gothicism has encouraged media consumers to suspect the monster hunters and rarely the monster, engendering sympathetic representations of queer monstrosity. Paranormal romance's meteoric rise is a second factor: Particularly in the young adult genre, paranormal romance normalized human/monster pairings as a heterosexual romance ideal, pushing queers out of even monstrosity's liminal spaces. In response to this second factor, in particular, fans (queer and straight alike) advocate for more representations of explicitly queer (not merely queer-coded) monsters (Elliott, 2016).

Numerous scholars have studied queer representation in supernatural genres (Benshoff, 1997; Owens, 2015), outlining how the LGBTQ experience aligns with paranormal depictions. Other scholars such as Julianne Myers (2023) have examined LGBTQ representation in all streaming teen dramas, with de Barros (2020), McCracken (2007) and Johnson (2016) specifically studying queer themes in teen supernatural dramas. A few scholars (Elliott. 2016; Espinoza, 2015) have focused on the use of slash fiction by queer supernatural teen audiences to reclaim their narratives. In this chapter, I add to this discussion by examining three more current teen supernatural television series: *Vampire Diaries* (CW, 2009–17) and its spin-offs (*The Originals*, 2013–18 and Legacies, 2018–22), *Teen Wolf,* (MTV, 2011–17), and *Shadowhunters* (Freeform, 2016–19). I consider their crucial roles in providing LGBTQ youth with similarly aged characters with identities to which they can identify, as reflected in their fans' online activities. But first, as context, let's consider what's known about social media, fandom, and LGBTQ youth.

Social Media, Fandom, and LGBT Youth

According to the Pew Research Center (2022), 97% of teens (13–17) use the internet daily. Of these, 46% say they use it constantly, as part of their daily habits. Black and Hispanic teens stand out for being on the internet more frequently than white teens. Some 56% of Black teens and 55% of Hispanic teens say they are online almost constantly, compared with 37% of white teens. All the cohorts most active online in the United States are enthusiastically using mobile ICTs (e.g., smartphones, tablets) and social media (e.g., TikTok, Instagram).

LGBTQ youth might be spending even more time online. The Gay, Lesbian & Straight Education Network (GLSEN, 2013) undertook a study that compared online media usage of general youth population to an LGBTQ youth subgroup (ages 13–18). Findings suggest LGBTQ youth may spend significantly more time online than their non-LGBTQ peers (approximately 45 minutes more daily). The study is dated, but there is no other in-depth study specifically focusing on the online media usage of LGBTQ youth. However, Fish et al. (2022) conducted a study investigating LGBTQ's use of online platforms during the pandemic. Their findings reaffirmed GLSEN's, proving the importance of synchronous, text-based online platforms to enable LGBTQ youth to feel safe seeking support while at home. Researchers in another study speculated that LGBTQ youth in particular have the propensity to use social media for emotional support and development, general educational purposes, entertainment, and acquiring LGBTQ-specific information (Craig et al., 2021).

Because contemporary online engagement is a central part of young people's lives (Pew Research Center, 2022), it seems fitting that most youths, gay or straight, would engage online to learn more about their sexuality. This is especially true for gender and sexual minority youth, who identify as lesbian, gay, bisexual, or transgender. A fast-growing body of literature explores, analyzes, and documents the myriad ways gender and sexual minority youth use online media in their everyday lives (Lucero, 2017) to build social relationships as well as to access resources about sexual health, gender, and sexual identity (Berger et al., 2022). Not mere passive receivers of information, gender and sexual minority youth also produce online media, transmitting messages to their peers (Mayo, 2017). Online media thus command a substantial amount of power over how gender and sexual minority youth understand the world. Consequently, queer youth regularly seek out varied LGBTQ content online, including television programming, LGBTQ social media influencers on various platforms like TikTok and YouTube, and other online communities. According to Trevor Project's 2022

National Survey on LGBTQ Youth Mental Health, 89% of LGBTQ youth reported that seeing LGBTQ representation in TV and movies made them feel good about being LGBTQ.

However, the type of shows including LGBTQ characters and these characters' portrayals on the shows make a substantial difference in terms of the positive or negative self-complexity created by engaging in such content. Self-complexity is the number of unique self-aspects that compose an individual's self-concept; one such self-aspect can be an individual's sexual orientation. Bond and Miller (2017) reported that LGBTQ youth's exposure to mainstream television negatively correlated with positive self-complexity, which refers to the constructive, affirming aspects of an individual's self-concept. Mainstream television shows reduce LGBTQ characters to sanitized versions of their sexualities that lack complexity. Therefore, such characters are likely to voice their sexuality, but viewers are not likely to see them being sexual or to learn about other aspects of their identity, their likes, their fears, and so forth (p. 105). The authors argued that this absence of diverse depictions of LGBTQ people on mainstream television leads LGBTQ youth to decrease their positive self-complexity. Contrarily, the study also found queer youth's exposure to gay- and lesbian-oriented television was negatively correlated with negative self-complexity. Negative self-complexity refers to the deconstructive, disaffirming aspects of an individual's self-concept. So, the negative correlation to negative self-complexity indicates that when LGBTQ youth are watching gay-and-lesbian-oriented shows, they can disassociate negative self-aspects that have been instilled through years of heteronormative sexual socialization because the LGBTQ characters in those shows are central to the story and are not depicted in a demeaning fashion. This disassociation removes these negative self-aspects from viewers' self-concepts, thereby lessening the discrepancies between LGBTQ teens' actual and ideal selves and increasing their well-being (p. 106).

Studies suggest that when LGBTQ youth discover programming they believe positively depicts LGBTQ youth, they are more likely to purposely engage with the content because it affirms their identity and/or their sense of self, thus creating fandom. Fandom refers to individual "investment in a particular object or idea" (Seregina & Schouten, 2016, p. 107)—typically a personal connection with an aspect of popular culture manifested in popular media (Duffett, 2013). Fandom is a participatory process. Fans not only join communities of shared interest but often engage in the production and/or consumption of creative materials—or fanwork (e.g., fiction, art, music)—based on their media fascinations. Due to the continued lack of representation of LGBTQ identities, LGBTQ youth undertake fanwork activities to "queer" media narratives, often referred to as "slash fiction," and to engage with like-minded communities (Dennis, 2010; McInroy & Craig, 2017). Slash fiction is a genre of fan fiction that focuses on romantic or sexual relationships between fictional characters of the same sex. This is why fandom has the potential to promote the self-reflexivity, identity-building, and social functioning of youth, especially for those who struggle with belonging and connectedness in their primary (i.e., offline) socialization contexts (Dennis, 2010; Seregina & Schouten, 2016).

Duggan (2022) found that speculative fiction attracts queer youth because it plays a key role in providing imaginative horizons for their developing gender and sexual identities. The study's participants insisted speculative fiction and slash are valuable spaces in which "contingent possibilities [...] open up," allowing them both to "rethink the gendered and sexual possibilities latent even in the (painfully unmagical)" real world and to find pleasure in "escapist fantasy" transcending cultural–material constraints (p. 719).

Given queer youth's affinity for supernatural shows and the long history of monsters being apt for queer readings, and then often leading to the creation of slash fan fiction, *The Vampire Diaries* universe, *Teen Wolf,* and *Shadowhunters* all provide suitable subject matter for discussing LGBTQ youth's engagement in online fandom, particularly when they are dissatisfied with the way the creators navigate the LGBTQ characters and storylines. In this chapter, I will analyze each show, looking at their representations of LGBTQ characters; the slash associated with each series created by queer fans; and how both the series' LGBTQ themes and characters and the fan fiction have affected queer viewers' sexual identity development. I examine social media campaigns, postings, and fan fiction from numerous fan sites and message boards to frame the influence and impact of each show.

Analyzing Supernatural Series and Fan Reception

For my analysis, I selected teen supernatural television series that aired on networks targeting younger audiences and inspired fandoms and/or fan fiction. These shows' target audience (generally teens and young adults, ages 14–34) is the typical demographic of those beginning to explore their sexualities. Through fandoms and fan fictions, viewers can reclaim queer perspectives that get lost or ignored within the current storylines while also exploring their own sexual identities; therefore, I also explore fan reactions to canonical developments within these shows.

The fan comments included in this chapter were sourced from various fan sites and fan pages on social media sites, including Tumblr, Twitter, and Facebook. I only compiled comments that mentioned the viewer's opinion of the LGBTQ characters on each show and how the show directly impacted their sexual identity, including their coming out process or affirmation of their sexual orientations. One limitation of the study is that I only collected comments from fan sites, which are heavily trafficked by individuals who have had positive experiences with the shows; therefore, the content is skewed toward those who have an affinity for the selected shows. However, for this study, such sites were the most appropriate ones to find personal testimonials of how LGBTQ media affects viewers as they explore their sexual identities.

To understand these comments in relation to what is known about youths' sexual identity exploration, I use the six stages of sexual identity development (Cass, 1979) to explore why and how viewers engage in such fandoms, and how this engagement influences their sexual identities. Although dozens of experts have created what they believe to be unique models of sexual identity development, the six-stage model proposed by Cass (1979) has become the standard reference of sexual identity models. Briefly, the six stages are as follows:

1. Identity confusion. Individuals recognize that their sexual feelings, actions, or thoughts could be homosexual, but they are not yet prepared to accept this possibility.
2. Identity comparison. Individuals compare their sexual feelings with those of others and may tentatively accept that they might be gay/lesbian.
3. Identity tolerance. Individuals begin with the tentative belief that they are likely gay/lesbian and end this stage with near certainty but not full acceptance that they are lesbian/gay.
4. Identity acceptance. With acceptance, individuals gain a clearer and more positive image of themselves as lesbian/gay.
5. Identity pride. Incongruity between the homosexual and heterosexual worlds dichotomizes the universe into in-group versus out-group dynamics (Spears, 2011), inspiring a preference for associations with like-minded people to help engender a sense of pride in one's sexual identity.
6. Identity synthesis. Individuals integrate their sense of self as a sexual minority with other aspects of the self. Being lesbian or gay is an important but not exclusive aspect of the self.

In their analysis of this model, Horowitz and Newcomb (2001) determined that most sexual identity models can be reduced to four common themes: self-awareness, self-acceptance, disclosure to others, and integration into personal identity.

The model does have several limitations. For example, while many sexual minorities may experience the stages outlined in Cass' model, each person's experience is unique; therefore, certain steps could be skipped or they might not occur in the order prescribed. The model also doesn't account for differences in sex, socioeconomic levels, cohort, ethnicity, religion, race, or nationality. Despite such limitations, I chose to use this model in my research because it provides a steadfast blueprint that clearly outlines each step of the coming-out process, and while the model might not apply to all LGBTQ experiences, no one model ever could. As indicated in the model, individuals undergoing steps two through four often engage with media, including social media, because they are actively looking for others like themselves, and those outlets are easiest to access without much risk. This is particularly important for sexual minorities because, unlike racial, ethnic, and religious minorities, they are often not born into families like them, so having a place to turn to see others with what they perceive as similar sexual orientations to their own is crucial. The pride stage (step 5) is when individuals tend to outwardly show their differences, thus making a statement about who they are and what they like by creating fan fiction or staging social media protests.

Queer Representation and Reception in Supernatural Youth Media

In this section, I will analyze the selected shows, discussing the LGBTQ characters and themes in each one, while examining how audiences responded to the characters and storylines, particularly those first acknowledging their own sexual identities. I will also explore how some queer youth are drawn to the LGBTQ characters but don't approve of the storylines, so they find their own acceptance by creating their personalized versions of the show that they then share with the online world. Lastly, some shows are so beloved by the LGBTQ community that fans take to the web and beyond to save it.

The Vampire Diaries (TVD) Universe

The Vampire Diaries (*TVD*) universe, based on the novels by L. J. Smith, is an American media franchise consisting of several interconnected television series (*TVD*, *The Originals*, and *Legacies*) that all aired on The CW network.

TVD (2009–17) is set in the picturesque, fictional town of Mystic Falls, Virginia, a hotbed of supernatural events long before and since the founding of the town in the late eighteenth century. The series follows the life of 17-year-old Elena Gilbert as she falls in love with a 162-year-old vampire named Stefan Salvatore, drawing her and her friends into a world of vampires, werewolves, witches, doppelgängers, and Original vampires. A spin-off of *TVD*, *The Originals* (2013–18), centers on the Original vampire family from the turn of the eleventh century. Continuing the tradition of *TVD* and *The Originals*, *Legacies* (2018–22) continues the story with the next generation of *TVD* supernatural beings at The Salvatore School for the Young and Gifted.

All three shows in the universe include LGBTQ characters and thus appeal to a large LGBTQ fan base. *TVD* introduces its first gay character, Luke Parker, in season 5. However, Luke dies when he falls victim to his brother Kai. It is not until season 7 that lesbian lovers Nora and Mary Louise are introduced. The duo is the first non-heterosexual couple featured on the show. Unfortunately, their union ends in tragedy when they sacrifice themselves in an explosion. Throughout the entire show's five-year run, Nora and Mary Louise are the only significant LGBTQ couple on the show.

The Originals slightly improved on its predecessors' shortcomings by introducing a supporting gay character, Josh Rosza, in the second episode. During his time on the show, Josh's role becomes more substantial after he transitions into a vampire, takes on a leadership role with the blood-sucking clan, and falls in love with a werewolf, Aiden. They are happy together for barely a season before Aiden is surprisingly killed. However, they do get their happy ending when Josh dies in the final episode and is reunited with Aiden in the afterlife. Like Nora and Mary Louise, their "happily ever after" ending is found in death and never fully realized on the show.

Subsequently, *Legacies* attempts to improve LGBTQ portrayals in the *TVD* universe. Many main characters (Hope, Josie, and Penelope) are sexually fluid, and this is made clear from the onset of the show. In the final season, werewolf Jed comes to terms with his sexuality and begins a gay relationship with demigod Ben, the only LGBTQ couple to get a living "happily ever after," proving the franchise can create LGBTQ characters who are healthy, well-adjusted and do not need to die tragically.

The online fandom associated with the *TVD* universe began early on, but it wasn't as popular with LGBTQ fans until the introduction of Nora and Mary Louise in *TVD*. Numerous sites were devoted to the couple's fan fiction, like fanfiction.net, which has over 50 selections (writing, poetry, artwork, etc.) of fanwork highlighting the couple. However, social media engagement intensified when the lesbian couple perished. There was already an outcry about LGBTQ characters, mostly lesbians, being killed on supernatural shows while their straight counterparts remained unharmed. This became known as the "bury your gays" (a.k.a. dead lesbian syndrome) trope (Waggoner, 2018; Snarker, 2016).

The #buryyourgays Twitter campaign began around February 2016, when the CW's *Jane the Virgin*'s Rose, a lesbian character, was murdered by being thrown off a roof. Over the following weeks, lesbian characters were also killed on CW's *The 100*, Syfy's *The Magicians*, and AMC's *The Walking Dead*. Adding those killings to the deaths of Nora and Mary Louise in *TVD*, the total count of lesbian characters killed in two months was an astounding six, four of whom were on the CW. Fans, many of whom were LGBTQ youth, showed their outrage on Twitter using the hashtag #LGBTFansDeserveBetter (Greenwood, 2016). Representative samples of their remarks include:

- "So The Vampire Diaries decide to use the 'Bury your gays' trope too. Two immortal vampires. Don't they see the harm this causes?" (Robyn, 2016)
- "I guess no.1 warned The Vampire Diaries that Bury your Gays is not acceptable anymore! #TVD went head long into dead lesbian syndrome!" (Brandee, 2016)
- "I CANT BELIEVE as were tweeting about the bury your gays trope the vampire diaries KILLED 2 MORE TONIGHT? UNBELIEVABLE." (We Deserve Everyone, 2016)
- "BURY TROPES NOT US LGBT FANS DESERVE BETTER than your lacking imagination and inability to treat us as dignified, multifaceted humans." (Bury Your Gays, 2016)

Thousands of similar comments expressed the same outrage on social media platforms, including Twitter, Redditt, and a Facebook group. The "bury your gays" trope is not new, and it prompted similar backlashes by fans when popular shows such as *Buffy the Vampire Slayer, Pretty Little Liars, House of Cards,* and *Supernatural* all killed lesbian characters in the 1990s; however, those retaliations never reached the intensity of the more current fan responses, due to the relative lack of social media in the 1990s (Framke, 2016).

The *TVD* fans' backlash did not go unnoticed, supporting the argument (Duffett, 2013) that fandom can influence creators and effect true change. Executive Producer Plec and *VD* actor Ian Somerhalder were impelled enough to apologize and acknowledge in her April 2016 blog that issues of representation reach beyond the parameters of escapist entertainment. They noted how death on the show is a probable outcome for any character in the *VD* universe, but they still acknowledge how the lesbian couple's tragic fate could have offended LGBTQ audiences.

> The conversation around this issue encourages me and hopefully the entire television landscape to do better on a larger scale as we all set out to tell stories that honor and are inclusive of the LGBTQ community. (Plec and Somerhalder, 2016 as cited in Lush, 2017, p. 298)

Getting any type of response from an executive producer of a major show would have been unheard of a few decades ago, but today's fans leverage social media to talk directly to show creators and producers, putting a spotlight on their decisions and forcing them to take notice and respond, which is exactly what these social media campaigns are designed to do. In this case, the fans received a positive response that will hopefully make other content creators think twice when they contemplate killing gay characters.

Even though the *TVD* universe includes queer characters and attracts many LGBTQ youth viewers, the shows, other than *Legacies*, do not always live up to their promise, sending the adolescents online to use their own agency to either create fanwork in which the characters, like Mary Louse and Nora, live happily ever after or to protest the mass television slayings of their favorite lesbian characters. Hundreds of stories featuring Mary Louise and Nora can be found on fan sites, including Wattpad, Fan Fiction, and Archive of Our Own.

Teen Wolf (TW)

Teen Wolf (*TW*) (2011–17), loosely based on the 1985 movie of the same name, is an American supernatural teen drama television series developed by gay-identified Jeff Davis for MTV. The supernatural show revolves around Scott McCall, whom an alpha werewolf bites the night before his second year of high school, forcing him to balance his new identity with day-to-day teenage life and ultimately leading him and his friends to become protectors of their fictional California hometown of Beacon Hills, a beacon for supernatural activity.

The series appears to have much promise regarding LGBTQ representation, especially since it is helmed by a gay creator (and given the werewolf "other" and LGBTQ parallels discussed at the beginning of this chapter). Debuting on June 15, 2011, the show posited a world where homophobia was nonexistent—a groundbreaking concept at the time. Viewers are quickly introduced to out-gay teen Danny Mahealani (played by Keahu Kahuanui), a supporting character on the show. Many critics applauded this innovative concept.

> His sexuality was treated no differently than differences in eye color. Instead of being taunted by the star jock of Beacon Hills High—Jackson (played by Colton Haynes)—Danny was his best friend. (Peeples, 2014, para 3)

Davis purposely shows boys flirting with boys as well as girls—most frequently Stiles Stilinski (played by Dylan O'Brien). Much of the LGBTQ fascination revolves around Stiles, due to the numerous hints the writers sprinkle into the show implying that he might be bisexual. Noticing the sexual chemistry between Stiles and the alpha werewolf Derek Hale (played by Tyler Hoechlin), viewers could not resist quickly coupling the characters, creating "Sterek," a type of neologism developed primarily in fan communities, using parts of both characters' names to signal a romantic relationship. This soon leads to an outpouring of fan fantasies in which the two are in a torrid romance, two of the biggest repositories being on Tumblr https://theofficialstereklibrary.tumblr.com and Wattpad (https://www.wattpad.com/stories/sterek).

Initially, series creator Davis was amused by the Sterek phenomenon. "I know certain reasons are the humor and the actors' chemistry together. And I know the actors themselves enjoy the scenes together" (Bricker, 2012, para 6). However, he was later shocked by how fervent the fans were to make Sterek a reality. "I had no idea that my Twitter account would be pummeled by pleas and requests to actually make Stiles and Derek a pair in the show itself, to become 'canon'" (Bricker, 2012, para 10). Promos are created with Hoechlin and O'Brien hugging and cuddling each other (https://youtu.be/oJo554Tiw1Y) for the Teen Choice Awards, heightening their fandom pairing. Yet the frivolity revolving around the unexpected pairing does not translate to the episodes' contents. When Sterek is at its height, scenes with only Hoechlin and O'Brien disappear from the show, causing much disappointment for fans.

The third season also fails to live up to LGBTQ-inclusive expectations. Danny begins a relationship with new gay alpha wolf twin Ethan (played by Charlie Carver), but the romance goes undeveloped and then non-existent when Ethan's character moves away from Beacon Hills. Fans grow weary of Stile's ambiguous sexuality, and it quickly goes from a draw for the show to a point of contention when some fans begin to accuse the show of "queer baiting" by continuing to tease viewers without any actual payoff. Queer baiting is a marketing technique for fiction and entertainment in which creators hint at, but then do not depict, same-sex romance or other LGBTQ representation to attract an LGBTQ or straight-ally audience. Numerous Reddit feeds discuss the queerbaiting on the show, particularly focusing on Stiles. One user posted:

> Jeff Davis has been asked many times if Stiles was bi and he always replied by calling it "spoiler territory." If they weren't baiting, he would have just said no. (ravenclaw1991, 2015, [online forum post])

The show tries to redeem its LGBTQ representation in the fourth season, but that does not come to fruition when Stiles becomes romantically involved with the female werecoyote Malia (played by Shelley Henning). Danny disappears from the show with no explanation, and a new gay teen of color named Mason (played by Khylin Rambo) is introduced; however, he receives very little character development, essentially becoming a token character.

Depicting LGBTQ characters in authentically is particularly troubling for the younger LGBTQ community. *Advocate* TV critic Peeples pointed out how generational differences played a significant part in the eventual negative reception of the queer *TW* characters:

> For a generation that has never known a time when LGBT people were not represented on the small screen in some form, limited visibility and queer subtext are no longer enough to hold their interest. (Peeples, 2014, para 12)

Since the creators were not going to provide the content fans longed for, annoyed fans created their own "Sterek" fanwork. Fan fiction "shipping" the two (e.g., creating a romantic relationship between them) flooded the show's fan sites. One legion of fans began The Sterek Campaign, which started the hashtag #cookiesforsterek. The initiative aimed to show Davis how much fans wanted Sterek to have a canonical story arc. "[W]e want an 'established will-they-won't-they, scripted' relationship," read the campaign's mission statement, "and to get that we need to make our voices heard" (Romano, 2012, para 4). Other fans took to social media sites like fanfiction.com, but particularly Tumblr, where there are communities devoted to Sterek fanwork, like "Sterek All the Way," "Sterek Stories" and "The Official Sterek Library." Years later, fans are still tweeting about their devotion to the pairing, especially after the announcement of the 2023 *TW* movie. As a couple of the posts requesting the pairing stated:

- "If I was a billionaire [...] I would be paying Tyler Hoechlin and Dylan O'Brien all kinds of money to actually reenact the stuff that the Sterek fandom comes up with!" (Raven, 2022)

- "OMG it's the final SHIP-tember and it's going to be these two because I'm still obsessed with them and a few days ago the #TeenWolf movie was announced! I need more #sterek." (Anonazure, 2021)

The posts above are a small sample of the immense discourse online associated with "Sterek." Numerous fan pages, websites, and YouTube Channels are devoted to highlighting the sexual chemistry between the two characters, illustrating just how widespread this fandom has become. The initiative *TW* fans took to see their fantasies come to life demonstrates the importance of LGBTQ youth searching for and/or creating positive images of themselves and their lives as sexual minorities, allowing them to effectively progress through the steps of sexual orientation identity.

Shadowhunters

The television show *Shadowhunters* (2016–19) follows Clary Fray who on her 18th birthday learns she comes from a long line of Shadowhunters, or human-angel hybrids who hunt down demons. Simultaneously, she is dealing with the struggles of forbidden love. The show, based on *The Mortal Instruments* book series by Cassandra Clare, aired on the Freeform Network. The show is racially diverse and includes several LGBTQ+ characters -- bisexuals, lesbians, and asexuals. Magnus Bane and Alec Lightwood are two popular LGBTQ characters on the show, also known by their shipping name "Malec." Season one explores their relationship, allowing viewers to watch as Alec comes to terms with his sexuality and begins dating the warlock Magnus. Watching characters grapple with their sexuality can be powerful for queer youth who are coming out themselves, realizing they are not alone and that others are going through the same experiences -- correlating to stage four in the sexual orientation identity process.

Fans and critics alike have heralded how *Shadowhunters* offers diverse storylines and depictions of LGBTQ and female characters with complexity unrivaled by other current young adult shows on TV. The Gay and Lesbian Alliance Against Defamation (G.L.A.A.D.) praised the show's depiction of lesbian characters with a review noting, "Ollie and Samantha's relationship has been treated the same way they would have if Ollie was a guy who had been dragged into the crazy world of angels and demons." (McDermott, 2018, para 7).

Shadowhunters' writers don't tokenize their characters when it comes to representation; instead, the characters are inclusive and incorporate previously marginalized sexualities, genders, and races without patronizing or stereotyping (Webb, 2020, paras 8, 16). Given these accolades, the show's cancellation announcement after its third season in 2018 sparked an unprecedented online campaign amongst fans to save it. People from all over the world came together on social media prepared to fight for their show, gathering under the hashtag #SaveShadowhunters. Posts fill these Twitter feeds either urging the network executives to save the show or lamenting that the shows with the most authentic LGBTQ characters are usually canceled:

- "I wish someone would #SaveShadowhunters or make a sequel with the SAME actors. Look at what a treasure you have. The #LGBTQ community needs shows like this. Love is love. It has and still helps those with trauma, mental health & more." (Kat~ BTS OT7 ~ #LoveMyself, 2019)
- "Typical. An all white, straight show like #Supernatural goes on forever, and a diverse, very #LGBTQ inclusive show like #Shadowhunters gets cancelled after three seasons." (Wilde Chase, 2019)
- "Finally, finally an #LGBTQ couple who got together in the beginning and felt with all obstacles together without having to sleep with other people to get their HEA! This is what we need more of!!! #Malec #Shadowhunters Other shows NEED TO TAKE NOTICE!" (Politically Drunk, 2019)

These posts' passion and urgency demonstrate fans' commitment to saving a show they felt a personal connection to and wished other shows could emulate.

In addition to sharing disdain online, *Shadowhunters* fans raised substantial funds to hire a #SaveShadowhunters pedicab that circled the 2018 San Diego Comic-Con. Fans flew a #SaveShadowhunters banner over the Netflix headquarters, purchased a billboard in Times Square to promote their campaign, leased posters on double-deck buses in London, and placed ads in Seoul subway stations (Franklin, 2019). They also started a petition that gathered over 200,000 signatures (Webb, 2020). Although the fans' campaign did not save the show, their initiative raised the creators' and networks' awareness of fans' power and ignited a bustling community of *Shadowhunters* fans and fandom that continues as of this writing. Fans are still creating and posting work for this show, including artwork on Pinterest, fan fiction on wattpad.com and fanfiction.net, and posts on Tumblr. They have even started Twitter rewatch parties as of March 2023 at @SHRewind and continuous *Shadowhunters* chat and nostalgia at @returntotheshadows.

Shadowhunters' extreme fandom suggests that when young LGBTQ viewers connect with a series that finally offers genuine and accurate LGBTQ representation, they feel as if these characters mirror their own lives, and they won't refrain from voicing their outrage when the network cancels that show. By identifying with these LGBTQ characters, viewers can see aspects of themselves and begin to develop pride in their own sexual identities as they synthesize their orientations into their full selves, aligning with stages five and six in the sexual orientation identity process. The fandom sites also create a safe space for youth to interact with each other by not only discussing their admiration for the show but also sharing personal experiences. As a *Shadowhunters'* master's thesis noted:

> Shadowfam has been and continues to be a safe space [. . .] The fandom spreads knowledge, opens for discussion among people with different backgrounds, and boosts resilience in people who might need it in their everyday lives. (Jenssen, 2021, p. 88)

Discussion

TVD and its spin-offs, along with *TW* and *Shadowhunters*, follow a long line of supernatural television shows going back to *Buffy the Vampire Slayer*, *True Blood*, and *Walking Dead* that feature LGBTQ characters, though some did a better job with queer representations than others. *TVD* distressed young LGBTQ fans by failing to include much queer representation and then introducing two prominent lesbian characters only to murder them. Joining the "bury your gays" campaign, *TVD* fans flocked to social media to communicate their dismay and frustration. This illustrates LGBTQ images' impact on queer youth, especially on those for whom the media is their only outlet to see others like themselves. To find characters they can relate to and then have them suddenly ripped away is exactly why they resort to fandom: It allows them to explore their own feelings and development while keeping the characters they love and admire alive.

Multiple scholars and LGBTQ organizations have noted the importance of queer youth having the ability to see representations of themselves in the media, particularly when progressing through the sexual orientation identity process stages. Steps one through three often lead them to become devoted fans of the show, leading them to want to connect with others who also find validation in these representations. Given adolescents' frequent internet usage, they would naturally be drawn to online communities where they can easily interact with peers from all around the globe. However, the quality of the LGBTQ portrayals and storylines they are exposed to is also significant, encouraging them when they see positive and life-affirming representations, and leaving them depressed and frustrated when LGBTQ characters are not treated like their straight counterparts, as evidenced by the queerbaiting many LGBTQ youth experienced with *TW.* Fan site posts revealed their intense frustration, especially from a show primed to be so gay-positive, in response to the gay characters being tokenized and two prominent characters' sexual chemistry never fully realized.

In this instance, the youths' activism appears to have succeeded because it prompted *TW* creator Jeff Davis and MTV to create the new series *Wolf Pack* and make the LGBTQ characters as clear-cut as possible, without queerbaiting. From the first episode, queer characters' storylines are just as prominent as their straight counterparts. Looking at the reviews on the show on Twitter (the social media platform rebranded in 2023 as X), it is working: As one fan wrote, "So. You know how the *Teen Wolf* series was super queer baitey? Well, the showrunners clearly decided to give us decent rep with a very hot very gay werewolf character in *Wolf Pack*" (Liz[7] 'Ghost King Trash' de Jager, 2023).

Unfortunately, the same success does not apply to the shows examined in this chapter, creating such disgruntlement that it propelled LGBTQ youth to take matters into their own hands. They first share their disdain for character development and story arcs, like in *TVD* and *TW*, or the cancellation of a show that they truly revere, like *Shadowhunters,* by creating campaigns to share their disapproval with series creators and/or networks. When it seems their voices are not heard, they engage in fandom by creating fanwork that mirrors the characters they would like to see: characters who are accepted by friends, who overcome obstacles, and who find love and live happily ever after (sexual orientation identity stages 4–6). Such portrayals affirm their identities, which is why the cancellation of a show like *Shadowhunters* that provided them with diverse, inclusive, and authentic characters was so devastating. The outpouring of fans and the social media campaigns launched to save the show signify the strong connection audiences, specifically LGBTQ viewers, had to these characters, prompting them to band together to communicate their outrage over its termination to the network.

In conclusion, the importance of queer youth having access to LGBTQ media images cannot be overstated. This research affirms how invested LGBTQ youth are seeking out such content, especially as they are coming to terms with their sexual identities. Supernatural shows have had a long history of including characters who reside outside the mainstream, which is why they attract so many LGBTQ audiences. Combining the inclination for queer youth to seek out characters like themselves and the fact that speculative shows have been known to have strong cult followings, it makes perfect sense that fandom is often the natural result. Fandom is a way for fans to express their admiration for these characters, create romantic storylines for the characters that the creators will not, and/or completely change the plotline, particularly when characters are unceremoniously killed off.

Creators and networks alike are seeing firsthand the powerful influence viewers have when they take to social media to criticize not only the representation within specific shows but also shows' arbitrary cancellation, especially beloved ones that feature characters who truly resonate with viewers. If creators learn anything from such fans' revolt, i.e. *Shadowhunters*, it should be the importance of writing their LGBTQ characters as they would their straight counterparts, valuing their input and showing all the experiences an LGBTQ individual encounters. Ultimately, LGBTQ teens' use of social media helps them explore their sexual identities while also having a meaningful impact on the content of media. Most importantly, thanks to fandom, queer youth know where to go to find or create their own happy endings when creators do not listen.

References

Anonazure [@anonazure]. (2021, September 29). *OMG it's the final SHIP-tember and it's going to be these two because I'm still obsessed with them and a few days ago the #TeenWolf movie was annouced! I need more #sterek.* [Tweet]. Twitter. https://mobile.twitter.com/anonazure/status/1443260957178753031

Benshoff, H. (1997). *Monsters in the closet: Homosexuality and the horror film.* Manchester University Press.

Berger, M. N., Taba, M., Marino, J. L., Lim, M. S. C., & Skinner, S. R. (2022, September 21). Social media use and health and well-being of lesbian, gay, bisexual, transgender, and queer youth: Systematic review. *Journal of Medical Internet Research, 24*(9). https://doi.org/10.2196/38449.

Bond, B. J., & Miller, B. (2017). From screen to self: The relationship between television exposure and self-complexity among lesbian, gay, and bisexual youth. *International Journal of Communication 11*(2017), 94–112.

Brandee, B [@JustBrandee]. (2016, April 1). *I guess no1 warned The Vampire Diaries that Bury your Gays is not acceptable anymore! #TVD went head long into dead lesbian syndrome!* [Tweet]. Twitter. https://twitter.com/JustBrandee

Bricker, T. (2012). 'Teen Wolf' boss talks Stiles and Derek's popularity, shipping and more. E! Online. https://www.eonline.com/news/338932/teen-wolf-boss-talks-stiles-and-derek-s-popularity-shipping-and-more

Bury Your Gays [#buryyourgays]. (2016, May 10). *LGBT FANS DESERVE BETTER than your lacking imagination and inability to treat us as dignified, multifaceted humans.* [Tweet]. Twitter. https://twitter.com/BuryYourGays

Cass, V. (1979). Homosexual identity formation: A theoretical model. *Journal of Homosexuality, 4* (3), 219–235

Craig, S. L., Eaton, A. D., McInroy, L. B., Leung, V. W. Y., & Krishnan, S. (2021). Can social media participation enhance LGBTQ+ youth well-being? Development of the social media benefits scale. *Social Media + Society, 7*(1). https://doi.org/10.1177/2056305121988931; https://www.mirror.co.uk/tv/tv-news/vampire-diaries-slammed-killing-lesbian-7678021

de Barros, A. C. (2020). "Gay now": Bisexual erasure in supernatural media from 1983 to 2003. *Journal of Bisexuality, 20*(1), 104–117. https://doi.org/10.1080/15299716.2020.1732258

Dennis, J. P. (2010). Drawing desire: Male youth and homoerotic fan art. *Journal of LGBT Youth, 7*(1), 6–28. https://doi.org/10.1080/19361650903507734.

Duffett, M. (2013). *Understanding fandom: An introduction to the study of media fan culture.* Bloomsbury Publishing USA.

Duggan, J. (2022). Worlds. . .[of] contingent possibilities: Genderqueer and trans adolescents reading fan fiction. *Television & New Media, 23*(7), 703–720. https://doi.org/10.1177/15274764211016305

Elliott, J. (2016). Becoming the monster: Queer monstrosity and the reclamation of the werewolf in slash. *Revenant: Critical and Creative Studies of the Supernatural.* https://www.revenantjournal.com/contents/becoming-the-monster-queer-monstrosity-and-the-reclamation-of-the-werewolf-in-slash-fandom/

Espinoza, J. J. (2015). *Re-examining resistance: Fan-produced queer readings and Teen Wolf.* [Master's Thesis, University of Texas at El Paso]. DigitalCommons@UTEP.

Fish, J. N. et al. (2022). I'm kinda stuck at home with unsupportive parents right now: LGBTQ youths' experiences with COVID-19 and the importance of online support. *Journal of Adolescent Health, 67*(3), 450–452. https://doi.org/10.1016/j.jadohealth.2020.06.002.

Framke, C. (2016). *Queer women have been killed on television for decades. Now The 100's fans are fighting back.* Vox. https://www.vox.com/2016/3/25/11302564/lesbian-deaths-television-trope

Franklin, D. (2019). *Save 'Shadowhunters': Data doesn't lie, so why hasn't it been saved yet?* Film Daily. https://filmdaily.co/obsessions/saveshadowhunters-data-saved/

G.L.A.A.D. (2022). *Accelerating acceptance 2022.* https://www.glaad.org/publications/accelerating-acceptance-2022

GLSEN, CiPHR, & CCRC. (2013). *Out online: The experiences of lesbian, gay, bisexual and transgender youth on the internet.* GLSEN. http://glsen.org/sites/default/files/Out%20Online%20FINAL.pdf

Greenwood, C. (2016, January). The Vampire Diaries slammed for killing off lesbian characters amid #BuryYourGays backlash against U.S. TV shows. *The Mirror.*

Halberstam, J. (1995). *Skin shows: Gothic horror and the technology of monsters.* Duke University Press.

Horowitz, J. L., & Newcomb, M. D. (2001). A multidimensional approach to homosexual identity. *Journal of Homosexuality, 42*(2), 1–19. https://doi.org/10.1300/J082v42n02_01

Jenssen, I. L. (2021). *Out of the shadows: LGBTQ+ representation in the television show "Shadowhunters."* [Master's thesis, UIT The Artic University of Norway]

Johnson, M., Jr. (2016). The homoerotics and monstrous otherness of Teen Wolf. *Studies in the Humanities, 43*(1–2), 65+. https://link.gale.com/apps/doc/A478140581/LitRC?u=anon-53781e75&sid=bookmark-LitRC&xid=c02059c7

Kat~ BTS OT7 ~ #LoveMyself [@KathrynLaprade]. (2019, May 3). *I wish someone would #SaveShadowhunters or make a sequel with the SAME actors. Look at what a treasure you have. The #LGBTQ community needs shows like this. Love is love. It has and still helps those with trauma, mental health & more.* [Tweet]. Twitter. https://twitter.com/KathrynLaprade/status/1124208947240554497

Liz7 'Ghost King Trash' de Jager [@LizUK]. (2023, February 8). *So. You know how the Teen Wolf series was super queer baitey? Well, the showrunners clearly decided to give us.* [Tweet]. Twitter. https://twitter.com/LizUK/status/1623411405167681540

Lucero, L. (2017). Safe spaces in online places: Social media and LGBTQ youth. *Multicultural Education Review, 9*, 117–128.

Lush, R. M. (2017). Original sin: Frontier horror, gothic anxiety, and colonial monsters in 'The Vampire Diaries.' *Horror Studies, 8*(2), 293–312. https://doi.org/10.1386/host.8.2.293_1

Mayo, J. B. (2017). LGBTQ media images and their potential impact on youth in schools. *Social Education, 81*(5), 303–307.

McCracken, A. (2007). At stake: Angel's body, fantasy masculinity, and queer desire in teen television. In E. Levine & L. Parks (Eds.), *Undead TV: Essays on Buffy the Vampire Slayer* (pp. 116–144). Duke University Press. https://doi.org/10.2307/j.ctv120qt6f

McDermott, A. (2018). *Why we, the stans, love 'Shadowhunters.'* G.L.A.A.D. https://www.glaad.org/amp/why-i-stan-shadowhunters

McInroy, L. B., & Craig, S. L. (2017). Perspectives of LGBTQ emerging adults on the depiction and impact of LGBTQ media representation. *Journal of Youth Studies, 20*(1), 32–46.

Myers, J. (2023). *Queer representation in teen drama streaming service TV shows.* (Publication No. 1794/29018). [Dissertation, University of Oregon]. Scholars' Bank.

Owens, A. J. (2015). *Desire after dark: The queer culture of contemporary supernatural media.* (Publication No. 3724341). [Dissertation, Northwestern University]. ProQuest Database.

Peeples, J. (2014, September). Op-ed: The trouble with *Teen Wolf. Advocate.* https://www.advocate.com/commentary/2014/09/17/op-ed-trouble-teen-wolf

Pew Research Center. (2022). *Teens, social media and technology 2022.* Pew Research Center. https://www.pewresearch.org/internet/2022/08/10/teens-social-media-and-technology-2022/

Politically Drunk [@hiswhiskeysumer]. (2019, May 6). *Finally, finally an #LGBTQ couple who got together in the beginning and felt with all obstacles together without having to sleep with other people to get their HEA! This is what we need more of!!! #Malec #Shadowhunters Other shows NEED TO TAKE NOTICE!* [Tweet]. Twitter. https://twitter.com/hiswhiskeysumer/status/1125582267408056320

Raven, A. J. [@tempest071990]. (2022, December 24) *If I was a billionaire[.].I would be paying Tyler Hoechlin and Dylan O'Brien all kinds of money to actually reenact the stuff that the Sterek fandom comes up with!* [Tweet]. Twitter. https://mobile.twitter.com/tempest071990/status/1606766037575553026

Ravenclaw1991. (2015). *I'm a bisexual male, so you can understand my want for Stiles to be bisexual so that I can have.* [online forum post]. Reddit. https://www.reddit.com/r/TeenWolf/comments/3gab5b/gay_baiting_with_teen_wolf_say_what/?rdt=51758

Rigby, M. (2017). "'Do you share my madness?'." In *Queering the gothic*. Manchester University Press. https://doi.org/10.7765/9781526125453.00008

Robyn [@RobynNotBatman]. (2016, April 2). *So The Vampire Diaries decide to use the 'Bury your gays' trope too. Two immortal vampires. Don't they see the harm this causes?* [Tweet]. Twitter. https://twitter.com/RobynNotBatman

Romano, A. (2012). *Behind cookies for Sterek: A "Teen Wolf" fan campaign for gay romance*. Daily Dot. https://www.dailydot.com/upstream/cookies-sterek-campaign-qhuinn-interview/

Seregina, A., & Schouten, J. W. (2016). Resolving identity ambiguity through transcending fandom. *Consumption Markets & Culture, 20*(2), 107–130. https://doi.org/10.1080/10253866.2016.1189417.

Snarker. D. (2016, March 21). Bury your gays: Why 'The 100,' 'Walking Dead' deaths are problematic (guest column). *Hollywood Reporter*. https://www.hollywoodreporter.com/tv/tv-news/bury-your-gays-why-100-877176/

Spears, R. (2011). Group identities: The social identity perspective. In J. Schwartz et al. (Eds.), *Handbook of identity theory and research* (pp. 201–224). Springer. https://doi.org/10.1007/978-1-4419-7988-9_9.

The Vampire Diaries universe. (n.d.). *Vampirediaries.fandom.com*. https://vampirediaries.fandom.com/wiki/The_Vampire_Diaries_Universe

Trevor Project. (2022). 2022 national survey on LGBTQ youth mental health. *Trevor Project*.

Waggoner, E. B. (2018). Bury your gays and social media fan response: Television, LGBTQ representation, and communitarian ethics. *Journal of Homosexuality, 65*(13), 1877–1891. https://doi.org/10.1080/00918369.2017.1391015

We Deserve Better [@komclexakru]. (2016, March 31). *I can't believe as were tweeting about the bury your gays trope the vampire diaries killed 2 more tonight? Unbelievable. Bury tropes not us.* [Tweet]. Twitter. https://twitter.com/komclexakru

Webb, D. (2020). *'Shadowhunters' is an LGBTQI love letter, so why has it been axed?* Film Daily. https://filmdaily.co/obsessions/shadowhunters-is-a-lgbtqi-love-letter-so-why-has-it-been-axed/

Wilde Chase [@HouseofSense8]. (2019, February 26). *Typical. An all white, straight show like #Supernatural goes on forever, and a diverse, very #LGBTQ inclusive show like #Shadowhunters gets cancelled after three seasons.* [Tweet]. Twitter. https://twitter.com/houseofsense8

12

Welcome to the Witching Hour: *The Craft* as a Neuroqueer Allegory of Legibility

DESIRÉE ROWE

In recent years, a growing list of media has drawn audiences into narratives centered on women, witchcraft, and danger—often featuring young, attractive ciswomen. Examples include a popular reboot of *Sabrina: The Teenage Witch* as *Chilling Adventures of Sabrina* (2018–2020); the exploits of young adult witches on *Legacies* (2018–2022); a kid-friendly depiction of young girl witches on *The Worst Witch* (2017–2020); niche television shows featuring young men and women discovering the enchanting dangerous of magic (i.e., *The Magicians* 2015–2021); *Hocus Pocus 2* (2022); and Dahl's *The Witches* (2020). In other words, there is no shortage of media that focuses on the relationship between women, witchcraft, and danger. But how are these representations in discourse with the public imagination, which generally perceives witches as violent and dangerous, but with a hint of intrigue?

The 1996 film *The Craft* offers unique insight into popular perceptions of witches. In the world of *The Craft*, four teenage ciswomen members of a coven use their powers of the occult to form a summoning circle, cast spells, and to invoke "Manon," a deity described by Nancy (Fairuza Balk) as, "If God and the Devil were playing football, Manon would be the stadium that they played on. It would be the sun that shone down on them" (Filardi & Fleming, 1996). The film blends practices from a variety of traditions including Wicca, Druidism, and Shamanism because the on-set Wicca advisor admonished that "the cultural impact of the film would cause teens to run out to beaches and invoke an actual deity" if it was authentic. This caution speaks to the cultural allure of witchcraft, especially for teen girls, to reclaim power and agency in the face of cultural torment for finding pleasure in being boldly themselves. And, in some ways, the advisor was right. The film was wildly popular among teen girls, and still resonates today. As *Teen Vogue* explained in 2016, "When *The Craft* appeared in theaters twenty years ago, it gave a generation of mystics and spellcasters a modern story of the power of magic, women and friendship—and showed us all the ways those things could get dark" (Houseman, para. 1). Today, the film is seen as a cult classic. *Time Magazine* (2020) frames the film within the cult classic genre because "it premiered to middling reviews," but then "captivated both experienced witches and total acolytes with its authentic portrayal of adolescent girls who dabbled in witchcraft to improve their lives and gain power" (Aloi, para. 1). The legacy of the film is secure and safe in the hands of generations of future witches. And, as *Vulture* agrees, it's not just because of the film's 90's nostalgia; *The Craft* "taps into the primal American fear of female power and what happens when women are alone together, forming hothouse bonds that seem to only occur in adolescence in ways that are both profound and contradictory, liberating and limiting" (Bastién, para. 2).

As a cult classic, *The Craft* offers an aesthetic of rebellion, torment, and ritualized teen girl performances. It is a narrative that is all too common—teen girls are bullied, remade through some frame of magical realism to be beautiful, and then live happily ever after. Rather than succumb to this typical narrative frame offered by most depictions of witchcraft, *The Craft* offers us another narrative thread, and one that I want to expand here—one of the neuroqueer leader who revels in her unbelonging and is punished for it. Building from discussions of a neuroqueer politic of understanding, I position the 1996 film *The Craft* as an allegory for exploring neuroqueerness and the ruptures of legibility. This chapter unpacks *The Craft,* and its depictions of deviance and witchcraft, as an allegorical frame for understanding a neuroqueer politic of legibility. Or, in other words, *The Craft* shows the audience what happens to a neuroqueer subject who demands to be recognized for their complete personhood.

Witchcraft in the Popular Imagination

As context for my analysis, it is important to consider the cultural context surrounding the public perception of witches. When a woman calls herself a witch, she is making a declaration of visibility—a declaration that can be dangerous, empowering, and threatening to her audience. In today's global political climate saturated with white supremacist, Christo-fascist rhetorics on social media and within popular culture, a person who declares an embrace of a seemingly "dark" supernatural force can be punished with threats (or more) of violence and intimidation. Making such threats is tacitly encouraged by conservative media. In November 2021, the Christian Broadcasting Network warned its readers that, as believers, they would be "shocked at how wide spread and accepting these dark practices have become, even within the church" (Aaron, para. 8).

The incitement of fear in modern Christian discourse has long historic roots. As Grossman (2020) notes in their forward to *Major Arcana*, a visual catalog of modern witches, a witch is a deviant which is laden with "centuries-old baggage of straight cis-male, desire, fear, and control" (p. 3)—especially for cis and trans women. The fear from their families, hiding of their beliefs and practices, and ostracization from society are experiences that many of the witches Grossman profiled describe. For example, as Juliet Diaz, an Indigenous Taino Medicine Woman and *bruja* wrote, "I didn't want to be that person. I wanted to shut it off and for me to be normal. I tried to commit suicide a couple of times until I realized I wasn't supposed to go. It wasn't my time. Who I was, was not changing. I needed to accept my witch and protect myself. So instead, I started to use my gifts to help people" (Denny, 2020, p. 104). Diaz felt like a tormented outsider so painfully she was pushed to attempt to end her own life. Other witches like Judika Iles note similar struggles: ". . . .while in an abusive marriage, whenever I gave the slightest indication of leave-taking or standing up for myself, my then-husband would threaten to tell the court I was a witch, telling me that because of this I would lose custody of our children. I took his threats seriously" (Denny, 2020, p. 20).

The reclamation of their witch identity after trauma and tragedy links the experiences of cis and trans woman witches together. As many of Grossman's participants note, using witchcraft openly is a powerful act of rebellion. Lenore Tija explains, "In a culture as racist and patriarchal and transphobic and homophobic and materialistic as ours is, if you don't see the way witchcraft is radical and revolutionary, you have some waking up to do" (Denny, 2020, p. 10). Tija's clear marking of witchcraft as politically radical is resonant within these real witches' lives and is a salient point in their own evolution as witches who are out and practicing in the Western world. Media representations of witches reflect a perception of witches as violent and dangerous (but with a hint of intrigue) within the public imagination. Depictions of witches and witchy behavior within popular media is received with curiosity, hesitancy, and acclaim.

Neuroqueerness

Witches Be Crazy

To support framing out the disruptions of neuroqueerness present within *The Craft*, let's first unfold what neuroqueerness means within communities of neurodivergence. Centrally, neuroqueerness marks resistance at the intersections of compulsory able-bodied assumptions and heteronormativity. Neuroqueerness diverges from neurodiversity with the desire to depart from "one's own cultural conditioning and one's ingrained habits of neuronormative and heteronormative performance" (Walker, para 17, 2015). Walker first coined the term publicly on her website in 2015, exploring the pairing of neuro and queer as primarily a verb, or a doing, but also opening the possibility of neuroqueer as an adjective, describing social identity. Walker's catalog of eight ways we can play within neuroqueerness offers a path to explore all the disruptive dimensions of a neuroqueerness with an emphasis on embodied disruptions and distortions of the status quo. Doing neuroqueerness is an intentional decentering of neuronormativity within cultural practices, performances, media, and traditions. As Walker (2015) proclaims, "you're neuroqueer if you neuroqueer" (para 13). In 2021, Walker expanded on the potentiality of neuroqueerness in ways that are especially important for understanding the characterization of Nancy within *The Craft*. She notes "neuroqueer is choosing to actively engage with one's potentials for neurodivergence and queerness, and the intersections and synergies of those potentials" (Walker, 2021, p. 175). As this piece works to frame *The Craft,* and particularly the performances of Nancy as an allegory of neuroqueerness, it's important to remember that neuroqueerness, through Walker's lens, rests on an active *doing* of neuroqueerness, rather than a masking of neurodivergence and/or queerness.

Since Walker, scholars have taken up the framework of neuroqueerness within a wide range of disciplinary applications. Most notably, Egner (2018) pulls together an archive of understanding the neuroqueer community project, one that as Walker mentioned above, actively resists normative frames of ability with an understanding of the intersectional dynamics of power and privilege in that recasting. As Egner (2019) explains, "A neuroqueer project not only questions typical conceptions of gender but also pivots away from normative gender categories altogether. Neuroqueer is a queer/crip response to normative discussions about gender, sexuality, and disability as pathology" (p. 124). Building upon Muñoz's (2013) germinal theorization of disidentifications, Egner asks scholars to decenter neurotypicality within analysis and reject centering oppressive ableist narratives, "Neuroqueer suggests that we, as gender scholars, recognize what it means to identify with a particular gender, and the way gender socialization is taken up does not just vary based on gender identity, sexuality, and sexual orientation but also varies by neurology" (p. 143). Egner (2019) also adds that neuroqueerness is under-explored within the development of Crip Theory (McRuer, 2006), an important moment of neuroqueer recognition that is later taken up by Johnson (2021).

Johnson (2021) calls upon a recasting of Borderline Personality Disorder (BPD) as a neuroqueer embodiment, continuing the turn away from the pathologizing within a neurodiverse frame to an emphasis on the queerness of embracing (with pride) neurological atypicality. Johnson explains that "I would add that neuroqueer could be defined as being unapologetically neurodivergent—being (or aspiring to be) fearless in disclosing one's psychological quirks" (p. 641). This emphasis is important for this project, because as seen earlier, "quirks" or other behaviors that are labelled as deviant are cast in opposition to either masking divergence or the status quo.

Witchcraft and Neuroqueerness

Importantly, there are clear ties between both neuroqueerness and witchcraft within popular culture and beyond. Both are seen as communities of deviance, as the unknown, and shrouded in secrecy. Sollée's poetic framing of "witch" marks the intertwining of the communities: "The witch is at once female divinity, female ferocity, and female transgression. She is all and she is one. The witch has as many moods and as many faces as the moon. Most of all, she is misunderstood" (2017, p. 17). As Sollée poetically explains, there is a link between public displays of neuroqueerness and public displays of witchcraft, where both perspectives reject exclusions and binaries in favor of a public performance of self without the mask. Media has also made this connection salient in the public imaginary. Depictions of witches are often represented within a frame of a "discourse of defectiveness" where those practicing witchcraft don't conform to interpersonal codes that require upholding normative conventions. As Cole (2021) explains in their invocation of neuroqueerness within interpersonal communication scholarship, neuroqueerness allows for disruption and possibility where interpersonal communication is centered on ableist codes of normative practices.

This forms the foundation for a neuroqueer politic of legibility. First noted by Egner (2019), a neuroqueer politic is "a politic in which those who experience exclusion from identity-based spaces can participate without needing to present themselves as a prototypical member" (p. 135). A neuroqueer politic of legibility is a thunderous call for recognition in a world dominated by neuronormativity. Neuronormativity is a frame that dominates all aspects of social life, including, "embodiment, development, cognition, expression, communication, comportment, conduct, and interaction" that create a "habitual *performance* of internalized social norms" (Walker, 2021, p. 180). The use of *The Craft* within this analysis hopes to offer a popular culture case study that is emblematic of the pitfalls of neuroqueerness within a neuronormative world when someone, in this case Nancy, attempts to live as legibly loud and neuroqueer. The neuroqueer politic of legibility is pulled together through both Egner (2018) and Walker's (2015, 2021) engagement with performances of a neuroqueer self.

"You don't even exist." Framing a Politic of Legibility Through Nancy and Sarah

Before we dive into an exploration of neuroqueer legibility within *The Craft*, it is important to understand the importance of Nancy and Sarah as central characters within the film. Nancy, played by Fairuza Balk, is the leader of the group of high school age women. Naming themselves as a coven and practicing witchcraft, these four are social outcasts. As discussed below, the women each come to the circle burdened by a marker of social undesirability. Sarah (Robin Tunney) arrives as the new girl to the school and is quickly taken up by Nancy's coven when they notice her potential supernatural prowess. The relationship between Nancy and Sarah is the driving force of the film. The witches get to know each other and become close friends, then, as detailed below, the relationship crumbles.

The Craft is marked within a neuroqueer politic of legibility. Legibility, for this analysis, emerges from the characterization of Nancy and her performances of a public neuroqueerness that don't mask or hide her supposed deviance. A neuroqueer politic of legibility is represented through embracing discourses of defectiveness without (a seeming) concern for rejection, a performance repeated throughout the film by Nancy. Legibility, when understood within a framework of a neuroqueer politic, reimagines legible personhood outside of neurotypical standards of behavior, relationality, and performance of self. For many neurodivergent people, learning performances of normality is a way to mask or hide neuroqueerness and become the norm for survival. You don't want others to see, or know, that you are different.

In *The Craft* we can see two competing performances of neuroqueerness that illustrate the differences in legibility. Throughout the film, Sarah can be read as rejecting a neuroqueer legibility while Nancy performs an open politic of neuroqueer legibility. Nancy is a stark contrast to Sarah's perfect hair, upper middle-class home, and pious commitment to monogamy. Nancy has sex (with perhaps both men and women), laughs loudly, and rebels against her poor/working-class background through her late 1990's goth clothes and the occasional petty theft. Nash's (2015) discussion of *The Craft* also positions Nancy and Sarah in opposition and considers Sarah's "birthright" magic in contrast to Nancy's learned magic. For Nash, this also marks Nancy's spells as "manifesting through horror" because of her "trashy genes" while Sarah is good because "her magical power is inborn" (2015, p. 16).

To continue to see the contrasts in performances of legibility, the first performance is that of Sarah (Robin Tunney) who carries all the performative markers of straight, cis, white, upper middle class, popular girlhood. Sarah is conventionally pretty, kind, and as the new girl in town, tries to make friends at her new private Catholic school and she eventually is befriended by a group of outcast girls who practice witchcraft. We have already seen in the film that each girl in the outcast group has some type of "deviance" that marks their outsider status; Bonnie has scars from a car accident, Rochelle is constantly bullied for being Black by the popular white girls, and Nancy lives in a trailer with her mother and her an abusive stepfather. Sarah joins the group within the trope of the new girl, who does not want to embrace a politic of visibility. Throughout the film, Sarah masks her witchy abilities and anything that might be perceived as outside of normative understandings of neurotypicality and able-bodiedness. Sarah quickly falls for the popular guy in school, Chris (played by Skeet Ulrich) and they go on a date. As the camera pans to Sarah and Chris sitting alone on a rooftop, they engage in silly banter. Chris holds Sarah's face and leans in for a kiss. Interrupted by Chris' friends saying goodbye, the kiss abruptly stops. Sarah wipes her bottom lip and looks around—as if making sure everyone is gone. Chris asks Sarah, "C'mon, let's go to my house. Nobody's there" and she replies with a hesitant "I . . . I don't want to go. I can't. I gotta go home." Noting Chris' disappointment she asks, "Are you mad?" and says softly "I'm sorry." As voyeurs into this early intimate moment between Sarah and Chris, Sarah continues to be framed as representative of conventional understandings of femme performances of self. Wiping her bottom lip to erase the traces of a sloppy kiss while refusing the sexual advances of the popular lead male character situates her wholesomeness in contrast to Nancy. Sarah, as we see here, is a "good girl." One that doesn't sleep around, and doesn't want to make anyone, especially popular boys, mad at her. With her upper-class upbringing, her whiteness, and the cleaning of the messiness of a kiss, she holds up our normative cultural ideals that reify how a "good girl" should behave.

The scene then cuts the inside of a classroom, where the three other teens ask Sarah about her date. The shot is centered on Nancy. Sarah finds out, from Nancy, that Chris is "going around the whole school saying" (and here Nancy leans in close to Sarah and pretends to whisper), "you were the lousiest lay he's ever had. And coming from him, that's pretty bad." "No he didn't," Sarah responds, as she notices (popular, blonde, white) girls staring at her and laughing. Rochelle (played by Rachel True) interjects, "He said the same thing about Nancy" and Nancy quickly responds while staring at Sarah, "Told you he was a jerk." This key sequence marks one of the central stories of *The Craft*. Nancy and Chris were "hooking up," but the relationship abruptly ended when Chris started spreading rumors that Nancy gave him a sexually transmitted disease (when in fact Chris transmitted the disease to Nancy). Later in the film the entanglements between the three escalate as Sarah casts a love spell on Chris, leading to him stalk, and then attempt to rape Sarah.

The setup of Sarah's sexuality in comparison to Nancy's is an important marker of legibility. Sarah is framed as not only the beautiful one, but the pure/virginal teen who demurs the popular boy's advances. This performance of sex and pleasure is a clear marker of white womanhood—one that is both virginal and demure. As Carlson (2020) explains, white womanhood is centered in an understanding of purity that is "encompassed a variety of "innocent" attitudes and behaviors, including sexual innocence" (p. 535). Sarah is removed from the discourses of deviance not just because of her refusal to go home with Chris, but also because of her stark comparison to Nancy in the next scene. Nancy is read as the opposite—a promiscuous, possibly diseased, maybe queer, witch.

As Sollée (2017) argues, and as Nancy demonstrates, there is a long historical connection between witches and sex. Since the fourteenth century witches, sex, bodies, and pleasure have been intertwined. "Portrayals of the woman-as-witch have thus reflected an unquenchable desire for the female sex mixed with fear, straddling horror and pleasure, disgust and arousal" (Sollée, p. 98). As the film progresses, we see Nancy play with the power and pleasure of sex to use both witchcraft and sex for revenge against Chris for his attempted rape of Nancy.

At a house party where Chris is clearly drunk, Nancy uses a glamour spell to look like Sarah and seduce Chris. After pushing him on to the bed, she towers above Chris and (looking like Sarah) demands, "make love to me Chris." At the same time, the three other witches enter the party through the front door and start looking for Nancy, commenting that she is probably up to something. Sarah opens the door to the bedroom and sees herself and Chris possibly having sex. Nancy removes the glamour spell and laughs loudly. Chris jumps up and, bewildered, says, "You're a witch. They were right." After making a faked shocked face, Nancy responds: "They usually are."

Before moving forward in this important scene, it's important to again mark the comparisons of legibility here. Nancy is already read as dangerous, and her friends remark as they get out of the cab, "we should not be here [at the party]" and Sarah retorts, "Neither should Nancy." Sarah again is performing the role of the calm and capable good girl and, even though she is the victim of the attempted rape, implores Nancy, "Look, you scared the shit out of him and thank you very much, let's go." In these two scenes Sarah works to manage Nancy's erratic behavior and protect Nancy, presumably, from herself even in the face of her own trauma. As another marker of normative constructions of womanhood, Sarah is performing maternal protection to Nancy and working to tame Nancy's deviance into conformity even though she herself has suffered at the hands of Chris. Valuing Nancy over her own revenge, Sarah is seen as truly altruistic and beyond any seemingly petty need for retribution. The difference in the representation of the cultural values of two woman is stark. Sarah continues to perform the good girl in her own self-abnegation of self-care (she is going to confront the man that attempted to rape her) and in her fervent desire to protect Nancy from Nancy. Sarah cares for others more than she cares for herself. Sarah as a "good girl" is a bold difference from Nancy's performance of identity within this scene. At this point, we are seeing Nancy for the first time as truly dangerous in her fight for legibility that pushes away from normative performances of girlhood.

Nancy's performances of neuroqueerness are big and bold in this scene and beyond. Nancy fights for legibility *and* recognition of her neuroqueerness, while Sarah actively hides her witchcraft practices, performs neurotypicality, and remains pure. While the audience is privy to Nancy's secrets, her peers see Nancy as someone unafraid to be her whole, witchy, poor, queer, self. And that is scary. Nancy consistently recognizes, and embraces, this outsider status with her dress and her interactions with others. In a particularly memorable scene, the four teens get off a local bus. The driver turns to them and cautions, "You girls watch out for the weirdos." Nancy, performing the role as leader, slowly turns and lowers her sunglasses, replying to the driver as he closes the door, "We are the weirdos, Mister." This is a clear performance of a politic of legibility within the counterpublic space of neuroqueerness, and Nancy privileges not the dominate public as the audience, as Sarah does, rather Nancy privileges creating spaces where you don't have to mask or perform "normalcy." Nancy, in this moment, pushes back against the invisibility of her own legibility as subject and demands to be seen. She is the weirdo and is going to let you know. Ultimately, however, *The Craft* teaches the viewer that attempting legibility through a politic of neuroqueerness like Nancy is wrong.

Returning to the scene in the bedroom, Nancy refuses Sarah's pleas to leave. Pushing back against Sarah's wishes to make it all go away, Nancy embraces retribution. After Chris accuses Nancy of being jealous of Sarah, Nancy replies, "Jealous? Jealous? You don't even exist to me. You don't even exist. You are nothing." The shot centers on Nancy as the background music reaches a higher and higher pitch, foreshadowing some imminent doom. The notion of being "seen" here is paramount in discussions of legibility. Nancy, the outsider witch, is talking back to the handsome popular jock and marking him as invisible, something Nancy has experienced her whole life and, through a politic of neuroqueer visibility, is physically pushing back against him. As Cisneros and Gutierrez (2018) explore in their discussions of undocuqueer immigration, being invisible to normative structures of sociality is a barrier to legibility faced by people across marginalized statuses.

But here, Nancy is demanding to be seen. Nancy is framed in the shot with her dark hair wild, and her head pointed down while her black-lined eyes look up. The camera moves in close and then quickly pulls back from Nancy, as if the viewer is running away as she says, "You are shit. You don't exist." We see the toes of Nancy's boots levitate quickly across the floor; Chris is backing up towards a window. She now catches up to the camera and we see her mouth wide as she yells, "The only way you know how to treat women is by treating them like whores. When you are the whore! And that's gonna stop!" The music continues to give the viewer the sense of impending dread when, for the first time in this scene, the camera moves back to Sarah for a brief moment. The positioning of Nancy versus Sarah within this pivotal scene is also explored by Moseley (2002) who succinctly notes, "In the figure of Nancy as tough feminist avenger, glamour as conventional feminine attractiveness and glamour as female power are insistently separated out" (p. 415). Sarah says nothing as she stands with tears in her eyes and looks frightened of Nancy, observing the ongoing horrors.

"Do you understand? Do you understand what I'm saying?" Nancy hisses to Chris as the camera moves back to her—with the shot even tighter on her face than before. Clearly, we understand that Nancy is casting something on Chris as he solemnly says, "I'm sorry." This apology triggers Nancy as she wildly shakes her head back and forth over and over and rushes backwards while screaming, "Oh, he's sorry. He's sorry! He's sorry!" over and over. The film quickly flits between different angles of Nancy. She grasps the sides of her head, seemingly unable to keep her rage bound inside her own body. This moment, with Nancy shaking her head violently and screaming while the music continues to rise, is seen as Nancy's psychotic "break" within the film. As Sarah (finally saying something) yells, "No!" Nancy screams and, presumably using telekinesis, pushes Chris out the window to his death. After the fall, the scene cuts to Sarah crying in her bedroom to her father about Chris' death.

In act 2 of the film, we see how this pulls Sarah away from the other witches as Nancy, Bonnie, and Rochelle become more powerful after Chris' death. The three witches use magic and force Sarah to self-harm. As Sarah is bleeding on the floor she calls upon the "spirit of three" and the spirit of her deceased mother to "make them see." Rochelle and Bonnie have pushed back against Nancy, and while searching for Sarah they run as they "see" themselves in the mirror burned and scarred. Sarah has come into her own power now and faces off against Nancy alone. The fight, which utilizes the same close-ups of Nancy screaming wide-mouthed and frantic and Sarah calmly responding, ends with Nancy unconscious after being kicked into a mirror. This moment is the first that we see Nancy overcome by Sarah and sets the stage for the shifting of legibility in the final act of *The Craft*.

The Glamour of Normativity and Disgust of Deviance

As an allegory, the ending of *The Craft* uncovers a final level of signification within the frame of a neuroqueer politic. As mentioned earlier, a neuroqueer politic embodies a "discourse of deviance" and must be corrected through the film. However, by the end of the film Sarah, the only witch in the coven we clearly see marked as pure example of good girlhood is the only one to retain her power and high school popularity. The final two scenes unravel the film's central conflict between Nancy's brash performance of neuroqueer legibility and Sarah's neurotypical performances.

First, we see Sarah at the trunk of (presumably) her father's car at their large begonia-covered house. She's peeking into the shopping bags from The Limited (a popular 90's store for teens) that also have a bouquet of lavender hydrangeas poking out. This immediate depiction of social class again marks Sarah as financially privileged, a stark contrast to our earlier witnessing of the violence in Nancy's messy, cigarette-smoke filled, double-wide trailer.

Rochelle and Bonnie stroll up the driveway and nervously ask Sarah how she is and if she still has her powers. It's here that we witness, for the first time, the true shift in Sarah. She has embraced her own power and, as the film is framed as an allegory, this power reads as her neurotypical legibility within a normative-privileging world. Sarah is, understandably, cold to both Bonnie and Rochelle. Two important details emerge. First, we realize that Sarah has cast a binding spell on all three witches prohibiting them from doing magic. We saw the start of the spell during her earlier fight with Nancy, but with Bonnie and Rochelle missing their powers as well we realize Sarah has "bound" everyone. Sarah, with her beauty, purity, and powers intact has won against the perceived darkness of Nancy's attempts at legibility, and Sarah revels in it. After Bonnie asks if Sarah would like to hang out Sarah responds with an uncharacteristically quick retort, "Maybe. Hold your breath until I call" as she whips her perfect hair around to walk away. The two girls whisper that Sarah probably doesn't have any powers left, and overhearing them, Sarah responds with a look of vengeance as the sky darkens. It's important to pause here and note that, as viewers, we are encouraged to be rooting for Sarah in this scene as lighting cracks, breaking a large tree branch onto Bonnie and Rochelle and knocking them backwards. But, isn't the violent act of a branch falling just as vindictive when Sarah does it as when Nancy seeks revenge? We are meant to believe that no, it is not. Sarah's need for revenge here is uncontaminated by the deviance that overtakes Nancy's yearning for revenge. While Nancy's wild neuroqueerness is marked by deviance and must be stopped, Sarah's fight is to be perceived within the structures of normativity. Sarah's revenge is palatable because Nancy has always been outside the structures of normativity. Nancy deserves to be punished. Sarah, because of her purity, should never be punished.

Sarah's final act of revenge on Nancy is even more brutal. The closing scene of the movie is a high aerial shot of Nancy, the neuroqueer witch, strapped down to a table in a hospital, thrashing against her restraints. Nancy's spellcasting power is gone, binded by Sarah. This powerful image illuminates her own neuroqueer rage against medicalization, and evokes the historical violence performed on women deemed crazy or hysterical. Inspired by Johnson's call to "sit with subjects who unravel, reading these disclosures on their own terms, that is, as sites/forms of embodied theorizing," this scene highlights the articulations between a politic of neuroqueerness and the ultimate expectation of the failure of that politic. We are first drawn into Nancy with her sarcastic retorts, a deep loyalty to her coven, and a sympathy for her abusive home life. But by the end of the film, Nancy is the villain, a psychopath who is hungry for power and revenge and it is Sarah, the normative, beautiful girl that put her there. Nancy has been disciplined throughout the film for her neuroqueerness, and in this final scene, as the nurse slide the door shut, we know she is paying the ultimate price for her disobedience.

As film critic Sollée notes, "What begins as a promising show [*The Craft*] of female bonding descends into a sexist circle jerk around the idea that girls just can't handle power" (Sollée, 114). And while that might be true too, reading *The Craft* as an allegory of neuroqueer legibility recognizes the breakdowns and failures a neuroqueer politic within multiple marginalized coalitional spaces. As Hill-Collins has theorized, we create monsters out of what we fear most. And, as a popular cult classic, *The Craft* helps us explore one type of monster. Here, the cruel object of Nancy reflects the hierarchical boundaries imposed by normative constructions of sexuality, gender, race, class, and ability. It's not that Nancy can't necessarily handle power, it's that others can't handle her having autonomy and revel in her own monstrosity—her own neuroqueerness. Embracing discourses of defectiveness signals a yearning for a neuroqueer legibility, not with the neurotypical community necessarily, but in a desire for a space of belonging where you don't have to perform or mask. Discarding the discourses of the status quo, however, has consequences.

Nancy, as the leader of the group and then coven, is the representation of this neuroqueer politic. She is powerful, angry, fallible, kind, traumatized, and the prototypical bitch. She exemplifies this politic precisely because she is dangerous to those on the outside. Dangerous because she is unpredictable, unknown, and her behavior, including her devotion to witchcraft and her coven, falls outside of the logics of performed neurotypicality. She embraces her deviances within normative spaces, and calls into question the legibility of those that are uphold majoritarian identities ("You don't even matter to me!" She screams in the face of the popular jock). There is pleasure in this for Nancy, and for a moment for her coven members, within the weird, the abnormal, the unbelongingness that is co-created by their neuroqueer community.

But, we are left with a screaming and thrashing Nancy strapped to the table as a nurse injects her with a sedative. So then, where does that leave the allegory for a politic of legibility within neuroqueer community? Nancy pushed too far for legibility and was punished. To be clear, Nancy was being seen as defective long before she was being sedated in a bed. Far before she "pushed" Chris out the window or tormented Sarah, Nancy was cast as poor, queer, white trash with an edge of witchiness, who draws the audience in with her sarcastic retorts and wild hair. As soon as Sarah entered the scene, all hope for visibility was lost. For Nancy, and for many like Nancy, that yearn for a neuroqueer politic of legibility- failure is inevitable because the dominant structures of understanding are too entrenched to allow for alternative sense-making to open up as a possibility.

While *The Craft* remains within the cult classic canon of teen girl witch films, it is critical or mark the clear disciplinary move within the end of the film. Nancy, the weird outcast witch, refused to balance her supernatural powers within the structures of traditional femininity. Sarah, on the other hand, was the good witch and was rewarded. Though both sought revenge, Sarah, not Nancy, was redeemed in the film. This leaves the audience with a clear message—the outcast will be punished. This failure of neuroqueer community, even within a community of witches, is a solemn reminder that there is work to be done in creating truly inclusive spaces—spaces where women, like Nancy, can be powerful and proud of their neuroqueer status.

References

Aaron, C. (2021). "They were releasing spells over the viewers": Ex-witch warns witchcraft everywhere from Hollywood to church. *CBN News*. https://cmsedit.cbn.com/cbnnews/us/2021/october/they-were-releasing-spells-over-the-viewers-ex-witch-warns-witchcraft-now-everywhere-from-hollywood-to-the-church

Aloi, P. (2020, October 28). *The Craft* inspired a generation of teenage witches. Now a sequel is poised to do the same. *Time*. https://time.com/5904701/the-craft-legacy-witches/

Bastién, A. J. (2017, October 27). The profound, enduring legacy of The Craft. *Vulture*. https://www.vulture.com/2017/10/the-craft-its-enduring-legacy.html

Carlson, A. C. (2020). Whiteness of a darker shade: Reclassifying Italian-Americans in the trials of Maria Barbella. *Western Journal of Communication*, *84*(5), 528–549. https://doi.org/10.1080/10570314.2020.1779336

Cisneros, J., & Gutierrez, J. S. (2018). "What does it mean to be undocuqueer?" Exploring (il)legibility within the intersection of gender, sexuality, and immigration status. *QED: A Journal of GLBTQ Worldmaking*, *5*(1), 84–102. https://doi.org/10.14321/qed.5.1.0084

Cole, K. (2021). Neuroqueering interpersonal communication theory: Listening to autistic object-orientations. *Review of Communication*, *21*(3), 187–205. https://doi.org/10.1080/15358593.2021.1961849

Denny, F. (2020). *Major arcana: Portraits of witches in America*. Andrews McMeel Publishing.

Egner, J. E. (2018). "The disability rights community was never mine": Neuroqueer disidentification. *Gender & Society*, *33*(1), 123–147. https://doi.org/10.1177/0891243218803284

Filardi, P., & Fleming, A. (1996). *The Craft*. Columbia Pictures.

Grossman, P. (2020). "Foreword." *Major arcana: Portraits of witches in America*. New York: Andrews McMeel Publishing, pp. 1–4.

Houseman, H. E. (2016, May 3). 10 witchery lessons learned from The Craft. *Teen Vogue*. https://www.teenvogue.com/gallery/the-craft-teen-witch-lessons

Johnson, M. L. (2021). Neuroqueer feminism: Turning with tenderness toward borderline personality disorder. *Signs, 46*(3), 635–662. https://doi.org/10.1086/712081

Moseley, R. (2002). Glamorous witchcraft: Gender and magic in teen film and television. *Screen, 43*(4), 403–422. https://doi.org/10.1093/screen/43.4.403

McRuer, R. (2006). *Crip theory: Cultural signs of queerness and disability*. NYU Press.

Muñoz, J. E. (2013). *Disidentifications: Queers of color and the performance of politics*. U of Minnesota Press.

Nash, I. (2015). The princess and the teen witch. In M. Forman-Brunell & R. C. Hains (Eds.), *Princess cultures: Mediating girls' imaginations and identities* (pp. 3–23). Peter Lang.

Sollée, K. J. (2017). *Witches, sluts, feminists: Conjuring the sex positive*. Threel Media.

Walker, N. (2015). *Neuroqueer: An introduction*. NEUROQUEER • THE WRITINGS OF DR. NICK WALKER. https://neuroqueer.com/neuroqueer-an-introduction/.

Walker, N. (2021). *Neuroqueer heresies: Notes on the Neurodiversity Paradigm, Autistic Empowerment, and Postnormal Possibilities*. Autonomous Press.

Notes on Contributors

Lori Bindig Yousman, Ph.D. is a Professor and Chair of the Department of Communication Studies in the School of Communication, Media and the Arts at Sacred Heart University. She earned her doctorate in Communication at the University of Massachusetts Amherst. Her research interests include feminist television studies and critical media literacy. Dr. Bindig Yousman has published three monographs on teen television with Lexington Books and her media literacy research has appeared in edited volumes and journal articles. She is the co-editor of the award-winning 5th and best-selling 6th edition of *Gender, Race, and Class in Media* published by Sage.

Victor Evans, Ph.D. is Assistant Professor of Communication at Seattle University where he teaches media analysis and journalism courses. He has published numerous articles and produced the documentary series, *Curved TV*, which all focus on LGBTQ media images and how they affect queer youth as they come to terms with their sexual identities. Find his work and learn more about him at victor-devans.com.

Cory Geraths (Ph.D., The Pennsylvania State University) is Assistant Professor of Communication and Leadership at Eureka College. His research focuses on the intersections of feminist and queer rhetoric and popular culture. Cory's scholarship has been published in multiple peer-reviewed journals, such as *Critical Studies in Media Communication, Rhetoric Review, Communication Teacher, Journal of*

Contemporary Rhetoric, and *Advances in the History of Rhetoric*. He has published additional research on rhetoric, gender and sexuality, and popular culture in edited collections such as *The Routledge Handbook of Queer Rhetoric*, and *A New Handbook of Rhetoric: Inverting the Classical Vocabulary*.

Rebecca C. Hains, Ph.D. is Professor of Media and Communication at Salem State University. She researches children's media culture from a critical/cultural studies perspective, taking an intersectional approach to exploring media representation, identity, and meaning-making. She is the author of *The Princess Problem: Guiding Our Girls Through the Princess-Obsessed Years* (Sourcebooks 2014) and *Growing Up With Girl Power: Girlhood on Screen and in Everyday Life* (Peter Lang, 2012). She also co-edited the books *The Marketing of Children's Toys: Critical Perspectives on Children's Consumer Culture* (Palgrave, 2021), *Cultural Studies of LEGO: More Than Just Bricks* (Palgrave, 2019), *Princess Cultures: Mediating Girls' Identities and Imaginations* (Peter Lang, 2015). She holds a Ph.D. in Mass Media & Communication from Temple University, a Master of Science in Mass Communication from Boston University, and a Bachelor of Arts degree in English and Communication Arts from Emmanuel College.

Rockia Harris is a fourth-year doctoral student in the Manship School of Mass Communication at Louisiana State University. Her research explores race, gender, and activism, identifying how black and brown bodies' realities are captured in mass media, specifically through entertainment and news media. Rockia is also interested in mentorship and public policy, inspiring her efforts with Louisiana Sea Grant to develop the REACH Mentor-Training for Inclusion Certificate. This training focuses on building mentoring philosophies and approaches for researchers working in diverse academic settings. Prior to LSU, Rockia received her B.A. in Gender & Women Studies, minor in African American Studies, and Global Studies Certificate from the University of Kentucky. Rockia continued her education at the University of Cincinnati, receiving her M.A. in Communication.

Hope Hickerson is a Ph.D. student at the Manship School of Mass Communication at Louisiana State University. Her research focuses on health communication and the perception of health messaging in marginalized communities. Hope has 15 years of experience as a health educator working primarily at higher education institutions such as Louisiana State University and the University of Maryland, College Park. She earned an undergraduate degree and master's degree in health education and promotion from East Carolina University and a master's degree in counseling from Louisiana State University before pursuing a doctoral degree in communication at Manship.

Kyra Hunting, Ph.D. is an Associate Professor of Media Arts and Studies at the University of Kentucky. Her research focuses on children's film and television, with a special emphasis on gender, fandom and technology. Her work has appeared in journals including the Jou*rnal of Popular Communication, Annals of ICA, Feminist Media Studies, Mass Communication and Society,* and *Critical Studies in Media Communication* as well as in numerous edited collections including anthologies on Children's Toy Culture and LEGO.

Eric M. Kennedy Jr. is a doctoral student in the Media and Communication Ph.D. program at Temple University's Lew Klein College of Media and Communication. His research applies textual and genre analysis to study serial, intertextual, and transmedia narratives in popular media texts. He is particularly interested in exploring how these complex texts impact issues of audience reception, representation, adaptation, authorship, and collective memory. He teaches interdisciplinary seminar courses that challenge students to engage creatively with texts and concepts beyond the limits of their academic and professional fields.

Ilana Nash, Ph.D. is Associate Professor of Gender and Women's Studies at Western Michigan University, specializing in gender and youth-media. She is the author of *American Sweethearts: Teenage Girls in Twentieth-Century Popular Culture* (Indiana University Press, 2006). Her work has appeared in *Feminist Media Studies* and the *Women's Review of Books,* as well as in several edited collections, including *Princess Cultures: Mediating Girls' Imaginations and Identities* (Peter Lang, 2015), and *The Cambridge Companion to American Crime Fiction* (Cambridge University Press, 2010).

Gwendelyn Nisbett (Ph.D., University of Oklahoma) is an associate professor of public relations at the Mayborn School of Journalism, University of North Texas. Dr. Nisbett's research examines the intersection of mediated social influence, political engagement, and popular culture. Her research incorporates a multi-methods approach to understanding the influence of fandom and celebrity in social and civic engagement. She has published in journals such as *Political Communication, Health Communication,* and the *Atlantic Journal of Communication.* She teaches courses in social influence, social media, and ethics in strategic communication.

Newly Paul (Ph.D., Louisiana State University) is a media and politics researcher and Assistant Professor of journalism at the University of North Texas in Denton. Her research areas include intercultural communication, race and gender in politics, and gender in entertainment. She has taught various journalism classes such as principles of news, news reporting and writing, copyediting, political reporting, and minorities in media. Her research has won grants and awards and has been published in top journals such as *Political Research Quarterly,* and *Journalism and Mass Communication Quarterly.* Before joining academia, she was a journalist and wrote stories on city government, crime, education, and politics.

Desirée D. Rowe (Ph.D., Arizona State University) is an Associate Professor in the Department of Communication Studies at Towson University. Desirée's research explores critical qualitative and interdisciplinary art-based research methods, failure, and negativity. She has published articles in *Women and Language, Text and Performance Quarterly, Cultural Studies -Critical Methodologies, Rethinking History: A Journal of Theory and Practice, Qualitative Inquiry, Western Journal of Communication Studies*, and many book chapters. In 2019 she was named a Fulbright Scholar to Kyushu University in Fukuoka, Japan.

Hope L. Russell earned her doctorate in Global Gender Studies from the State University of New York at Buffalo. She teaches in the Women's Studies Program at Niagara University. Her research focuses on girlhood, personal narratives, and the processes of coming of age and coming to feminism in the late twentieth and twenty-first centuries.

Meghan S. Sanders is an Associate Professor and the Associate Dean for graduate studies in the Manship School of Mass Communication. She specializes in media psychology, exploring the underlying cognitive and affective processing and mechanisms associated with using mediated communication. Her research focuses on popular culture and entertainment, morality, narrative engagement, and positive media psychology. Her work has been published in *Communication Theory*, the *Journal of Communication, Mass Communication & Society*, and in several edited volumes. She earned her undergraduate degree in mass communication at Dillard University, her master's degree in media studies from The Pennsylvania State University and her doctorate in mass communication from The Pennsylvania State University.

Jana K. Schulman is Professor of English at Western Michigan University, where she teaches Old English and Old Norse language and literature as well as medieval, epic, and British literatures. Recent essays include: "Minnesota Medieval: Dragons, Knights, and Runestones," in *The United States of Medievalism*, ed. T. Pugh and S. Aronstein (2021); "*Beowulf* in the Context of Old Norse," in *Teaching Beowulf in the Twenty-first Century*, ed. H. Chickering, B. Yeager, and A. Frantzen (2014); "Old Norse-Icelandic Sagas," *Oxford Bibliographies Online: Medieval Studies* (2014); and "Retelling Old Tales: Germanic Myth and Language in Christopher Paolini's *Eragon*," *Year's Work in Medievalism* 25 (2010): 33–41.

Tiffany R. Smith is a second-year doctoral student in Media and Public Affairs at Manship School of Mass Communication. Her research explores intersectionality, race, media representation, and the African diaspora. Before attending LSU, Tiffany was a higher education professional focusing on diversity, equity, and inclusion. In addition to her academic experiences, she has held positions with Amnesty International, The Walter Rodney Foundation, Atlanta Jobs with Justice, and is a trainer of Nonviolence365 at the King Center in Atlanta, GA. She is a Founding Member at the National Center for Civil and Human Rights. She received her B.A. in communication at Bowling Green State University and M.A. in Global Communication at Kennesaw State University.

Erika M. Thomas (Ph.D., Communication, Wayne State University, 2011) is an Associate Professor and the co-Director of Forensics in the Department of Human Communication Studies and Queer Studies Minor Affiliated Faculty at California State University, Fullerton. Her areas of study include rhetorical criticism and theory, argumentation, and representations of gender, sex, and sexuality in popular culture. Her work has been included in *Transmedia and Public Representation: Transgender People in Film and Television* (2021, Peter Lang), *Beyond Princess Culture: Gender and Children's Marketing* (2019, Peter Lang), and in the journals, *Women & Language* (2018) and *Relevant Rhetoric* (2017).

Asha Winfield, Ph.D. is an assistant professor at Louisiana State University's Manship School of Mass Communication, and a critical/cultural media scholar. Her research focuses on exploring the stories, rituals, and practices of Black individuals and communities as portrayed in media, culture, and society. Her work has been featured in several journals such as *Health Communication* and *Women's Studies in Communication*, as well as in various edited volumes, book chapters, and online academic forums. In 2022, she launched The Storytellers Lab at LSU, collaborating with students on documentary research projects. Her documentary, "Our Black COVID-19 Stories", which tracks the impacts of the pandemic on Black American families, is set to be released in 2026.

Index

ABC (American Broadcasting Company) 14, 110
activism 71, 77, 216
  see also hashtag activism
adaptation 13–15, 29–31, 35, 65–66, 68, 69, 80, 95–96, 126, 128–129, 132, 135
Addams Family, The 14
adolescence 4, 6–7, 29, 150
  see also coming-of-age
adolescents 11, 202, 215, 222
  as audience members 202
adulthood 4, 6, 48, 49, 50, 107, 119, 192, 198n1
adults 7, 8, 11, 12, 27, 28, 29, 30, 32, 38, 39, 41, 45, 48, 50, 52, 71, 73, 84, 91, 93, 97, 134, 164, 166–168, 172, 177, 194, 202, 204
African cinema 163, 164, 167–168, 177
African storytelling 168–169, 171
Afrofuturism 196

Amazon Prime 18, 19, 175
animation, children's 42, 109–110, 143–162
  see also cartoons, girls';
Archie Comics 7, 70, 109
Archive of our Own 210
audience 128, 185, 195, 205, 212, 144, 212
  and reception 65, 80, 87, 88, 94–98, 147, 164, 175–177, 185, 187, 195, 201
  see also fandom; fans; target audiences
Avengers: Age of Ultron 129

Baby Boomers 6, 11
BBC (British Broadcasting Company) 15, 88
beauty ideals 107, 195
Black Lightning 191
Black Panther 185, 186, 191–192, 197

Black youth
  media impact on 186–187
  representation of 36, 176, 184, 186, 192, 194, 195
    princesses 194–195
    STEM brilliance 188, 191–194, 197
    superheroes 190–191
    supernatural 36, 163–164, 166–171, 176–177, 188–190
Blair Witch Project, The 9
Blood and Chocolate 16
branding 30–31
Buffy the Vampire Slayer 9, 11, 12, 105, 106–109, 111–115, 117, 119–123, 215

Carrie 7–8
Cartoon Network, 32
cartoons, girls' 13, 14, 27, 31, 35, 37
  see also animation, children's
CBS (CBS Broadcasting Inc.) 12
Charmed 1, 11, 12, 13, 108, 112, 149
Chilling Adventures of Sabrina 1, 7, 14, 16, 33, 105–123, 189–190
Christian Broadcasting Network 223
Christianity/Christian
  and media 10
    see also culture wars
  and witchcraft 223
  references to 68, 112–114
Chronicles of Narnia, The 45, 46, 47, 50
"Circumstances, the" 47, 53–57
climate change 63, 64, 66, 71, 72, 77, 79, 80
comics *see* Archie Comics; Marvel: comics
coming-of-age 29, 39–41, 50, 72–76, 148, 150, 153, 155, 158, 159
conservatism 19, 223
Craft, The 9, 10, 17–18, 221–222, 226–234

Creed, Barbara *see* "monstrous-feminine, the"
Crip Theory 224, 225
cultural traditions 19, 64, 80, 164, 165, 171, 172, 177, 221, 224
culture wars, 19
CW (The CW Network, LLC) 1, 12, 32, 110, 195, 207, 209

"dark fantastic" 184, 186, 188, 189
Davis, Jeff 210–212, 216
demonic activity 9, 129, 130, 131
demons 10, 11, 83, 107, 108, 130, 131, 231
disability 79, 80–81
Disney media
  Aladdin 145
  Coco 145
  Encanto 149–152
  Lightyear (Pixar) 145
  Lion King, The 145
  Little Mermaid, The 8, 146, 148, 188, 194, 195
  Loki 18, 67
  Moana 145
  Mulan 145
  Owl House 5, 19
  Pocahontas 145
  Princess and the Frog, The 194, 196
  Strange World (Pixar) 145
  That's So Raven 13, 16
  Turning Red 152–158
Disney
  and adolescent girls 159
  and Black princesses 194–195
  and family-friendly programming 148
  and femininity 148
  and global influence 144
  and identity 144
  and stereotypes 144–145

and Western fairytales 174, 175
as transmedia 159
Disney+ 18, 67, 143, 144
Disney Princess brand 8
diversity 17–18, 19–20, 36, 66, 79–80, 84, 95, 96, 97–99, 127–128, 145, 146, 159, 176, 184–85, 213
see also neurodiversity

Education-Entertainment research 84, 85
embodiment 53–59, 146, 164, 168–170, 171
empowerment 16, 39, 105, 107, 111, 114, 119, 127, 137, 147, 186
Eurocentrism 165, 176–177
Extended Transportation-Imagery Model 84, 87, 89–93

Facebook 206, 209
fairies 3, 16, 28, 34, 38, 40–41, 132–133, 201
fairytales 165, 171–177
fandom
 and fan fiction 89, 99, 205, 207, 208, 210, 212, 214
 and influence on media creators 209–210, 216
 and LGBTQ 96, 202, 208, 216–217
 and online spaces 80–81, 89, 99, 202, 213
 see also fans
FanFiction.com 212
fans 30–32, 34–36, 204
 and reception 205–207
 and rejection 80–81, 94–95
 see also fandom
fantasy 17, 29, 146, 176, 184, 185, 197
Fate: The Winx Saga 14, 16, 27–44
fathers/fatherhood 74, 77, 78, 86, 90, 133, 187, 190, 191

see also masculinity/masculine
femininity/feminine 15–17, 37, 105–111, 114, 118–120, 122, 227–229, 234
see also "monstrous-feminine, the"
feminism/feminist 37–42, 76–78, 105–111, 118–123, 143, 159, 230
 New Wave 143–144, 149, 159–160
 girl power 13, 15–16, 106–107, 118–123, 164
film see movies
folklore 4, 19, 147, 164
Fox 31
Freeform Network 213

gender 8, 15–17, 37–38, 64, 67, 75, 76–78, 126–127
 see also feminism/feminist, masculinity/masculine, LGBTQ/LGBTQ+
generation(s) 6, 7, 11, 13, 18, 71, 202, 212, 222
 see also Baby Boomers, Gen X, Gen Y, Gen Z, Millennials
generic tropes
 delinquent, juvenile 71
 detective 85
 maternal 159
 mean girls 38, 70, 71
 monstrous womb 154, 157
 new boy/girl 70, 227
 post-feminist 108, 119
 princess 37
 strong Black woman 192
 subversion of 146
 virginity loss 70, 71
 Western fairytale 165, 173, 175
 woman as possessed monster 154, 157
 youth as saviors 114, 117, 118–119, 152, 195
 Zambian fairytale 173
genre 3, 6–7, 27–44, 49, 51, 64, 65, 72

and hybridization 32, 64–65, 80, 164–165, 171–174
Gen X 70
Gen Y 11, 12
   see also millennial generation
Gen Z 202
giants *see* mythology, Norse
Ginger Snaps 16
girl power
   see girl power under feminism/feminist
girls 16, 37, 95, 107, 119, 159, 176, 193, 222
   see also girl power
   see also tweens
gods *see* mythology, Norse
Good Omens 18
Grossman, Lev *see Magicians, The*

Harry Potter 5, 10–11, 12, 13, 51
   see also Rowling, J. K.
hashtag activism
   #BuryYourGays 76, 209
   #CookiesForSterek 212
   #LGBTFansDeserveBetter 209
   #MeToo 105, 107, 111, 119
   #SaveShadowhunters 214, 216
Hays Production Code 201
HBO Max *see* Max
Holmes, Sherlock *see Irregulars, The*
horror 7, 146–148, 150, 159, 201, 202
Hunger Games, The 176, 193–194, 195, 197

I Am Not a Witch 17, 163–180
"imagination gap" 176–177
IMDb (Internet Movie Database) 88–89, 99, 175, 195
inheritance, matrilineal 133, 135, 136
Instagram 203

intelligence 46, 90, 191, 192, 193, 197
   emotional, 46, 51
internet 4, 5, 10, 11, 203, 215
   see also social media
introspective analysis 187–188
Irregulars, The 15, 83–101
I Was a Teenage Werewolf 7, 9, 15

Jingle Jangle: A Christmas Journey 192–193
Joan of Arcadia 12

kairos 47, 53–57
Kristeva, Julia 126, 129, 130–1, 133–5, 136–137, 147

Legacies 208
Lewis, C. S. 45, 49–50, 58
LGBTQ (Lesbian, Gay, Bisexual, Transgender, Queer, and Questioning)/LGBTQ+ (Lesbian, Gay, Bisexual, Transgender, Queer, Questioning, and Others)
   characters 17, 19, 51–52, 75–76, 135–136, 201, 207–215
   representation, queer 145, 201–202
   youth 17, 202, 203–205, 215
liminality 4, 6, 112, 133, 202
Loki: Agent of Asgard 67
Loki *see Ragnarok* and Disney

magic 3, 4, 5, 8, 9, 14, 15, 45, 126–127, 130–137
magic school 5, 28, 37–38, 45, 46, 49–52, 57–59
magical realism 164, 165, 171–173, 174
Magicians, The 14, 45–62
marketing 7, 11, 12, 28, 37, 46, 50, 105, 106, 120n11, 211
Marvel

comics 65–67, 125–126, 128–129, 132, 135, 136–137, 138
films 63–67, 126–127, 129, 186
masculinity/masculine 76–78, 128–129
and STEM, 8, 126–127
Max 1, 13, 28
media fragmentation 14, 20
media multiplicities 30
menstruation 130, 133, 148, 150, 154, 160, 162
millennial generation 11–13, 50, 70
see also Gen Y
"monstrous-feminine, the" 126–127, 129–130, 131, 133, 135, 136–137, 147–156
mother/motherhood 77, 135–136, 154–155, 159
movies 12, 16, 68, 72, 83, 86, 87, 89, 128, 137, 147, 148, 154, 187, 194, 202, 204
MTV (Music Television) 16, 202, 216
My Best Friend Is a Vampire 9
mythology, Norse 63–82

Naomi 190–191
narrative engagement 86, 96
Netflix 1, 7, 18, 27, 28, 30, 32, 33, 34, 37, 38, 39, 41, 63, 69, 93, 99, 110, 118, 163, 188, 192, 214
neurodiversity 17–18, 224–226
neuroqueer 222, 224, 225, 229, 231, 232, 233
New Mutants, The 126, 131–132
New X-Men 132
Nickelodeon 31, 39
Nick Jr. 31–32
Norway 63, 69, 70, 72, 76, 79, 80, 81
nostalgia 34–37
Nyoni, Rungano 163–164, 173–174
see also *I Am Not a Witch*

Originals, The 208
Owl House 5, 19

Paganism 10
Paramount+ 16
patriarchy/patriarchal 76–77, 78, 111, 112, 119, 128, 135, 164
Pixar see Disney
Poetic Edda 64–65
Princess Culture 37
see also Disney Princess brand under Disney
progressive 16, 37, 48, 76, 78, 89, 144, 145, 149, 159
Prose Edda 64, 65, 66, 67, 68, 69, 73, 79
protagonists 1, 2, 3, 5, 6, 8, 9 16, 92, 145, 146, 148, 159, 196
psychoanalytic theory 144, 147, 148, 149

queer baiting 211–212

racism/racist 35, 66, 95, 98, 99, 144–145, 191, 192, 195, 196
Ragnarok 15, 63–82
Raising Dion 187, 190, 196
reception see audience: reception
religion see Christianity; Paganism; Satanism; Wicca
review bombing 89, 97, 195
Rings of Power 19
Ring, The 147
Riverdale 110, 118, 122
Rowling, J. K. 45, 49, 58
see also Harry Potter
Runaways 133–135

Sabrina the Teenage Witch 7, 9, 14, 15, 108, 109, 110, 112, 120
Salem Witch Trials 6

Satanic Panic 9–11
Satanism 10
science fiction 8, 27–28, 41, 67–68, 190–193, 196, 197
  distinct from supernatural 3, 18, 184
  see also superheroes
See You Yesterday 192
sex 46, 51–52, 57–59, 70–71
sexism/sexist 95, 119, 143, 145, 189, 233
sex magic 47, 55–59
sexual identity development model 206
sexuality/sexual 46, 130–131, 132, 134, 135, 153–155, 189, 211, 227–228
Shadowhunters 213–215
slash fiction 205
Snorri Sturluson see Prose Edda
social media 34, 128, 203, 207, 209, 210, 212, 214, 216, 223
  see also Archive of our Own, Facebook, FanFiction.com, Instagram, TikTok, Tumblr, Twitter, Wattpad
  see also hashtag activism
Spider-Man 67
superheroes 27–28, 67–68, 77, 125–142
  Black 186, 190–191, 196
  female or feminized 125–126, 127–129, 136–137, 190, 191
  see also Marvel: comics and Marvel: films
supernatural, concept of 3, 178n1, 184
  see also supernaturalism
supernaturalism 164, 165, 171, 172, 178n1
supernatural youth media
  as genre 2–3, 145–146
  conventions of 2–3, 32, 38–39, 83, 107, 58–59
  history of 6–13
  subgenres of 33, 38, 46, 49–50, 58–59
  see also teen drama
Syfy 14, 46–48

target audience 2, 3, 4, 8, 10–14, 18, 20, 29, 30, 31, 32, 34, 41, 42, 48, 50, 58, 84, 91, 96, 205
technology 3, 5–6, 126–127
teen drama 14, 15, 30, 32–33, 37, 39, 40, 41, 64, 70–72, 97, 105–109
Teen Witch 9
Teen Wolf (film) 9
Teen Wolf (TV) 210–213
television
  cable 11, 12, 14, 20, 106, 187
  network 1, 12, 187, 214, 216
  see also ABC, Amazon Prime, BBC, Cartoon Network, CBS, Christian Broadcasting
  streaming 13, 20, 31, 70, 110, 144, 163, 184, 187, 202
  Network, CW, Disney, Disney+ under Disney, Fox, Freeform, Max, MTV, Netflix, Nickelodeon, Nick Jr., Paramount+, Syfy, UPN, WB
That's So Raven 13, 16
Thomas, Ebony E. see "dark fantastic"; "imagination gap"
Thor 63–64, 65, 67, 68, 69, 72, 73–77
  see also Marvel: comics; Marvel: films
Thor: Ragnarok 63–64, 65, 67, 77
TikTok 203
transmedia 28, 83, 94, 137
transportation-imagery model 86
tropes see generic tropes
Tumblr 88–89, 97, 99, 206, 212, 214
tweens 2, 6, 12, 14

twitter 209
   and activism 214
   see also hashtag activism

UPN (United Paramount Network) 3, 12

Vampire Diaries, The 32, 176, 207–210
Völuspá 65, 66, 68

Wagner, Richard 65, 66
   and white supremacy 65, 79–80
Walt Disney Company *see* Disney
Wattpad 210
WB (The WB Television Network) 12, 105, 106, 107, 110
Wednesday 14, 188–189
werewolves 15, 16, 208, 210–211
Western culture
   and audiences 173, 175

   and beauty standards 107
   and femininity 147
   and girl power 164
   and worldviews 165
Whedon, Joss 16, 107–108, 120
Wicca 10, 15, 221–222
   see also witches
Winx Club 13, 14, 16, 27–44
witchcraft 10, 164, 165–168, 221
   and Christianity 223
witches 222–223
   as characters 10, 15, 133–135, 149–152, 189, 221, 226–234
   and neuroqueer 225–226
   see also Wicca
woke 19, 96, 97, 111
Wolf Pack 216

Young Avengers 135–136

Sharon R. Mazzarella
General Editor

Grounded in cultural studies, books in this series will study the cultures, artifacts, and media of children, tweens, teens, and college-aged youth. Whether studying television, popular music, fashion, sports, toys, the Internet, self-publishing, leisure, clubs, school, cultures/activities, film, dance, language, tie-in merchandising, concerts, subcultures, or other forms of popular culture, books in this series go beyond the dominant paradigm of traditional scholarship on the effects of media/culture on youth. Instead, authors endeavor to understand the complex relationship between youth and popular culture. Relevant studies would include, but are not limited to, studies of how youth negotiate their way through the maze of corporately-produced mass culture; how they themselves have become cultural producers; how youth create "safe spaces" for themselves within the broader culture; the political economy of youth culture industries; the representational politics inherent in mediated coverage and portrayals of youth; and so on. Books that provide a forum for the "voices" of the young are particularly encouraged. The source of such voices can range from in-depth interviews and other ethnographic studies to textual analyses of cultural artifacts created by youth.

For further information about the series and submitting manuscripts, please contact:

SHARON R. MAZZARELLA
School of Communication Studies
James Madison University
Harrisonburg, VA 22807
mazzarsr@jmu.edu

To order books, please contact our Customer Service Department at:

peterlang@presswarehouse.com (within the U.S.)
orders@peterlang.com (outside the U.S.)

Or browse online at WWW.PETERLANG.COM

www.ingramcontent.com/pod-product-compliance
Lightning Source LLC
Chambersburg PA
CBHW061710300426
44115CB00014B/2627